W9-BTM-103

ATHENIA
TORPEDOED

ATHENIA
TORPEDOED

The U-Boat Attack That Ignited the Battle of the Atlantic

FRANCIS M. CARROLL

Naval Institute Press
Annapolis, Maryland

Naval Institute Press
291 Wood Road
Annapolis, MD 21402

Library of Congress Cataloging-in-Publication Data

Carroll, Francis M.,
  Athenia torpedoed : the U-boat attack that ignited the Battle of the Atlantic / Francis M. Carroll.
    p. cm.
  Includes bibliographical references and index.
    ISBN 978-1-59114-148-8 (hbk. : alk. paper) — ISBN 978-1-61251-155-9 (e-book) 1. Athenia (Steamship) 2. U-30 (Submarine) 3. World War, 1939-1945—Naval operations, German. 4. World War, 1939-1945—Campaigns—Atlantic Ocean. I. Title. II. Title: U-boat attack that ignited the Battle of the Atlantic.
  D772.A7C28 2012
  940.54'293—dc23

                                                                    2012020768

20 19 18 17 16 15 14 13 12   9 8 7 6 5 4 3 2 1
First printing

DEDICATION

For all those still touched by the shadow of the Second World War

The unmentionable odour of death
Offends the September night.

—W. H. AUDEN

CONTENTS

PREFACE

For those of my generation the shadow of the Second World War has never fully lifted. The war lives with us in subtle and improbable ways. I was a child during the war, living in the middle of the United States, and in a sense I was physically untouched by it. But the war left its imprint on me, my family, my childhood friends, and the people I came to know in adulthood and as colleagues. I was too young to remember the events of the 1930s and Pearl Harbor, but I do remember coming down to breakfast and being told it was D-day and not understanding what that meant. I remember being sent home early from school when President Franklin D. Roosevelt died. I do not actually remember V-E day or V-J day, but I remember "the boys" coming home, sort of one by one. Particularly, I remember airplanes flying over our little town—a town then well out of the path of any airplanes in those days. But suddenly, literally out of the blue, preceded only by a roar of engines, a fighter plane or a bomber would fly low over the town and would return and crisscross above the streets; and everyone—all of us children, housewives in aprons, men in shirtsleeves—would rush out into the streets in great excitement and look up into the sky, and someone would say, oh, that was so-and-so's boy, he grew up on 10th Street.

Even as children, the war took over our lives and we played war all the time. Small hills became South Pacific beaches, front porches with railings became ships, and fuel-oil tanks on stilts and with pipes and ladders became submarines. Equipped with packsacks, belts, and helmet liners from the new army surplus stores and inspired by the Saturday matinee films we saw ourselves in turn as Marines, submariners, bomber pilots, and commandos. We collected shoulder patches and insignias, as well as airplane identification cards. The American Legion drum and bugle corps practiced along the streets on summer evenings, making stirring march music part of the experience. Eventually we had teachers who were living heroes who fought at Guadalcanal, flew fighter planes, were held prisoner by the Japanese, or landed at Normandy. We became obsessed with the details and the minutia—our favorite airplane, aircraft carrier, or general.

Now the war has become less obvious, less overt, but present, just below the surface nonetheless: Friends and colleagues who had been refugees and displaced persons forced to emigrate, colleagues on antisubmarine patrol out of Northern

Ireland, friends caught up in the holocaust, colleagues who had been bombed out in London, acquaintances torpedoed in the Atlantic. Almost everyone of my time period has a story about the war, was affected by the war, or is in close contact with someone who was. In that way, for people of my age, even as the actual soldiers and sailors themselves are going fast, the war is still very much with us.

As a historian also the war has been a major preoccupation for me. The Second World War was never my special area of research, but it was inescapable in most of the classes that I taught. The perspective was now different—what were the causes, who was responsible, when were the turning points, what were the key strategic decisions, who made the most irretrievable mistakes, why did the war end the way it did, what was the legacy of the war, what can be learned from the war to prevent a repetition? The micro of the favorite fighter plane gave way to the macro—the large picture, the command decisions, the causes and effects. But this too has its comfortable routine, its familiar "Time Marches On" litany—Ethiopia, Spain, Austria, Czechoslovakia, Poland, and Manchuria, China, Pearl Harbor! Numerous historians have attempted to answer the question of how the war started, and as a result quite a brilliant and insightful historical literature has been written. My own interest has increasingly focused on the question of where did the war start, and there is of course no real agreement about that matter either. I was, nevertheless, struck by the fact that the first shots fired in the Second World War for the English-speaking world—the beginning of the war in the West—involved the four countries in whose histories I have had a long-time interest: the United States, Great Britain, Canada, and Ireland. The first shot was fired by a German submarine on 3 September 1939, which sunk a British passenger ship, the TSS *Athenia*, sailing from Glasgow, Belfast, and Liverpool to Quebec and Montreal. It was carrying passengers of British, Canadian, and U.S. citizenship, as well as a number of refugees from Europe; and after the ship was sunk the survivors were brought into Galway, in Ireland; Glasgow, in the United Kingdom; and Halifax, in Canada. Thus within eight or nine hours of war having been declared, all four countries, and their citizens, were physically involved in the war with Germany. It was surprising to me that despite the enormous historical literature that exists about the Second World War there is only one book in English, and that written over fifty years ago, about this tragic incident. I am now attempting to tell afresh, and with sources not previously available, the story of the sinking of the *Athenia* and the beginning of the Second World War in the West. It is also my attempt to deal with the shadow of the war as it extends into our own times.

—FRANCIS M. CARROLL

PROLOGUE

The waves of the sea are mighty, and rage horribly.

—PSALM 93:5

This is an account of a disaster at sea. It describes the sinking of the passenger liner *Athenia*, loaded with Americans, Canadians, and European refugees who hoped to get across the North Atlantic. As such, it is filled with drama, tragedy, pain, suffering, and triumph—death and survival, separation, and joyful reunion. It is a story of compassion. But of course it is also a history of war and politics. Indeed, a unique element of this story is that this is actually where the Second World War began. This is where Germany, having already invaded Poland in what was expected to be a limited war, first struck the Western Allies, Britain and France. This is the first blow, fired without warning. For Britain, the sinking of the *Athenia* was seen as both a violation of international law and an immediate reversion by Germany to the kind of total war it had been fighting in 1918, at the end of the Great War. The sinking of the *Athenia* pushed Britain to adopt convoys by the end of the week as the means of protecting shipping, and it served from the first to shape British public opinion toward the war. The impact of the *Athenia* reached further still. In Canada the sinking of the ship and the death of the innocent, young passenger, ten-year-old Margaret Hayworth, became issues around which much of the nation could rally in support of the decision of Parliament and Prime Minister William Lyon Mackenzie King's government to go to war. In the United States the administration of President Franklin D. Roosevelt and the Congress were too wary to make the sinking of the *Athenia* the counterpart of the sinking of the *Lusitania* in the Great War. But the *Athenia* incident, together with other German actions, helped to expose Germany in the public mind as a serious threat to the United States, as well as to Europe, and provided the opportunity for President Roosevelt to open direct communication with Winston Churchill. The *Athenia* helped to change public opinion in the United States sufficiently to amend the existing Neutrality Laws to allow the country to sell munitions and supplies to Britain and France—a supportive first step to meeting the Nazi threat directly. So the sinking of the *Athenia* is a tale that deserves to be told, full of passion and meaning.

ACKNOWLEDGMENTS

E very book is something of a miracle and this book is the beneficiary of many "miracle workers." It is a pleasure for me to express my thanks for all those who have helped make possible the telling of the story of the *Athenia*. First and foremost I should like to thank those actual survivors of the sinking of the *Athenia* who were gracious enough to talk with me or correspond with me about their experiences. Dr. André Molgat, here in Winnipeg, and Hay "Scotty" Gillespie, in Brandon, Manitoba, talked with me about what they and their families experienced. Reverend Gerald Hutchinson and Rosemary Cass-Beggs Burstall corresponded with me and sent written accounts of their recollections and Mrs. Burstall was kind enough to allow me to use a photograph of her family. Melanie Brooks, the daughter of James A. Goodson, also corresponded with me and send photographs of her father. Cynthia Harrison deserves special thanks for rescuing at an estate sale, and then making available on Ahoy-Mac's Web Log, the only known copy of Judith Evelyn's vivid memoir of her experiences on the *Athenia*. Mackenzie J. Gregory in Australia created Ahoy-Mac's Web Log, which is an extensive compendium of naval and maritime information; he has a special *Athenia* page where he has amassed a substantial volume of information about the ship and its survivors.

Of course much of my research for this book was done through archives and libraries. I started work visiting The National Archives at Kew (formerly the Public Records Office) in London where it became apparent that there was a rich collection of *Athenia* documents. I knew that I could acquire much, although not all, of the State Department documents about the *Athenia* on five reels of microfilm from the vast collection at the National Archives and Records Administration in College Park, Maryland. The Library and Archives of Canada in Ottawa made most of their *Athenia* materials available to me on a CD that I could very conveniently read on my computer. The Mitchell Library in Glasgow provided me with vital documents about the relief effort, photographs of the ship, and plans and diagrams from the ship builder. Very early on Astrid S. Steen from Fred. Olsen & Company in Norway sent me data about the *Knute Nelson* and a photograph of the ship. I should like to give special thanks to the Joseph P. Kennedy Papers Donor Committee for allowing me first to examine material and then to quote extracts from Ambassador Kennedy's unpublished "Diplomatic memoir," a most insightful document. I was fortunate to be able to consult many other *Athenia*-related materials from libraries and archives in Britain, Ireland, Canada, and the United States. Librarians and archivists in all of these countries were enormously helpful in assisting me in viewing and obtaining the materials I needed. In particular I must mention Tim Hutchinson, archivist at the University of Saskatchewan Library, who, when I explained that I wanted to look at the papers of some survivors of the *Athenia,* said, "I think my uncle was on that ship," and then put me in touch with his cousin and uncle in Alberta. I am also especially indebted to Melanie L. Rodriguez, who photocopied for me extensive sections of the A. D. Simpson Family Papers in the Houston Public Library in Houston, thus making available the experiences of Rowena Simpson and many of her University of Texas friends.

At the University of Manitoba the staff of the Dafoe Library has been as helpful as ever. Barbara Bennell and her colleagues went to great lengths to obtain microfilms, articles, and books through inter-library loan. Mary-Jane Clear and Gaitree Boyd untangled for me the complexities of making photocopies from microfilm images. In the department of Information and Technology, Luc Desjardins converted both sketchy digital images and damaged photographs into the dramatic visual materials that the publisher could use. Diana DeFoort at St. John's College was always of great assistance in helping me with computer and printing problems. My colleague, Professor Richard Lebrun, guided me through Catholic Church materials and led me to the Oblate Archives for information about the life of Father Joseph V. O'Connor, one of the important figures in the story of the survivors of the *Athenia.*

It has been a pleasure for me to work with the Naval Institute Press. Particularly helpful and encouraging were Susan Todd Brook, Senior Acquisitions Editor, Susan Corrado, Managing Editor, and Claire Noble, Marketing Manager. They have led me by the hand, step by step. I am grateful for my copy editor, Jeanette Nakada, who has rescued me from countless embarrassing errors and omissions, although I take full responsibility for such lapses and defects that may remain. Thanks also to Henry Wilson of Pen & Sword for his early interest in this book. I should also like to thank two old friends in the publishing world, George Nicholson in New York and Linda Oberholtz Davis in London, for their encouragement and advice at the beginning of this project. Finally, homage to Janet Foster Carroll, who recognized early on that the story of the *Athenia* deserved to be told.

—*Francis M. Carroll*

CHAPTER 1

THE HINGE OF FATE

SAILING DELAYED   NOT WORRIED   RETURN FIRST AVAILABLE SHIP
STAYING CENTRAL HOTEL
—*NINO*[1]

It had been deceptively quiet, steaming through the Irish Sea and up the North Channel between Ireland and Scotland and into the Atlantic beyond. After all of the anxiety and excitement of getting away, the passenger liner TSS *Athenia* left Liverpool late Saturday afternoon under a steely gray sky. The ship, still in its traditional colors of black hull and white superstructure, cut through the water at just over sixteen knots, generating enough motion to send some people to bed with seasickness. In the middle of the night, the *Athenia* cleared Inishstrahull Island, off Malin Head, the northernmost point of Ireland in County Donegal. But while the following morning, Sunday, 3 September 1939, dawned bright and clear, clouds built up as the day went on and the temperature fell, the wind coming out of the south and shaping swells between four and six feet. She sped west on Sunday and, under instructions from the Admiralty, sped farther north than usual, out of the normal shipping lanes and closer to Rockall Bank, leaving Europe, newly at war, as rapidly as possible.

Sitting in the third-class lounge at about quarter past eleven in the morning was James Goodson, a young, seventeen-year-old American whose trip around the world had been cut short. After spending part of the summer with an aunt and uncle in Kent, Goodson had been told by the U.S. consul in Paris that he should return home immediately, and he managed to book a ticket on the *Athenia*. He listened to the prime minister's rather flat and anticlimactic remarks on the radio reporting that there had been no response to the British ultimatum to Germany to withdraw its forces from Poland and that therefore Britain and Germany were now at war. Borrowing T. S. Eliot's lines, Goodson commented, "This is the way the world ends: not with a bang but a whimper!" He concluded with some satisfaction that those on board the westward-bound ship, "were well out of it."[2] News of the declaration of war by Britain and France against Germany made its way around the ship following Prime Minister Neville Chamberlain's radio broadcast at 11:15 in the morning. Captain James Cook was notified immediately by the second radio officer, who received the broadcast from Valentia Island radio in Ireland. By noon the official announcement was posted by the purser's office. It confirmed the pessimism and depression that had touched many of the passengers.

As a precaution, Captain Cook ordered Chief Officer Barnet Mackenzie Copland to have the canvas covers taken off the ship's lifeboats; the gear for lowering the boats checked; the drainage plugs secured in place; and supplies and provisions, such as water and condensed milk, put in each of the boats. Two lifeboats, one on each side of the ship, were actually swung out on their davits, cranelike devices designed to lower lifeboats into the water, in order to be instantly ready for use. Work had already been under way to paint black the glass on portholes, to board up various other windows, and to screen outside doors, all of which might expose light from the ship at night. All of this added to a sense of foreboding that many passengers found oppressive, despite the fact that the ship was well out to sea before war had been declared. While something of the normal shipboard life was started—Sunday church services were held, dining room seating was assigned, lunch was served, shuffleboard and deck tennis were played—no radio messages or cables could be sent from the ship, no chart of the ship's progress was posted, a Sunday morning lifeboat drill was held, and the crew seemed annoyingly vague about the ship's route and when it was expected to arrive in Montreal. As evening approached the *Athenia* was steered in a zigzag course to confuse and elude a possible attack by submarines, the boatswain proceeded to darken ship, and only dimmed running lights were lit.

Because there were so many passengers on board, dinner was served in three sittings. Judith Evelyn, a beautiful young actress, born in Seneca, South Dakota, and raised in Moose Jaw, Saskatchewan, was too exhausted and emotionally wrung out by the news and the precautions to dress for dinner. Furthermore, the cabin she shared with three other women was too crowded with luggage to encourage a change into more fashionable clothes. Watching the covers being taken off the lifeboats, she had the morbid feeling that "we shan't be out of this without being in the life-boats." With only a quick wash and brushup, and still wearing her canvas tennis shoes, she was ready to go to dinner just after 7:00 p.m. for the second sitting. Miss Evelyn, who had been cast in several promising acting roles while in London, joined her fiancé, Andrew Allan, a young Canadian who had also been working in London producing radio programs. They sat at a table with Andrew's father, the Reverend William Allan, a popular Presbyterian minister in Toronto who had enjoyed some acclaim with devotional radio programs. The meal began with half a grapefruit and a lively, if rather forced, conversation about the most advantageous time to visit Scotland. September was thought to be best, after most tourists had left and the weather was still fine. The main course of chicken and rice was just served when the dining room was shaken by a loud report. The lights in the dining room and throughout the ship went out, followed by what sounded like a second explosion. The ship took a distinct list to the port side; glasses, dishes, and silverware fell to the floor; and chairs and tables slid across the room. With the windows and portholes painted black, the dining room was left in complete darkness and shock. The *Athenia* had been hit by a torpedo from a German submarine. "This is it," said Judith Evelyn, announcing to her stunned table companions what was in fact the first shot of the Second World War in the West and the beginning of what some have called the longest battle of the war, the Battle of the Atlantic.[3]

This was *it* for the *Athenia* and all of its civilian passengers and crew. One hundred and twelve people on board the ship would be killed, some in the explosion when the torpedo hit and some in the sea while people attempted to save themselves in the lifeboats. On a ship sailing from Great Britain to Canada, not surprisingly the largest proportions of deaths were among British subjects. Of these, as many as 48 of the 50 passengers killed holding British passports were Canadians, or British subjects living in Canada, while 18 of the 19 crew members killed were British and the 1 Canadian. Americans, heading home from Europe, were the next largest group among the *Athenia*'s passengers, and 30 U.S. citizens died in the sinking. Seven Polish citizens, 4 German citizens, and 2 officially "stateless" people made up the reminder of the fatalities. A very large number also would be injured or traumatized in the crisis. However, it was amazing that 1,306 people were actually saved from a ship sunk in mid-ocean as night was falling. Their rescue itself became an epic story of endurance and luck.

So this was where the war began. Within hours of the declaration of war a commercial passenger liner loaded with civilians, having put to sea before the war broke out, was torpedoed and sunk, taking with her American and Canadian, as well as British and European, victims. What would be the implications? Would international law—the London Naval Treaty and the Geneva Conventions—be observed? Would this be a total war from the start? Would the sinking of the *Athenia* prompt the United States to issue an ultimatum to Germany as President Woodrow Wilson had as a result of the sinking of the *Lusitania* in 1915? Would the deaths of American citizens ultimately bring the United States into the war? This was a dramatic and painful beginning to the Second World War.

War in Europe. It was hard to believe that only twenty years and nine months after the end of the Great War, the "war to end all wars," and less than a year since the Munich settlement, which was to provide "peace in our time," the great powers of Europe were again in conflict. Of course, Japan had been fighting since 1937 in China, if indeed not since 1931 in Manchuria. This ongoing crisis had done much to undermine the authority in the League of Nations, as Japan first ignored the League's resolutions and then withdrew from the League. Events in Europe, following the uneasy Versailles Peace Treaty ending the Great War, had also taken a decided turn for the worse in the 1930s. In Germany bitterness over the defeat in 1918, resentment over territorial losses and diminished great-power status, and economic chaos contributed to the emergence of a Nazi government in 1933 headed by Adolph Hitler. Almost every subsequent year saw dramatic moves to reassert Germany's position in postwar Europe. Hitler took Germany out of the League of Nations in 1933 also, and repudiated the demilitarization provisions of the Versailles Treaty by reintroducing conscription in Germany and establishing an air force in 1935. The following year he ordered reoccupation of the Rhineland with German troops, also in defiance of the Versailles Treaty, and began cementing German relations with totalitarian Italy and Japan. In early 1938 he manipulated events so as to successfully bring about the annexation of Austria by Germany. All of this had been preceded by the formation of a fascist government in Italy under Benito Mussolini in 1921 and paralleled by the overthrow of the Republic of Spain by the forces of General Francisco Franco and his Falange Party beginning in 1936. It is possible now to see a steady, seemingly irreversible, decline in international relations in Europe during the 1930s and the security of the democracies, reaching a climax during the twelve months between the Czechoslovak crisis in September 1938 and the outbreak of war in September 1939.[4]

The Czech crisis had its origin in the circumstance of three and a quarter million ethnic Germans (former Austrians, really) living in Czechoslovakia, most of them in the Sudetenland near the German border. In fact, Czechoslovakia, like a number of other central European countries, was created out of the old Austro-Hungarian Empire and was made up of a number of large ethnic groups, several of which would prove troublesome in the crisis. Led by Konrad Henlein, and subsidized from Germany, the Sudeten Germans agitated for more autonomy and then amalgamation with Germany. Hitler claimed they were a persecuted minority and made increasing demands—first, that they be given greater political rights and, later, that they and the land they occupied be annexed to Germany. This situation was more than a minor central European border problem because of the alliance structure that had been established to guarantee European stability. The "Little Entente" had been created in the early 1920s to provide protection for Rumania, Yugoslavia, and Czechoslovakia, linking its fate to several other central European countries. More to the point, however, through a 1925 treaty, France was pledged to defend Czechoslovakia, and Britain was committed to assist France in any possible conflict with Germany. In late May 1938 Henlein slipped over into Austria and as a result of German troop movements there was a general scare that Germany might simply invade Czechoslovakia. This led to a partial mobilization of the Czech army and also prompted a more active role by the British in an attempt to prevent events from boiling over into a general conflict.

British prime minister Neville Chamberlain, in common with many people in Britain at the time, felt that the Versailles Treaty had not been entirely fair to Germany and that in the 1920s Germany had been humiliated by the restrictions and limitations that had been placed upon it. Chamberlain saw the emergence of Hitler as an indication that Germany would no longer tolerate its inferior position and that some accommodation would have to be made to modify the provisions of the Versailles Treaty in order to undo the wrongs that treaty enforcement perpetuated. In short, Germany needed to be "appeased" by diplomatic concessions before it seized by force what were its reasonable demands. The awkward position of the Sudeten Germans in Czechoslovakia was a case in point. The problem was to extend to the Germans what was appropriate without appearing to yield to the threat of force. In July 1938 Lord Runciman was sent to Czechoslovakia as a mediator; however, his report was tailored to recommend that the Sudeten Germans be allowed to choose self-determination and annexation with Germany. The Czech president, Eduard Beneš, offered the Sudeten Germans most of their demands, but riots in several Czech towns in early September generated a new crisis and prompted Hitler to give voice to his plans, set in motion on 30 May, to invade Czechoslovakia. Chamberlain flew to meet Hitler at Berchtesgaden, the führer's mountain retreat, and Hitler agreed to the separation of the Sudetenland through a process of self-determination. Chamberlain returned to London with the task of convincing his cabinet, the French, and the Czech government. The French gave their support more or less on the condition that the three powers—Britain, France, and Germany—guarantee the newly configured Czechoslovakia. Beneš and the Czech government were pressured into accepting this arrangement. Public opinion in Britain, certainly as revealed in newspapers like *The Times* and the *New Statesman*, supported what looked like an effort to preserve peace.

Chamberlain returned to Germany on 22 September to meet with Hitler at Godesberg, but Hitler raised new conditions. Poles and Magyars living in Czechoslovakia had also voiced demands, and Hitler presented Chamberlain with a map of the territory to be ceded, which now included the carefully built Czech fortifications which would also be given up. He agreed to wait until 1 October, the date for his earlier invasion plans. The Czech army went to full mobilization. France agreed to support Czechoslovakia and Britain agreed to support France (although not Czechoslovakia). A war crisis settled on Britain and France. Bomb shelters were put up, trenches were dug in London parks, anti-aircraft guns were sited, gas masks were distributed, and plans for various evacuations were drafted. There was a sense of impending doom, especially with the recollections still fresh of such Spanish Civil War horrors as the bombing of Guernica. But Chamberlain sent Sir Horace Wilson, one of his advisers and confidantes, to Germany to talk again with Hitler, and after several stormy meetings Hitler agreed to guarantee the newly configured Czechoslovakia and to treat well the Czech people subsequently living in German territory. Chamberlain also urged Mussolini to use his influence with Hitler, and this too paid off. While in the midst of a speech in the House of Commons, Chamberlain was handed a note. It was from Hitler inviting the prime minister to a conference of the four powers—Germany, Italy, Britain, and France—in Munich on 29 September. Pandemonium broke out in the house, with members cheering and weeping with relief at having averted war.

It was the purpose of the Munich conference to make the arrangements for the transfer of those areas of Czechoslovakia where German, Polish, and Hungarian speakers were a significant population. The Germans worked out the formula that was presented by Mussolini and accepted by the British and the French in the early hours of 30 September. Plebiscites were to be held and a five-power commission—with representatives from Britain, France, Italy, Germany, and Czechoslovakia—was to administer the transfer of the areas to be surrendered by the Czechs. The four great powers also promised to guarantee the security of what remained of Czechoslovakia. Hitler agreed to move the deadline for all of this from 1 October to 10 October. The Czech representatives, who had come to Munich but had not been a party to the negotiations, had little choice but to accept the decisions presented by the four great powers. In Prague people wept; Beneš resigned. When the conference was all over Chamberlain asked Hitler to sign a statement that Britain and Germany "regard the agreement signed last night and the Anglo-German Naval Agreement [signed in 1935] as symbolic of the desire of our two peoples never to go to war with one another again." It was this document that Chamberlain waved at the airport when he returned home to England and announced that he had achieved "peace for our time."[5]

The Munich settlement should have resolved the major ethnic dislocations concerning Germany in central Europe and it should have established a lasting agreement among the four great powers. Whatever complaints one might have had about how Czechoslovakia had been treated in these procedures, the greater good of European stability seemed to have been assured. Chamberlain reported that Hitler told him that with the annexation of the Sudetenland all of Germany's territorial claims had been satisfied. There was tremendous relief that war had been avoided. However, disquieting events continued. In November violent actions against Jews in Germany, in what is now called "Kristallnacht," reinforced the image of the Nazi regime as brutal and lawless. Furthermore, the march of German troops into Prague on 15 March 1939, shattered any remaining British and French confidence in Hitler and the value of his agreements. Prompted by Hitler, the Slovakian provincial government had declared independence. Its dissolution by the Czech government and the proclamation of martial law gave Hitler the excuse to intervene, annexing Bohemia and Moravia and creating a new German province of "Czechia," making Slovakia a semiautonomous protectorate, and presiding over the cession of Sub-Carpathian Ruthenia to Hungary and Teschen to Poland. Czechoslovakia no longer existed; the four-power guarantee never came into effect. British and French public sympathy for Germany changed sharply. While the annexation of Austria and the Sudetenland brought German speakers into the Reich, no such ethnic justification could be made for Prague and its hinterland. There was a growing realization that the Western democracies had suffered a terrible defeat at the hands of the Nazis. "Munich" and "appeasement" became synonymous with naïveté and betrayal.

Subsequent events in 1939 continued the downward spiral into war. Before March was out Hitler had demanded and received the return of Memel, along the Baltic–East Prussian coast, which had been allotted to Lithuania by the Versailles Treaty and constituted that country's only major port. His foreign minister also raised the question of Danzig with the Polish ambassador, the German Baltic port made a free city by the Versailles Treaty and administered by the League of Nations. Although Poland had worked very hard to maintain good relations with Germany, it was clear that Danzig, the Polish Corridor (that strip of land linking Poland to the Baltic Sea and dividing East Prussia from the rest of Germany), and Poland itself became Hitler's next target. On 31 March, Chamberlain, who had earlier described Czechoslovakia as a country beyond the reach of British military assistance, now announced to Jozef Beck, the Polish foreign minister, and to parliament, that Britain and France would extend "all the support in their power" if Poland's independence were threatened.[6] Legislation for conscription in Britain was introduced and steps were taken to upgrade military preparedness. While Britain and France were still willing to make concessions to Germany in order to preserve peace in Europe, all of these actions were intended to make clear to Hitler that the West would not accept further German military expansion in central Europe. In the face of both pro-Nazi agitation among the German population in Danzig and diplomatic pressure from Hitler, the Polish government refused to be intimidated. However, by the end of April, Hitler repudiated both the German-Polish nonaggression pact of 1934 and the Anglo-German Naval Agreement of 1935, and he gave orders that the army make plans for an invasion of Danzig and Poland on 1 September. A month later Germany and Italy signed the "Pact of Steel" in which they agreed to support each other in the event that hostilities were opened with any other power.

As the prospect of war loomed between the West and Germany over central Europe, the position of the Soviet Union became increasingly important. Historically, Russia had been at various times allied with both Germany—under Bismarck—and Britain and France, in the Triple Entente. As the possibility increased of a German war with Britain and France over Poland, the situation presented Germany with the nightmare of a two-front war. However, if the Soviet Union were allied with Germany it would reduce the military problems of dealing with Poland and the West. If the Soviet Union were allied with Britain and France, on the other hand, it would expose Germany to major military confrontations on both fronts. But for both sides, the Soviet Union presented great obstacles. For the British and the French there was both the issue of ideology—the latent rivalry between bolshevism and capitalism—and the problem that the Stalinist purges of the late 1930s had decimated the upper levels of the Red Army—convincing some in the West that Poland was a more reliable military ally than the Soviet Union. The Poles were themselves unwilling to allow Soviet troops into Poland to resist Germany, given the history of Russian domination of Poland. The result was that the British and the French pursued their negotiations with the Soviet Union during the summer of 1939 in a lackadaisical and unconvincing manner, possibly with more of a hope of intimidating the Germans than with actually signing a pact with the Russians. The Germans, on the other hand, following up hints of a pragmatic arrangement by the Soviets, ignored their own ideological antagonisms with bolshevism and entered into serious talks with the Russians, acknowledging a Soviet sphere of influence in the Baltic countries, eastern Poland, and the Bessarabian province of Rumania, while obtaining a free hand from the Soviets for themselves in western Poland and Lithuania. On 23 August the German foreign minister flew to Moscow to sign the nonaggression pact. These negotiations had been conducted very much in secret, and the announcement of the agreement stunned the world. The Western powers had been pre-empted and upstaged by the Germans once again. Poland and Britain signed a defense agreement two days later, but it looked like another case of "too little too late."

While the United States was not an active participant in these events, President Franklin D. Roosevelt was not a disinterested observer. Roosevelt's suggestion to Chamberlain in early 1938—to hold an international security conference in which Germany might be brought to the table with the other great powers to openly discuss how her aspirations might be met—was turned down by the prime minister who was then hoping to pursue private talks with Germany. Roosevelt supported Britain and France in the talks leading to the Munich agreement, but he withdrew the U.S. ambassador to Germany following the Kristallnacht riots in November. In the course of 1939 Roosevelt attempted to extract some commitment to restraint by asking both Germany and Italy to declare that they had no territorial aspirations in a variety of countries in central Europe—a request that was met with derision by both Hitler and Mussolini. Domestically Roosevelt urged Congress to change the Neutrality Laws passed earlier in the decade that placed an embargo on trade with belligerent countries, changes that would allow the United States to sell munitions and strategic goods to countries whose policies the administration supported. However, the "isolationists," or "noninterventionists," in Congress, strengthened by modest Republican gains in the 1938 elections, were able to defeat these changes by preventing the measure from coming to a vote in the Senate during the summer session.[7] Public opinion in the United States throughout 1939 was largely in line with the preference of Congress. Although most Americans were suspicious of Germany and supported Britain and France, they were firm in their views that the United States should avoid getting involved and the current Neutrality Acts seemed to ensure that.[8] Thus the United States had almost no leverage in the international crisis of August 1939.

Throughout the summer of 1939 the Poles maintained an uncompromising position on the status of Danzig and the Polish Corridor, both of which were authorized by the Versailles Treaty. Talks were broken off and Germany began to prepare for war. Nevertheless by 25 August, Hitler learned that the Anglo-Polish treaty had been signed and was told by Mussolini that Italy would not be ready to go to war under the provisions of the Pact of Steel. The British attempted to devise a workable compromise over the next week, with economic inducements for Germany if war were avoided, but mostly they struggled simply to gain time. Polish foreign minister Beck agreed on 28 August to resume direct talks with the Germans, but refused Hitler's demand to come to Berlin immediately, a demand similar to that made to the unfortunate Czech foreign minister the year before. Although both official and unofficial talks went on in Berlin right through Thursday, 31 August, time ran out. German troops crossed the border into Poland in the early hours of 1 September 1939, and the German battleship *Schleswig-Holstein* fired on key fortifications around the city of Danzig. Britain and France warned Germany that they would go to war, but said that if the troops were withdrawn they would ignore the fact that fighting had been initiated. Both the British cabinet and the House of Commons were in turmoil. After a stormy session, the cabinet decided to send Germany an ultimatum on Sunday morning, 3 September, demanding that Germany agree by 11:00 a.m. (12:00 p.m. in Berlin) to withdraw its troops or war would be declared. The Germans made no reply. Chamberlain announced on the radio at about 11:15 that, the Germans having not complied with the ultimatum, a state of war then existed. The French followed later in the day. Europe was at war.

Could negotiations in late August or September possibly have worked, or was Hitler determined to conquer Poland by force of arms? Did Hitler believe that Chamberlain and the French would back down and accept the conquest of Poland, as in the end they had over Czechoslovakia, first at Munich and then after the seizure of Prague? Was Chamberlain too naïve and not really competent to handle negotiations in so complex a situation with so unscrupulous a counterpart as Hitler? Although the implications of these questions still shape international affairs, these are issues that continue to vex historians.

At the time people wondered what would happen next. Almost immediately after Chamberlain's announcement the air-raid sirens went off in London, sending everyone scurrying for bomb shelters. This proved to be a false alarm, but the questions remained: Would Germany respond to the declaration of war by bombing London or other cities in Britain? Would Britain and France attack Germany? Would they, or could they, come to the aid of Poland? If there was to be war, where would it start, who would strike the first blow?

For the second summer in a row a war crisis unfolded, leaving governments and private individuals to make their way as best they could. Although the prospect for a satisfactory negotiated settlement of the Polish question waxed and waned, the British government cautiously attempted to put the country on something of a war footing. During the interval since the Czech crisis the previous year, aircraft production was expanded from 240 planes per month in 1938 to 600 per month the following year. Royal Air Force fighter squadrons were increased from six to twenty-six by September 1939. Reserve officers were called into active service beginning in June of 1939, and conscription was legislated—for the first time during peace—to start on 1 July. The regular army and the territorials were increased to make a total of thirty-two divisions. On 9 August the reserve fleet began exercises, and with the passage of the Emergency Powers Defence Bill on 24 August the Royal Navy was put on a war alert. War plans were put into operation in anticipation of the likely outbreak of hostilities and the home fleet stood out to sea west of the Hebrides. With the actual German invasion of Poland on 1 September, roads and train stations were filled with troops and sailors on the move. Evacuation plans were also set in motion, and thousands of mothers and children, carrying cardboard boxes containing gasmasks, were removed from the major cities to what were held to be safer quarters in rural England.[9]

Among the steps taken by the government in late August was the requisition of commercial passenger liners for conversion to troopships and hospital ships. Several of the largest transatlantic liners were taken out of service and sent to shipyards to be refitted to carry enormous numbers of soldiers. This had the effect of causing the cancellation of bookings and the reduction of the number of berths available to those who were attempting to leave Britain and Europe as the war crisis reached its climax. Nations like the United States, which expected to remain neutral in the event of war, began to take precautions. Citizens were urged to return home if their circumstances permitted. In fact, the U.S. embassy had had contingency plans for the evacuation of citizens since at least the Czech crisis of 1938, and it circulated warnings to all the consulates in the United Kingdom as early as 21 March 1939. On 22 August specific public warnings were issued. The consul general in Glasgow reported to the embassy on 31 August that the *Athenia* would sail the next day with a large number of Americans, the freighter *City of Flint* would sail later the same day with about thirty American passengers.[10]

These warnings put additional pressure on the ships remaining in the transatlantic service to take as many passengers as possible. Florence Hargrave, an assistant high school principal, and Jeannette Jordan, a Latin teacher, both of Madison, Wisconsin, had been booked to sail on the SS *California* on 25 August, but the ship had been requisitioned. New arrangements were made by Miss Hargrave with the Donaldson Line and cables were sent off to family in New York: "CALIFORNIA CANCELLED SAILING ATHENIA FRIDAY LAND MONTREAL NEW YORK BY TRAIN HOME AS PLANNED." Miss Hargrave saw the *California,* being repainted in battleship gray, as she sailed down the Clyde out of Glasgow on 1 September. Alexander and Rebecca Park of Philadelphia and their eleven-year-old son Russell had also expected to return on the *California* from their visit to Ireland, but they were able to get last-minute tickets on the *Athenia.*[11] Herbert Spiegelberg, an instructor at Swarthmore College in Pennsylvania and also a German citizen, had similarly been transferred from the SS *Britannic* and sailed with his brother on the *Athenia* from Liverpool on 2 September. Mr. and Mrs. Henry DeWitt Smith were in Britain with their daughter Jeannette and her friend Caroline Stuart, all of Plainfield, New Jersey, and had intended to sail on to South Africa when the threat of war persuaded them to cancel their plans and return to America. "With much difficulty," Smith said, they were able to book cabin-class tickets on the *Athenia* on 28 August and joined the ship in Glasgow four days later.[12] John and Georgina Hayworth and their daughters Margaret and Jacqueline, from Hamilton, Ontario, had visited family in Scotland during the summer. John Hayworth had gone back to Canada early to return to work, but cabled his wife to hurry home as the international crisis deepened. Mrs. Hayworth was able to get a third-class booking on the *Athenia* out of Glasgow. In part prompted by the warning from the American embassy, the actress Judith Evelyn and her fiancé, Andrew Allan, decided to return home also. Allan's work in radio advertising in Europe had been suspended by the war crisis and coincidentally he had been offered a job with the Canadian Broadcasting Corporation at home. Although they had an opportunity to take a third-class passage on the SS *Antonia*, which was sailing in late August, they decided to wait and join Allan's father, the Reverend William Allan, who was booked to return from his visit to family in Scotland on the *Athenia* on 1 September.[13]

Eva Blair of Vancouver, British Columbia, had been in Britain and Northern Ireland on a religious holiday. She had attended the Keswick Conference in England and was visiting family in Bangor, County Down, staying at the Christian Endeavour holiday home, when news broke on Friday, 1 September, that Germany had invaded Poland. Praying for guidance, Miss Blair opened her Bible to Isaiah, chapter 52, and read verse 12: "For ye shall not go out with haste, nor go by flight; for the Lord will go before you; and the God of Israel will be your rereward." This was guidance enough for Miss Blair. Returning to Belfast she found that the Cunard Line, with which she had tickets on the *Queen Mary*, could do nothing for her; however, the representative of the Donaldson Line assured her of a berth on the *Athenia*, which would call in at Belfast that evening. Within an hour she had made arrangements to sail and was packing her bags and saying farewell to her relatives. Rev. Gerald Hutchinson, twenty-five years old and newly ordained as a United Church of Canada minister, had spent July and part of August as a one of several Canadian delegates of the Student Christian Movement at the World Council of Christian Youth meeting in Amsterdam. It had been an exhilarating experience, despite the international tension. However, after a brief visit with relatives in Scotland, he expected to sail for home on 25 August. When he got to Glasgow he found that his ship had been requisitioned but he was able to transfer his booking to the *Athenia*. Bernice Jansen from Red Wing, Minnesota, was a teacher at an Episcopal Mission school, St. Margaret's School, in Sendai, Japan, who was on a furlough and returning to the United States by way of a trip around the world. She had left Japan in June and had got as far as England, where she had reservations to sail for America on the *Scythia*, but when that ship was commandeered by the British government she obtained a third-class booking on the *Athenia* leaving from Liverpool.[14]

Dr. Rudolf Altschul and his wife, Anni, had been traveling across Europe for weeks. Dr. Altschul, who had trained in Paris and Rome, had been a professor of anatomy at the University of Prague when the Nazis invaded Czechoslovakia in March. The German occupation forced the Altschuls to flee, and Dr. Altschul negotiated appointments at both Queen's University Belfast and the University of Saskatchewan. The British Home Office refused to allow Altschul's settlement in Northern Ireland and so Saskatchewan became the choice. However, the process of obtaining a visa to Canada took some time, with the result that for safety's sake Dr. Altschul went to Rome and Anni to Hamburg and Antwerp. They were to have sailed on the Cunard White Star liner *Aurania*, Dr. Altschul joining the ship in Le Havre, France, and his wife in Southhampton. At the point of sailing, the ship was requisitioned by the British government for use as a troopship, leaving the Altschuls in different cities on the continent and unable to communicate with each other because of the international crisis. Nevertheless, relying on luck and intuition, they each made their way to London and were reunited at the National Hotel in Bloomsbury. The following day they were able to book tickets to Canada on the *Athenia*.[15]

Having concluded in the spring that war was not likely to break out, David and Barbara Cass-Beggs had negotiated a leave from the Technical College in

Oxford and a teaching appointment at the University of Toronto for the autumn of 1939. David, an electrical engineer, and Barbara, a musician and music teacher, had rented out their cottage for a year, sold their car, packed up their belongings, and booked tickets to Canada, also on the *Aurania*. However, when they went to pick up the tickets they found that their ship had been requisitioned by the government and they were assigned to the *Athenia*. They were sure the war scare was just a bluff. So, together with their three-year-old daughter, Rosemary, and her new Panda teddy bear, they proceeded to Liverpool to join the ship.

Eight-year-old Ruby Mitchell had spent "two glorious months" in the summer visiting her "darling" grandmother in Aberdeen. She had a wonderful time getting to know her aunts and uncles and cousins. Ruby's widowed mother in Toronto had a full-time job to support the family, so when a neighbor Isobel Calder and her young daughter, Margaret, Ruby's playmate, decided to go to Scotland for the summer, Ruby joined them to spend the holiday with Mrs. Mitchell's mother. They were all to return in mid-August, but the Calders were having such a pleasant visit that the return trip was delayed and passage was booked on the *Athenia*.[16]

Organized groups presented a special problem. Mrs. Annette Brock and Mrs. Gladys Strain ran European tours for college-aged girls. In the summer of 1939 they had led a party of eighteen young women students from the University of Texas, many of them from Houston and all graduates of Hockaday School in Dallas. The girls had paid $897 for the trip and had a wonderful tour, visiting nine countries in two months. They had acquired all sorts of treasures, including Paris dresses and china sets and wedding veils for their trousseaus. However, in late August, following both the warnings from the American embassy and the British government's requisitions of passenger liners, they were confronted with the problem of finding alternative passage for their young women. The girls had been booked to sail on the Anchor Line steamer *California* on 26 August, but the ship was requisitioned. Mrs. Brock got help from several parents in Texas. Burke Baker, the father of Anne Baker and president of the Seaboard Life Insurance Company of Houston, cabled a friend in the American embassy in London. A. D. Simpson, the father of Rowena Simpson and president of the Houston National Bank of Commerce, got in touch with the Chase National Bank of New York and their London office to find spaces on any available ships. He also contacted Jesse H. Jones, a Texas Democrat and chairman of the Reconstruction Finance Corporation in Washington, D.C. Jones may also have put some pressure on the embassy in London to do something for the Texas girls. Ambassador Joseph P. Kennedy certainly did what he could to help. The young women were advised to go to Glasgow, and Rowena "Nino" Simpson cabled her father that they were not worried and would take the next available ship. By 30 August the vice president of the Chase National Bank wired Simpson, "OUR LONDON OFFICE CABLES

THEY CONTACTED YOUR DAUGHTER WHO SAYS DEFINITELY BOOKED ATHENIA WITH SOME OF PARTY OTHERS BOOKED FOR AMERICAN TRADER STOP."[17] Fifteen of the eighteen girls obtained berths on the *Athenia*, while three were given places in the makeshift facilities on the American merchant freighter *City of Flint*. Rowena herself sent her father the reassuring confirmation on Friday morning, 1 September: "SAILING TODAY MONTREAL SHORTLY." Writing later the same day to his son in Schenectady, New York, Simpson said with premature optimism, "This is good news to all of us."[18]

A less formal group were the scientists attending the Seventh International Congress of Genetics in Edinburgh. This conference was particularly ill-starred. It had originally been scheduled to meet in Moscow, but difficulties with the Soviet government caused a shift to Edinburgh. The meeting there coincided with the deterioration of the international crisis. First, German and Dutch participants were called home by their governments, and then when war broke out the citizens of neutral countries were urged to leave as well. Charles Cotterman and Bronson Price were able to obtain passage on the *Athenia*, while six others found space on the merchant vessel the *City of Flint*.[19] Thus many plans were changed in reaction to the war crisis, and the *Athenia*, scheduled to sail from Liverpool for Montreal on 2 September, took on many extra passengers to accommodate the crush of people desperate to leave.

CHAPTER 2

IN ALL RESPECTS READY FOR SEA

Will ye no' come back again?
—TRADITIONAL SCOTTISH SONG[1]

T he *Athenia* began her journey in Glasgow on the morning of Friday, 1 September. Glasgow was the homeport of the Donaldson Line ships and the company had its own berths in the dock area where cargo could be taken on and where the ships could be outfitted for their voyages. It was here that the *Athenia* had come six days before, having completed a trip from Liverpool to Montreal and back. Here the Canadian cargo was unloaded, mostly food stuffs—grain, butter, eggs—but there was aluminium and copper as well, much needed for the manufacture of aircraft and munitions. In Glasgow also a new general cargo of some 880 tons was taken on, 472 tons of which were building bricks, surprisingly. Other items included good granite curling rocks from Scotland for a devoted Canadian winter sports community, as well as textbooks for the Toronto school system. Less weighty, but much more distinctive, were the paintings by the English illustrator Winifred Walker, the official artist for the Royal Horticultural Society, that were intended for her planned book, *Shakespeare's Flowers.*[2] A number of sealed steel boxes were brought on board, giving rise to the speculation that gold was being shipped, but they turned out to contain only new clothes that had been purchased in Europe by tourists, inspected by customs officials, and allowed to pass through Britain duty-free. The provisioning for the trip to Montreal was completed. With the growing demands for more berths on the *Athenia*, the crew was put to work constructing temporary facilities for 200 extra passengers and 41 extra crew. Both the third-class smoking room and the ship's gymnasium were converted to sleeping spaces, and bunks were built wherever space and privacy allowed. This meant that in many cases married couples were split up so that the staterooms could be filled with either men or women. On Friday, 1 September, the ship was moved a short distance to the Princes Dock, and the Board of Trade surveyor inspected the ship, paying particular attention to all of the firefighting and lifesaving equipment. As a demonstration and practice for the crew, all of the upper boats of the double-stacked lifeboats were swung out on their davits and lowered into the water. The ship was prepared to take on passengers and begin her perilous voyage. The *Athenia* was deemed in all respects ready for sea.[3]

———————————————

The TSS *Athenia* was one of the main passenger ships of the Donaldson Atlantic Line, servicing primarily the transatlantic route between Britain and Canada. The *Athenia*, together with her sister ship, the TSS *Letitia*, was built in Scotland in 1922–23 at the Fairfield Shipbuilding and Engineering Company, Ltd. yards at Govan, downriver from Glasgow on the Clyde. Fairfield was a huge shipyard, employing some seven thousand workers and with slip facilities to allow work on fifteen ships at once. The *Athenia* was 526.3 feet long (160.4 meters), with a 66.4-foot beam (20.2 meters), drew 38 feet of water (11.5 meters), and displaced 13,465 tons. She was powered by six steam turbines driving twin screws and was capable of cruising speeds in excess of fifteen knots. Her designation, TSS *Athenia*, identified her as a "Twin-Screw Ship." The ship had watertight bulkheads throughout the vessel with watertight doors that could be sealed by controls on the bridge. This construction created a series of watertight vertical compartments throughout the ship. However, the open boiler rooms and engine rooms, that housed the huge machinery, formed a vulnerable space within the ship below the waterline. Distinguished for its engineering and steam technology, Fairfield had built many of the great Cunard liners. The keel for this ship was laid down in 1922 for Cunard, although the ship was purchased by Donaldson and completed with the help of a loan from the Commercial Bank of Scotland, and went into service in April 1923 at a cost of £1,250,000. She was built along the lines of a Cunard Class "A" vessel and was distinguished by a cruiser stern. The hull was painted black and the upper decks were white, while the single funnel was black with a narrow white stripe, and she carried two large masts, which supported the radio antennas. In short she was a handsome, efficient, modern-looking ship. Ironically an earlier *Athenia*, built in 1904, was sunk by a German submarine, also off the northwest coast of Ireland, in 1917, with a loss of fifteen lives. The *Athenia* typically sailed 2,625 miles (4,224.5 kilometers) from Glasgow, Belfast, and Liverpool to Quebec City and Montreal and back on a twenty-four-day cycle.[4]

Transatlantic passenger liners were really floating hotels. The new *Athenia*, although originally intended mainly for the immigrant trade to Canada, was within that tradition. She was built to carry 516 cabin-class passengers and 1,000 third-class (immigrant) passengers. With a falling off of immigration and the growth of tourism by the late 1920s the ship was refitted in 1933 to carry 314 cabin-class passengers, 310 tourist-class, and 928 third-class. In 1939 the price of a roundtrip tourist-class ticket cost $225. A cabin-class ticket cost significantly more. Thus, the ship became essentially three hotels, with first-class luxury facilities, economy tourist accommodations, and boarding house immigrant fare. Not as well known or as glamorous as the large, fast Cunard White Star passenger liners sailing between Southampton and New York or some of the French and German ships, the *Athenia* was a comfortable vessel with numerous lounges, bars, smoking rooms, writing rooms, a library, and recreational facilities. There was a ladies' hairdresser and manicurist, as well as a men's barber. Both a doctor and a nurse staffed the ship's hospital, and several of the clergymen on board were asked to hold denominational services on Sundays. Musicians would provide afternoon concerts and dinner music and would play for dances in the evening. "Grand Concerts" were held in the evenings in which both passengers and members of the ship's company entertained. Distinguished passengers in the cabin class would be invited to join the "Captain's Table" at dinner. The meals generally were quite elegant and elaborate, with several courses and many choices. Even the tourist-class dinner menu would feature a choice of such items as prime ribs, sirloin of beef, roast leg of pork, or tenderloin of mutton for a main course. In the extravagant tradition of the transatlantic liners, the cream-colored cabin-class dining room was decorated in the Renaissance style, with marble columns, mirrored walls, and a domed ceiling. The *Athenia* was regarded as "a very happy ship," and she was advertised, certainly for her cabin-class passengers, as having "all the comforts of a first class hotel."[5]

The Donaldson Line was one of many small- and medium-sized steamship companies that operated both coastal and transoceanic service in the years before modern airline travel. Originally founded in 1855 by James Donaldson, a successful Glasgow cotton broker who had earlier helped to back Samuel Cunard, the company operated sailing packets from Scotland to South America. By 1878 the firm had established regular steamship service between Glasgow and Quebec and Montreal. In 1916 the company merged with the Anchor Line (partially owned by Cunard) to form the Anchor-Donaldson Line, but in the 1930s the company was reorganized as the Donaldson Atlantic Line. The company also maintained a link with Cunard White Star, which helps to explain how so many of the stranded Cunard passengers were transferred to the *Athenia* in late August 1939. While holding only a small portion of the transatlantic passenger traffic in the 1930s— 2.8 to 4.89 percent compared with the Cunard White Star line, which held between 40.45 to 55.46 percent—the *Athenia* and the *Letitia* enjoyed something of a niche market sailing into Canadian ports and competing primarily with the Canadian Pacific Railway's steamships. Nevertheless, the world economic depression of the 1930s, competition with government-subsidized steamships, and the crisis of the Second World War created financial problems for the company. After the war the company resumed service to Canada and into the Pacific, eventually extending routes into the Great Lakes in the 1950s. However, as the result of the rapid expansion of international airline travel and the costly development of container ships and container terminals, in 1967 the ships of the Donaldson Line were sold and the company closed down.[6]

The officers on the *Athenia* were all Scots and were well-experienced sailors. The ship was commanded by Captain James Cook, who was making his fifteenth trip on the ship as skipper. Cook was from Glasgow, was married and had one son, and had grown up in family that was prominent in the world of professional yachting crews. His father was Captain John Cook, skipper of the *Joel* and the steam yacht *Doris*; his uncle, Captain James Cook, ran the steam yacht *Phalassa*. Captain Cook went to sea himself as a boy of sixteen, working on the boats of Prentice Service & Henderson and Thomas Dunlop. During the Great War he joined the Royal Navy and served as a lieutenant on destroyers and minesweepers until 1919. After the war he joined the Donaldson line, commanding the *Gracia* and the *Salacia*. He was appointed captain of the *Athenia* in April 1938. Captain Cook was a cautious man, well into his middle age, and well aware of his responsibilities for the ship and the lives of those on it. While at sea he stayed close to the navigation bridge, often taking his meals and sleeping in the small chartroom just off the wheelhouse. He was described as a typical sea captain with "steel-blue eyes and very regular, weather-beaten features"—one of the company's best captains and the "personification of reliability." Captain Cook was particularly anxious about the dangers presented by the outbreak of war and the possibility of an attack from German forces. He did think that by getting under way well before the declaration of war the *Athenia* should be out of the danger zone by late afternoon on 3 September.[7]

The chief officer was Barnet Mackenzie Copland. He had served on the *Athenia* even longer than Cook, this being his twenty-first trip. Copland came from Dundee, was thirty-two years old, and was unmarried. He had gone to high school in Stepps, near Glasgow, and to the Royal Technical College in Glasgow, but he went to sea when he was fifteen and was a seasoned sailor. An energetic young Scot with a bright smile, Chief Officer Copland served as Captain Cook's right-hand man. John Emery, from Ayr, was the first officer. He was a tall bachelor engaged to marry a former passenger, a young Canadian. The second officer was K. G. Crockett, a Glasgow man. The third officer was Colin Porteous, also from Glasgow, a young officer of only twenty-eight years who was to have a long career with the Donaldson Line. Emmery, Crockett, and Porteous all joined the ship in 1938. The size of the ship's crew varied with the season and the number of passengers; it ranged from as few as 150 to as many as 285. The deck crew remained at about 63 men and the engine crew at about 29, but the cabin crew serving the hotel function of the ship was varied to meet the current need. When the *Athenia* sailed in September of 1939 with a large number of 1,102 passengers, the cabin crew numbered 220, making a total of 316 in the ship's company.[8] Given the Glasgow origins of the Donaldson Company, the building of the *Athenia* on the Clyde, and the Scottish links of most of the crew, it was not surprising that Glasgow took special pride and interest in the ship. Early on Friday morning members of the crew who had been on leave returned to board the ship, along with some 41 new cabin crew members hired to help with the additional number of passengers. They could begin making beds and putting out linens and generally making the ship's accommodations ready for the arriving passengers. As the morning passed a number of local Glasgow wives came down to the dock in an attempt to persuade their husbands in the crew not to go to sea in circumstances where Britain was likely to go to war with Germany. Feelings were quite mixed as to what might happen, whether Britain would actually go to war, whether the ship would be out of harm's way by the time war broke out, whether Germany would abide by the rules governing submarine warfare. Although members of the crew did make fatalistic remarks, even to the passengers from time to time, very few were convinced to leave the ship that Friday morning.

Ticket-holding passengers and numerous hopefuls had been arriving in Glasgow for several days, filling all of the city's hotels and guesthouses. Holidays were cut short and family visits were ended abruptly. There were desperate attempts at booking offices and travel agencies all over the United Kingdom to make alternative arrangements, and the *Athenia* was one of the alternatives. All of these people, particularly students, tourists, and expatriates, wanted to return to the United States or Canada before the European crisis boiled over into genuine hostilities; and of course in the early hours of that very morning, 1 September, Germany had invaded Poland, thus setting in motion events leading to the Second World War.

Passengers began joining the ship just before 11:00 a.m. People had been in Glasgow for several days in anticipation of getting on the *Athenia*, but the overnight trains from other parts of England and Scotland brought additional numbers. Something of a crisis developed during the morning as taxis in the city were commandeered to facilitate the movement of mothers and children being evacuated from urban centers that were thought to be probable targets for German bombers in the event that war broke out. People had to get to the Princes Dock as best they could. Rev. William Allan, who was returning to Canada because of his wife's illness, had hired a car to take him to Glasgow from rural Scotland, where he had been visiting his eighty-six-year-old mother, and was able to pick up his son Andrew and Judith Evelyn at the station. One bus arrived at the ship loaded with European refugees. Many of these were Jewish, some from Poland and some from Germany. A number wore traditional peasant costumes—such as long skirts and headscarves—and carried their worldly goods in wicker baskets, blanket rolls, and bundles. Some were even barefoot.

But others were well educated and cosmopolitan. Dr. Rudolf Altschul, a neurologist, and his wife, Anni, had fled Prague, taking with them five trunks filled with medical research materials. Dr. Altschul had been educated in Prague, Paris, and Rome and spoke five languages. It was left to Andrew Taylor, the assistant purser, to sort out the confusion of rooms and luggage. In many cases families were split up so that staterooms could be filled with all women or all men. More luggage found its way into the staterooms than could be comfortably accommodated with the large number of people in these quarters. While there were problems and complaints, most people were grateful to have actually got on board and under way before war broke out. Altogether 420 passengers boarded the ship in Glasgow, of which 241 were in third class, or "steerage" although that term was no longer used, and 143 were American citizens.[9]

Just after noon on 1 September, in order to catch the tide, the lines were cast off and the *Athenia* was eased out of Princes Dock by two tugboats and into the narrow confines of the Clyde. Captain Cook yielded control of the ship to the pilot, although he remained on the bridge, and Chief Officer Barnet Copland kept watch on the docking bridge at the stern of the vessel to see that the ship did not stray from the main channel. Even at midday the Clyde was shrouded in a thick fog. As was the custom with departing Donaldson ships, a piper on the dock played the traditional Scottish lament,

> *Will ye no' come back again?*
> *Will ye no' come back again?*
> *Better lo'ed ye canna be,*
> *Will ye no' come back again?*

Meanwhile, nearby shipyard workers taking their lunch break shouted "Cowards!" at the ship leaving Britain on the eve of war, whereas in fact a high proportion of the passengers were American or Canadian tourists or mothers with children who had visited family during the summer. Judith Evelyn remembered hearing the words "What are ye runnin' from?" as she stood at the railings.[10] It was enough to put one on edge.

Once in the Clyde, with one tugboat forward and one aft, the ship slowly worked its way past the SS *Caledonia*, which was being refitted as an armed merchant cruiser and the SS *California*, which was being painted battleship gray, past the Harland & Wolff shipyards, past the John Brown yards, where work was still being done on the enormous new Cunard White Star liner *Queen Elizabeth*, and past the Fairfield yards at Govan where the *Athenia* herself was built in 1923. From the river, Glasgow was a fairly grim industrial town, and its grayness and sooty chimneypots added to a sense of gloom within the ship. Once beyond Greenock the Clyde widened and the lines to the tugs could be cast off and the ship was able to proceed under her own power at an increased speed. Shortly after four o'clock they dropped the pilot near Gourock and Captain Cook resumed command of his ship. Here also work could be seen putting in place a submarine boom in the estuary to protect the shipbuilding and harbor facilities on the Clyde should war come. As the ship gathered speed, the first of several lifeboat drills was organized, a reminder of the perils of the sea. All of the passengers were instructed about putting on their lifejackets and were called to their assigned lifeboat stations, and the boarding procedure was explained to them. On this leg of the trip there remained only the narrow passages around Great Cumbrae and Little Cumbrae and the ship would be in the open waters of the Firth of Clyde and the North Channel.[11]

Shortly after eight in the evening, under broken clouds and a southerly breeze, the *Athenia* steamed into Belfast Lough, in Northern Ireland, anchoring off Black Head. This was well out from the city and docks of Belfast and beyond Carrickfergus. There she was met by a tender and took on another 136 passengers, of whom 65 were U.S. citizens. George Calder of Long Island City, New York, watched from the deck as the passengers and their baggage came aboard, including the anxious and devout Eva Blair, praying to get back to her family in North Vancouver, and the young and hopeful Ernest Smith, bound for the Princeton Theological Seminary. Twenty-eight-year-old Father Joseph V. O'Connor and his father, Charles O'Connor, climbed on board the ship also. Father O'Connor, an Oblate priest and a recent graduate of Catholic University of America, had been ordained earlier in the year in Wilmington, Delaware, by Cardinal Dennis Dougherty, and he and his father had gone to visit family in County Tyrone. Alexander and Rebecca Park from Philadelphia had crossed to Ireland on the *Transylvania* with Father O'Connor and were pleased to see him again when they joined the *Athenia* off Belfast. Their son Russell noticed that the ship looked somewhat ominous, completely blacked out, although he associated steamers with lights and celebrations.[12] The Belfast passengers brought the day's newspapers with glaring headlines describing Germany's invasion of Poland. War seemed much closer. By ten o'clock all the new passengers were on board and the anchor weighed. Chief Officer Copland inspected the ship for the night, checking to see that all lights were blocked from view and all doors and hatches closed. Another nine hours' sailing would bring the ship into Liverpool by seven o'clock in the morning of 2 September.

Dawn broke gray and overcast on Saturday as the *Athenia* entered the Mersey estuary, picking up a pilot and threading her way through the channel markers into Liverpool. Captain Cook anchored the ship in the river, rather than bringing her up to the pier, in order to facilitate a faster departure when loaded with the remaining passengers and cargo. Before noon Captain Cook went ashore to confer in the Royal Liver Building with Naval Control about the sailing procedures to be employed with the prospect of war looming. Merchant vessels were now sailing under the authority of the Admiralty and many new sailing regulations had been put in force since 25 and 26 August. The most important of these were that ships must exercise antisubmarine procedures by pursuing a zigzag course and travel with their lights darkened at night. Passenger ships were also instructed to sail north of the usual trade routes to avoid possible waiting submarines or surface vessels. There was speculation that Captain Cook had demanded an escort for the ship, although there is no evidence that this was considered. Passenger George Calder, for one, worried whether the *Athenia* would even be allowed to sail, but Patricia Hale was assured by a crewmember that the ship was going—he had a date with a girl in Montreal.[13] The captain returned to the ship by four o'clock in the afternoon.

In the meantime the ship began taking on cargo as the tender *Skirmisher* came alongside. Passengers watched fascinated as a large number of automobiles were winched up from the tender by the ship's derricks and placed in the hold. Vast cargo nets full of luggage were similarly hoisted from the tender and, as the hold space was gradually filled, placed on the deck. The remaining passengers began joining the ship at about one o'clock. They too came out from the pier on the *Skirmisher* and climbed on board by the gangway lowered over the side. The decks were quickly crowded with suitcases and trunks, creating a tangle for both passengers and crew—the purser undertaking to settle people in their quarters and the boatswain attempting to see that the luggage got to the right place. The new passengers numbered 546, of whom 101 were American citizens. The ship now carried a total of 1,102 passengers, rather more than usual but not beyond her capacity. Together with the 316 crew members, there were 1,418 on board. Of the passengers, 469 were Canadian citizens, 311 were Americans, 172 were either British subjects or Irish citizens, and 150 were European refugees, most of whom were Jewish and 34 of whom carried German passports. Now there was a sense of some overcrowding. All staterooms were shared, and many rooms that had been intended for two people now had four. Husbands and wives, such as the Cass-Beggs from Oxford were separated, David to one side of the ship in a cabin with a man and his two sons, and Barbara and Rosemary to the other side with a mother and her infant son. Temporary facilities in the lounges were also filled. Donald Wilcox, a boy of fourteen returning to Montreal with his mother, remembered a lot of confusion and having to stand in a queue to be assigned accommodations. The Donaldson firm circulated a letter to each passenger stating that, "in view of the present emergency and the many urgent appeals made to us, the *Athenia* is carrying more passengers than usual on this voyage." The steamship company said that it would do its best to serve all of the passengers and their needs, but asked that people be understanding and appreciate the exceptional circumstances. This was an admission that would later give rise to accusations.[14]

Liverpool, even more than Glasgow, betrayed the approach of war. Many of the passengers heading for the *Athenia* had found the train windows blacked out and the carriages packed with soldiers and sailors being sent to their assignments. Mothers and children were being evacuated from urban centers also. As many as three million people left London alone in the first week of September. Thus trains were crowded and it became impossible to find seats. Most of the northbound passengers for Liverpool passed through, or had to change trains at, the large rail junction at Crew, which was packed. Dorothy Dean, returning to Canada with her mother after a visit in England with family, was kept awake in her hotel room by the sound of soldiers marching in the streets below. Hotels across the city were filled, and many people simply spent the night in the train station. The Saturday Liverpool newspapers printed bold headlines announcing the German invasion of Poland. When passengers managed to get on board ship it was possible to look back at the city and see the large, strange-looking barrage balloons, intended to force enemy bombers so high as to interfere with their accuracy, floating over the skyline. Eva Blair said the balloons "emphasized the grim proximity of war," and for her, Liverpool "resembled a city of the dead."[15]

The *Athenia* weighed anchor at 4:30 on Saturday afternoon, 2 September, and started down the River Mersey for the Irish Sea. Even before the ship had left the Mersey estuary another lifeboat drill was called. The pilot was dropped at the Bar Light and Captain Cook resumed command of the *Athenia*, and by six o'clock the ship was into the Irish Sea. Passengers began going to dinner. Barbara Bailey complained to her table companion, Chief Radio Officer David Don, that the ship was crowded; he replied flippantly, "Don't worry, there'll be a lifebelt for you."[16] As the sun went down the portholes were shut, the exterior lights on the ship were closed down or shut off, and no one was allowed to smoke on deck. By about nine o'clock the vessel cleared "The Chickens," the lighthouse at the southernmost point of the Isle of Man and could steer a course north by northwest into the North Channel, now through increasing rain squalls and heavier swells. The motion of the ship was enough to make some people seasick and perhaps contributed to the serious fall of Mrs. Rose Griffin of Toronto. She had just finished dinner and missed her step on the stairway of the dining room and landed on her face so hard that she broke her nose and was knocked unconscious. Chief Officer Copland helped carry her to the ship's hospital ward, where she was looked after by the ship's doctor, Albert Sharman of Glasgow, and nurse A. D. Weir. The North Channel took the *Athenia* up past the Mull of Galloway and the Firth of Clyde, once again, and past the Mull of Kintyre on the coast of Scotland to starboard, and past Belfast Lough and the Antrim Coast of Northern Ireland to port. The *Athenia*, making a speed of over fifteen knots, then edged out into the Atlantic, northwest along the coast of Ireland, clearing Inishtrahull Island off Malin Head, County Donegal, at about 3:40 in the morning 3 September 1939.[17]

Sunday dawned cloudy and cool. There was a mild breeze, but the four- to six-foot swells and occasional whitecaps meant that quite a number of people stayed in bed with seasickness. The *Athenia* seemed likely to make safe her passage to North America. Something of a normal shipboard life began to appear. The Reverend Dr. G. P. Woollcombe, the headmaster of Ashbury College in Ottawa, Ontario, had been appointed the shipboard chaplain for the voyage as he returned to Canada. At 7:30 in the morning he held Holy Communion for nineteen communicants and at 10:30 a regular Church of England service for about two hundred people in the tourist lounge. He preached his sermon on the text of Psalm 93:5, "The waves of the sea are mighty, and rage horribly, but yet the Lord, who dwells on high, is mightier," which Miss Blair said held the congregation in "respectful attention." One of the hymns was appropriately, "Eternal Father strong to save, whose arm doth bind the restless wave, Oh hear us when we pray to Thee, for those in peril on the sea," which reinforced the sense of danger. Mary Louise Kelly of New York said she could never hear that hymn again without thinking of the *Athenia*. Father Joseph V. O'Connor held Holy Mass for at least thirty Catholic passengers on both Saturday evening and Sunday morning. After the services a third lifeboat drill was called. Andrew Allan thought his fellow passengers put on their lifejackets and went through the drill "more devotedly than is usual in such cases."[18]

Not long after eleven o'clock the ship's Second Radio Officer Donald McRae picked up the broadcast, by way of Valentia Island radio station in Ireland, of Prime Minister Neville Chamberlain announcing that Germany had not complied with the British ultimatum and that therefore war now existed between Germany and Great Britain. McRae informed Captain Cook immediately. Passengers, like young James Goodson, in several lounges also heard the broadcast from the public radios there. Under the captain's orders a typed announcement was put up by the purser's office stating that Britain had declared war on Germany. Not long afterward the text of Chamberlain's speech to the nation was added. News traveled quickly around the ship, with many people reduced to tears by fear and anxiety. Judith Evelyn was stopped on deck by a woman who grasped her arm and asked, "Have you heard? War has been declared." A steward explained to Mrs. Wilson Levering Smith of Baltimore County, Maryland, that the excessive heat about which she complained was the result of the engines making "top speed to get us past the danger zone." Barbara Bailey, who was going to Canada to look after her brother's infant girl, was also distraught by having broken up with her long-time boyfriend. It was all too much. She broke down over lunch, and the later boasting by a German woman on deck did not help.[19]

Captain Cook called a meeting of his senior officers after being handed the news that war had been declared. It was decided that the news of war should be officially posted, but that every effort should be made to reassure the passengers and put them at ease. "The important thing, of course," the captain said, "is not to alarm the passengers."[20] However, all of the safety equipment, fire extinguishers, lifesaving equipment, and watertight doors were to be inspected and checked. The lifeboats particularly were to be made ready for possible use. The covers were to be taken off, supplies and provisions placed in the boats, and all of the drain plugs were to be put in place. After the meeting broke up all of the deckhands were called out to work on the lifeboats. By one o'clock in the afternoon the boats had been made ready for use, and one boat on each side of the ship had been swung out on its davits, ready to be lowered into the sea in an instant. Passengers out walking the decks saw the preparations of the lifeboats as a sign that trouble was expected. Reverend Woollcombe thought it was merely a precaution; after all, the ship had sailed before the declaration of war and was not carrying contraband. Judith Evelyn was not so sure, however, and her fiancé, Andrew Allan, speculated as to what it might be like to be at sea in one of the boats.[21]

The afternoon unfolded undramatically. Lunch was served. Deck games were played. Parents, mothers mostly, sat with their children on deck or took them for walks around the ship. Children sang popular songs, such as "South of the Border, Down Mexico Way." Russell Park was told to put on his oldest clothes—knickerbockers, a sweater, and sneakers—so that he could freely explore the ship. The sky clouded over and the wind, out of the south, picked up a bit, but many people still walked along the decks and watched the sea as the ship surged westward. Many of those who were still seasick stayed in their beds, some attempting to read. Frank Connolly, a mechanic from New York, was looking after his three seasick young boys in their cabin. A stewardess gave Eva Blair a tour of the third-class quarters and the temporary sleeping quarters that had been put together for this voyage. With a bit of forethought, Patricia Hale and her friend Margaret Patch, two recent McGill University graduates, laid out some warm clothes and put them in small packsacks. They then went through their own drill of getting from the deck down to their cabin to fetch them, timing themselves in the process. "We weren't taking any chances," Hale said later; but as for the ship being attacked, "we never thought it really would happen." Douglas Stewart, a manager of a branch of the Bank of Montreal in Montreal, and his wife decided in view of the captain's worried look to take some precautions. Before going down for dinner, Stewart placed their passports, all of their banknotes and money orders, and his wife's old jewelry in his vest pocket. They also set out their lifejackets and a throw rug, and they intended to pack a small handbag after dinner just in case.[22]

Seats were assigned for dinner, although it being Sunday, formal dress was not expected, even for the cabin-class dining room. Nevertheless, for the first sitting Barbara Bailey changed into her deep red dinner dress and put on her brown leather shoes that matched her handbag. Mrs. Kate Ellen Hinds, a house-wife from Houston, Texas, was also getting dressed for dinner in her cabin on C Deck. Lobster and cold salmon were served, among other delicious entrees. Margaret McPherson, a housewife from White Plains, New York, went to the first dinner sitting and after walked the deck with her three children. W. Ralph Singleton of Hamden, Connecticut, also finished dinner and went up the stairs to read the announcements on the wall near the purser's office. George Calder quickly finished his meal in order to look after his seasick wife in her cabin. H. DeWitt Smith, a New York stockbroker, arranged for tea and sandwiches to be served in an enclosed section of the promenade deck for his wife, his daugh-ter, and his daughter's friend. Ellen Hutchinson, a housewife from Cambridge, Massachusetts, was waiting to go to dinner in the third-class dining room.[23]

Captain Cook joined the captain's table at a little after seven o'clock. On his way to dinner Captain Cook talked with Gustav A. Anderson, a Chicago passenger who had taken the *Athenia* on earlier trips. "It's bad now," he told Anderson. "I have hardly left the bridge since Liverpool. See me in three or four days," he said. Even so, the captain hoped that by about three that afternoon the ship would be far enough west to be out of any danger zone around the British Isles, so he allowed himself the luxury of joining his passengers. At his table were Sir Robert Stuart Lake, the former member of parliament in Canada and for-mer lieutenant governor of Saskatchewan, and Lady Dorothy Lake. The British actress on her way to Hollywood, Pax Walker-Fryette, asked whether there was any likelihood that they would be attacked. She was assured by a veteran of the Great War that the ship was in greater danger when it came back across the Atlantic loaded with supplies. The New York rare book collector and literary fig-ure Montgomery Evans completed his lobster and had just got a bottle of wine. Dr. Charles Wharton Stork, an English professor at Harcun Junior College in Vermont, Pennsylvania, and distinguished scholar in Scandinavian and German literature, was enjoying his meal in the main dining saloon and was just order-ing desert.[24]

After the first sitting a number of young people gathered in one of the lounges, and when someone sat down at the piano and began to play, everyone joined in singing. James Goodson remembered that the international character of the passengers was reflected in the songs. "My Old Kentucky Home," "Land of Hope and Glory," "Scotland the Brave," "Men of Harlech," "Danny Boy," and many more. One young boy about Goodson's age stood out, singing in a clear tenor voice all of the sentimental old songs about home and love and going far away. It brought tears to many eyes.[25]

The third officer, Colin Porteous, was the officer of the watch in command on the bridge. Assisting him were two quartermasters, the boatswain, and six able-bodied seamen. Seaman M. Mackinnon was the lookout in the crow's nest on the foremast. The order had been given to darken ship and the boatswain had switched on the dimmed running lights and checked that no other lights were visible. The weather was clear, with moderate swells of four to six feet and a steady breeze out of the south. The sun was low in the western sky and it would soon be dark. Although a moon was due to rise, the night sky would give the *Athenia* seven to eight hours of darkness—a perfect cover for the ship to make between 105 and 112 miles before daylight came once again. The *Athenia* was at a position approximately latitude 56° 42′ North latitude, 14° 05′ West longitude, or 250 miles west of Inishtrahull Island and 60 miles southwest of Rockall Bank, an isolated rock formation in the sea—well out into the Atlantic and well on the way to being clear of Europe and the war that gripped it.[26]

CHAPTER 3

SURFACE SHIP SIGHTED

Open hostilities against England immediately.
—ORDERS TO GERMAN SUBMARINES, 3 SEPTEMBER 1939[1]

T
he British declaration of war on Germany did not come as a surprise to the *Kriegsmarine*, the German navy. Fourteen German *unterseeboots*, or U-boats, had put to sea from Wilhelmshaven on 19 August, and five more left before the end of the month. Their mission was to be on station in the Atlantic and the waters around the British Isles if a general war broke out when Germany invaded Poland on 1 September. Among these nineteen vessels was the *U-30*, commanded by *Oberleutnant* Fritz-Julius Lemp, which sailed on 22 August. Born in Tsingtau, China, in 1913, Lemp was the son of an army officer, so his military career was in the family tradition. He had joined the navy in 1931 at eighteen and had advanced very quickly, praised by his superiors and admired by his men, receiving command of the *U-30* in November of 1938 at a very young age. Lemp was an eager and aggressive young officer who had a spectacular, although clouded, career.[2]

The *U-30* was a Type VII submarine, the workhorse of the early U-boat war, built in 1936. She was 206.75 feet long (63 meters), 19 feet wide (5.8 meters), and weighed 500 tons, the kind of vessel that was often described as a steel cigar. The ship was powered by two 1,160-horsepower diesel engines while on the surface and two battery-powered electric motors generating 375 horsepower while submerged. She was capable of speeds of about 16.5 knots on the surface and 8 knots under water. The *U-30* carried ten 23.5-foot-long torpedoes (6.2 meters) of two types, an older compressed air–powered torpedo with either impact or magnetic firing mechanisms, or pistols, and a new battery-powered torpedo, which showed no wake of bubbles on the surface, with magnetic pistols. While these torpedoes and their firing mechanisms were not completely reliable, they carried a warhead of 616 pounds of explosives and were extremely destructive if they worked. The ship had four torpedo tubes in the bow and one in the stern. On deck she had a fast-firing 3.5-inch gun and on the conning tower an oerlikon antiaircraft gun and several machine guns. The Type VII submarine had a crew of four officers and forty men. They lived and worked in incredible conditions, crammed in among the ship's machinery, torpedoes, and food supplies for the voyage, with almost no personal space and absolutely no privacy. The ship was almost always cold and damp, the stale air was heavy with engine smells and personal odors, and the boat's motion, while surfaced, was violent because the vessel was tossed by North Atlantic seas. Despite all of these discomforts, the crew ate reasonably well and regarded themselves as the elite force in the German navy.[3]

The *U-30* was one of six submarines which formed the *Salzwedel* Flotilla stationed in a sweeping arc around the west side of the British Isles. Their purpose, in the event of war, was to attack ships of the Royal Navy, troop transports, and military craft under escort. Lemp took his U-boat north from Wilhelmshaven along the coast of Denmark and Norway almost to the Arctic Circle and then out into the Atlantic beyond the Faeroe Islands before heading south of the Rockall Bank to a sector about 280 miles west of Scotland, or 250 miles northwest of Ireland. Much of this travel was to be done at night on the surface, while during the day the craft moved underwater to avoid detection. During this time radio messages from naval headquarters kept all the submarines informed of the Nazi-Soviet Pact, the failure of talks about Poland, and the invasion of Poland by Germany on 1 September. On 3 September Lemp kept his boat on the surface, now searching for British shipping. News came just before twelve noon of the British declaration of war, but orders to commence hostilities were still needed. In the meantime the Norwegian freighter SS *Knute Nelson* was seen and had also observed the submarine on the surface and moving fast. Several coded radio instructions from naval headquarters in Germany were received in short order. The first, at about two o'clock in the afternoon, instructed "U-boats to make war on merchant shipping in accordance with operations order," meaning the rules and conditions under which submarines could and could not attack and sink merchant vessels. The second came about an hour later and authorized the submarines to "open hostilities against England immediately. Do not wait to be attacked first," although the submarine commanders were also warned to not yet attack French ships. These were orders to attack British shipping, although under the rules of warfare to which Germany had agreed. However, prior to sailing Grand Admiral Karl Dönitz, U-boat commander in chief, gave verbal instructions to his submarine captains that they should be particularly alert to the probability that the British would use armed merchant cruisers, that is, fast merchant vessels such as passenger liners, armed with 4- to 5-inch guns, sent to patrol the waters around the British Isles.[4] Thus, while hostilities were to begin, there were numerous and complicated conditions that were intended to restrict or limit submarine warfare, but which also sent a mixed message.

Apart from the *Knute Nelson*, Lemp had seen no other ships on 3 September, until by midafternoon, about three thirty, he made out first the smoke and then the shape of a second vessel on the horizon, heading on a northwesterly course. This ship appeared quite large and was moving fast although in an antisubmarine, zigzag pattern. The vessel was on the starboard side of the *U-30* and both to the north and east, but by anticipating the ship's course and moving at full speed on the surface, the submarine could expect to intersect with her in just over three hours. By seven o'clock the sun was just going down and in the gathering dusk Lemp brought the *U-30,* now submerged, to a position close enough to view the approaching ship through the powerful magnification of the Zeiss lenses of his periscope. What he saw was a large ship with a high superstructure, running without lights in a zigzag pattern at a speed of about fifteen knots and well north of the usual trade routes. Lemp's conclusion was that this was a British armed merchant cruiser probably on a patrol west of the British Isles, just as Admiral Dönitz had predicted. Lemp brought the *U-30* to battle stations and maneuvered the submarine into an attack position. The distances, angles, and speeds were entered into the fire control instruments to derive the accurate settings for the torpedoes.

At 7:40 p.m., when the ship was about 1,600 yards away (1,472 meters), Lemp fired two torpedoes at the ship. One torpedo struck the ship on the port side and exploded. *Oberleutnant* Lemp in the *U-30* had fired the first shot in the Second World War in the West and had begun the Battle of the Atlantic, barely eight and three quarter hours after the declaration of war. Just before the moment of impact, the lookout in the crow's nest of the *Athenia,* seaman M. Mackinnon called out and pointed to the water on the port side of the ship. Several passengers on deck looked into the water and could see the streak of bubbles in the ocean surface—"a white kind of ripple on the water," remembered Mrs. Hugh McDonald. One young man saw "a pipe" upright in the ocean some distance away, but for most people on the ship, including those on the bridge, there was no warning. The U-boat detected the second torpedo running in an erratic course; it missed the target and was in danger of circling back and striking the *U-30.* Lemp took the submarine down to greater depth until the running time of the torpedo had expired. He then brought the *U-30* back up to the surface, about a half hour after the initial attack, to have a look at the stricken ship now less than a half mile away. One of the crew members, Adolph Schmidt, witnessed the event from the bridge and later recalled, "I have seen the ship with my very eyes, but . . . I do not think that the ship could see our U-boat at that time because of the position of the moon."[5] Lemp had positioned the U-boat on the east side of the ship with the hope of avoiding detection, but with the moon up about ten degrees in the sky numerous people on the ship said they clearly saw the submarine. H. DeWitt Smith, the New York lawyer, saw the U-boat about 300 yards away in the "bright moonlight," as did John Cobb Coullie of Chicago: "I saw a submarine clear above the water about a quarter of a mile off, as near as I could judge." Mrs. Isobel Bruce from Montvallo, Alabama, identified "the conning tower and part of the deck of a submarine at a distance of less than a mile from the *Athenia*." "Looking out to the port side, I saw the submarine breaking the surface," observed Duncan F. M. Stewart of Glencoe, Scotland. Douglas Stewart of Montreal said that the submarine was visible when he reached his lifeboat station and that it fired two shells, one hitting a mast and the second hitting the *Athenia* on the port side on the waterline.[6]

The *Athenia* did not appear to be sinking, so Lemp fired two more torpedoes. One torpedo got away but failed to hit the ship, the second did not leave the torpedo tube. Lemp took the *U-30* down deep to try to dislodge the malfunctioning torpedo under greater compressed air pressure. This did not work, although it released a large bubble of air that boiled over on the surface, and only on a second attempt was the torpedo ejected from the boat. Many of the *Athenia* survivors in lifeboats observed a turbulence or vibrations or swishing in the water, one person in a lifeboat likening the sensation to that of an earthquake in the water, the cause of which might have been either the submarine itself or a runaway torpedo passing beneath the lifeboats or the large air bubble. In any case, the sight of a periscope, often described as a stick moving through the water, was also reported by numerous people. Did the *U-30* also fire its deck gun at the *Athenia*? Neither the submarine's records nor the surviving crewmembers mention firing the deck gun, but numerous survivors of the *Athenia* claim to have seen a gun flash from the submarine and heard a shell hit the mast of the ship with the probable intention of disabling the radio antennae.[7]

At this point Lemp brought the submarine closer to what was by now a clearly sinking ship, dead in the water and down at the stern. In a moment of triumph and excitement at sinking the first Allied ship in the war, he brought several members of the crew to view the vessel through the periscope. However, he also saw people getting into the lifeboats that were being put over the side of the now brightly illuminated ship. Somewhat anxiously, Lemp climbed down to the radio room from the control tower where he been looking through the periscope. Radio operator Georg Högel remembered that the captain consulted the *Lloyds Register of Ships* and found that the TSS *Athenia* bore a close resemblance to the vessel he had attacked. "He was, of course, shocked." Högel also told him that he was receiving on the shipping frequency uncoded distress signals from the *Athenia* stating that it had been torpedoed and was sinking. Instead of an armed merchant cruiser or a troopship, Lemp had sunk a civilian passenger liner, contrary to both Hitler's order and international law. "What a mess," Lemp said to his gunnery officer, *Leutnant* Hans Peter Hinsch, and asked the rhetorical question "But why, why, was she blacked out," as he clearly thought a warship would be.[8]

Oberleutnant Lemp had fired the first shot, but for Germany he had got the war off on something of the wrong foot. In this respect the submarine was itself a troublesome weapon. While the use of submersible craft is part of the history of the American Revolution and the American Civil War, and in one form or another can even be traced back to ancient times, the modern submarine emerged as a formidable weapon during the First World War. However, the focus of naval theorists in the early twentieth century was not on submarines but on the decisive engagement of battle fleets led by early dreadnoughts or battleships. In this respect, the Royal Navy had an overwhelming superiority. The naval building race between Britain and Germany prior to the First World War had not changed the fact that the Royal Navy retained the predominant surface fleet. A variety of circumstances kept the British and German fleets from meeting on the high seas, other than at the Battle of Jutland and that proved inconclusive. What was conclusive was that despite Britain's losses at Jutland, it still was the dominant surface force. The result of this apparent stalemate was that the submarine gradually evolved from its intended role in defense of port facilities and in scouting and screening for the fleet, to emerge as an attack weapon. However, Germany's initial submarine operations in August 1914 were not very promising. One U-boat was sunk in a minefield and a second attempted to attack three British battleships but missed and was later rammed and sunk by a cruiser. Nevertheless on 5 September 1914 the HMS *Pathfinder*, a light cruiser, was sunk and just over two weeks later, on 22 September, the armored cruisers HMS *Aboukir*, *Hogue*, and *Cressy* were all sunk by one U-boat. The submarine had effectively demonstrated its offensive potential. Roughly a month later, on 20 October, the *U-17* sunk the British merchant ship *Giltra*, after allowing the crew to abandon ship in accord with the existing rules of naval warfare. Indeed the submarine emerged as an even more effective offensive weapon when directed against merchant vessels.[9]

To exploit the potential of this weapon, and in retaliation for the British blockade of German maritime trade, Kaiser Wilhelm's government declared in February 1915 the seas surrounding Britain to be a "war zone" in which merchant vessels would be sunk on sight. In fact the submarine blockade was expected to end the war quickly by starving Britain of food and supplies. The sinking of ships on sight and without warning, "unrestricted submarine warfare," was contrary to the procedures of search and seizure that had been customary international law since the early nineteenth century. These were procedures in which merchant ships and their papers were inspected by naval officers from surface ships to determine whether the vessels were neutral or belligerent and whether they carried any contraband goods (or war materials), in which case the ships were brought into port and their fate determined by a prize court. This form of warfare against the merchant commerce of an enemy nation was known as *guerre de course* and had been a legitimate form of hostilities in the nineteenth century. However, the likelihood of armed belligerent merchant vessels attacking the submarines, and the very fragility of the submarines themselves, made the procedures impractical and dangerous. The number of merchant vessels sunk by U-boats, including a well-marked ship intended for Belgian relief, rose dramatically in the first half of 1915. Both the American government and the American public reacted in horror at the ruthlessness of sinking freighters and passenger liners with no provisions for the civilian crews and passengers. The first American civilian killed in the First World War—Leon C. Thrasher, a mining engineer returning to West Africa on the British liner *Falaba* when it was sunk by the *U-28* in the St. George's Channel on 28 March 1915—prompted a protest from the U.S. government. However, outrage and indignation reached a high point when the Cunard liner *Lusitania* was sunk by the *U-20* off the Irish coast on 7 May with the loss of 1,198 people, 128 of them American citizens. President Woodrow Wilson declared that the United States would hold Germany to "strict accountability" for similar sinking in the future. A break in diplomatic relations, if not war, seemed a possibility. Germany reacted by halting attacks on passenger liners in June and by September 1915 ending unrestricted submarine warfare in British waters.[10]

The submarine, however, had proved to be so effective in sinking merchant vessels that when the land war reached a stalemate in the course of 1916, the German government decided by January of 1917 to disregard the possibility of American entry into the war by waging an all-out U-boat blockade of Britain in the expectation of forcing her out of the war before the United States could influence the conflict. German U-boats did indeed do frightful damage to the ships bringing foodstuffs and war material to Britain during the winter and spring of 1917. The United States broke diplomatic relations with Germany in February and, after American ships were sunk, declared war on Germany on 7 April 1917. During April alone 860,000 tons of shipping were sunk, but by May the first convoys were formed and now merchant ships were protected by both U.S. Navy and Royal Navy destroyers. U-boats continued to sink ships right up to the Armistice in 1918, but the submarine blockade failed to bring England to its knees. Moreover the submarine campaign also brought the United States into the war at a decisive moment with all its economic and industrial strength and manpower potential. In short, the submarine could be seen as both one of the most innovative weapons of the First World War and also as one of the direct causes of Germany's defeat.[11]

The potential of the submarine was recognized only with reluctance, criticism, and outrage in military, legal, and political circles. From the early years of the First World War, through the disarmament conferences of the 1920s and 1930s, and right into the Second World War, controversy raged about the practicality, legality, and morality of the submarine. The sinking of unarmed merchant ships was really a new form of piracy, some said, although committed by the uniformed servants of the state. Many people had urged that it be abolished, while some argued that the vessel was just another naval weapon and its use merely needed to be defined and controlled. Actually treaty agreements in the 1930s worked out a set of rules under which submarines might engage both naval and merchant ships. As for Germany, the Versailles Treaty specifically prohibited the German navy from having any submarines.

Throughout most of the first half of the twentieth century the naval profession continued to regard the heavily armored, large-gun battleship as the ultimate weapon. "The big gun was, however, still regarded as the principal arbiter in naval warfare," British naval historian Captain Stephen W. Roskill concluded in his commentary on the interwar years. The tremendous firepower of the battleship, supported by cruisers and escort ships, gave decisive force to the concept of the battle fleet, as described by the American naval theorist Capt. Alfred Thayer Mahan. This was an idea that shaped the thinking of professional sailors and naval strategists until the middle of the Second World War. The submarine, by contrast, was seen by many naval officers as an unreliable, dangerous technological innovation that might at best have a role in coastal and harbor defense or in scouting in advance of the fleet. Its offensive capabilities were largely downgraded—despite the fact that the submarine almost brought Britain to her knees in 1917 by an all-out attack on merchant ships—until convoys were instituted and the United States entered the war and contributed its ships to combating the U-boat threat. In the years after the First World War German naval officers turned again to the concept of the "capital ship," first with the building of "pocket battleships," really super cruisers armed with six 11-inch guns (like the *Admiral Graf Spee*), and eventually the constructing of proper battleships, with eight 15-inch guns (like the *Bismarck*). The German navy had been led by Hitler to believe that it need not expect to go to war with Britain until the mid-1940s, by which time a sufficient number of battleships would be built to challenge those of Great Britain. The result was that in 1939 the German navy was less well equipped with a surface fleet that it had been in 1914. It really had only two battleships, two battle cruisers, and three pocket battleships. The British navy, by contrast, had thirteen battleships and three battle cruisers and several more under construction. Thus as a result of having expended considerable resources on a limited number of capital ships, Germany went to war in 1939, as she had in 1914, with a relatively small number of submarines. In fact in the summer of 1939 Germany had fifty-two U-boats, only thirty-nine of which were capable of offensive operations and a mere twenty-five that could be used on the North Atlantic.[12]

The legal issues surrounding the submarine were very elaborate. Attempts to make the submarine illegal failed at the Second Hague Peace Conference in 1907 and later. The leaders of countries that were not in the race to build battleship fleets saw that the submarine was a very effective weapon and a very inexpensive weapon—at least, compared with a battleship. So in the Versailles

Peace Treaty in 1919 and the Washington Naval Treaty of 6 February 1922, the submarine was recognized to have the status of a legal weapon of war. However, the tremendous loss of largely civilian life and property that resulted from the German submarine campaign in the First World War by the indiscriminate sinking of passenger ships and unarmed merchant vessels demanded that some restrictions be placed on the possible use of the submarine in wartime. The 1922 Treaty in Relation to the Use of Submarines and Noxious Gases included the provision that submarines could legally stop merchant vessels on the high seas only by using the customary international law procedures of visit, search, and seizure, and that failure to follow those procedures, whether on the orders of the submarine's government or not, would render the crew subject to prosecution "for an act of piracy." In 1930 the major powers negotiated the London Naval Treaty, Article 22 of which, among other things, declared that submarines were entitled to sink without warning warships, troopships, ships sailing in a protective convoy, and ships taking part in belligerent actions. On the other hand, restrictions specified that submarine commanders visit and inspect merchant ships suspected of carrying contraband cargoes. Even if contraband were found, the submarine "may not sink or render incapable of navigation a merchant vessel without having first placed passengers, crew, and ship's papers in a place of safety"; and safety here meant not simply placing people in lifeboats unless those boats were within a half hour from shore. In practical terms, because of the vulnerability of the U-boat while surfaced and stopped, complying with these rules made it almost impossible for a submarine to engage a merchant vessel. The Anglo-German Naval Treaty of 18 June 1935 agreed to German capital ships built to a ratio of 35 percent of the British fleet and also permitted the German acquisition of submarines. Germany subsequently signed the London Treaty on 6 November 1936, including Article 22, referred to as the "Submarine Protocol," and therefore was thereby bound by its restrictions.[13]

Politically the submarine was also a very real problem. During the First World War the German use of the submarine to sink merchant vessels and particularly passenger ships reinforced the image of the Germans as barbaric Huns. The numerous passenger liners and ferryboats that were attacked—the *Falaba*, *Lusitania*, *Arabic*, *Sussex*—were a public relations disaster for Germany. The deaths of so many civilians, completely unrelated to the war, generated so much indignation and disgust that Germany never really recovered from it. President Wilson sent Germany a virtual ultimatum to cease its attacks on unarmed merchant vessels or the United States would hold Germany "to strict accountability." What this demand actually meant was unclear. However, when the German High Command decided to resume unrestricted submarine warfare in 1917, in a desperate bid to end the war by isolating and starving the British Isles in a matter of weeks, Wilson had very little option but to declare war on Germany, especially after American merchant ships were also sunk on the high seas. America's entry into the war provided great support to the Allies, shifted the balance of power, and led directly to the collapse of Germany by the autumn of 1918. To many in Germany the submarine failed to defeat Britain in the predicted matter of weeks, and it also brought the United States into the war.

Hitler was particularly aware of the role of the submarine in bringing the United States into the war in 1917 and was anxious not to set in motion the same sequence of events. After months of propaganda attacks against President Roosevelt (called an "honorary Hebrew," among other things) and the United States, the German media eased up during the summer of 1939 with the expectation of keeping the United States neutral in the international crisis. "On land I am a hero. At sea I am a coward," is a statement that accurately reflects Hitler's anxiety about the possible complications that could grow out of an aggressive naval program.[14] The naval command had therefore sent out specific orders to observe the 1936 Submarine Protocol, to focus on military targets, to avoid passenger liners, and to take special care in attacking merchant ships to make provisions for their crews. Hitler wanted to keep the war confined to Poland and he hoped for a negotiated settlement with Britain and France after Poland was defeated. The U-boat war was initially intended by the high command to intimidate the Allies, not push them to retaliate. However, as it became clear that Britain and France would not acquiesce in the conquest of Poland, the submarine restrictions created by the protocol were gradually lifted by the German naval staff. As early as 13 November 1939 Hitler began to break from his orders of 3 September and started to expand the scope of the submarine campaign. The international law for submarine warfare that had been worked out in the several treaties during the interwar years was quickly torn to shreds. Although the term "unrestricted submarine warfare" was never used, by mid-November of 1939 it was for all practical purposes being implemented.[15]

Thus the submarine campaign began during the first hours of the war. Whatever mistake or miscalculation, "fog of war" or opportunism, had prompted *Oberleutnant* Lemp's attack, and whatever inconvenience it might have been for Hitler's immediate wartime objectives, the effect was unmistakable. Germany appeared to have begun the Second World War exactly where she ended the First World War, with a ruthless submarine campaign. Indeed, the submarine campaign and the Battle of the Atlantic, of which the sinking of the *Athenia* was the first blow, were a grueling ordeal for Great Britain, Canada, and eventually the United States. Winston Churchill later wrote that "the only thing that ever really frightened me during the war was the U-boat peril."[16] Of course worse was to come, but the *Athenia* was the beginning.

As darkness fell, Lemp now turned away from the sinking *Athenia* and steered for the easternmost sector of his patrol area. He made no provision for, nor offered assistance to, the survivors bobbing in lifeboats in a widening circle around the stricken ship. It is possible that he knew from intercepting radio signals to and from the *Athenia* that several ships, including the *Knute Nelson* sighted earlier in the day, had answered the distress calls and were speeding to rescue the survivors. In any case he made no attempt to comply with either the letter or the spirit of the 1936 Submarine Protocol. Lemp also maintained radio silence, as he was under orders to do, although the attack on the *Athenia* had for all practical purposes revealed the presence of a submarine in the area. However, the result was that the German High Command knew nothing of his actions and only learned of the sinking of the *Athenia* through the British radio. Even without specific information, however, in light of the sinking of the *Athenia*, Hitler had the message sent to the whole submarine fleet: "By order of the Führer. Passenger-ships until further notice shall not be attacked even if escorted."[17] Clearly the enormity of his actions became apparent to Lemp.

The cruise of the *U-30* went on for two and a half more weeks. Despite a run of bad weather, Lemp sank the freighter *Blairlogie* on 9 September. This time he attempted to comply with the rules of submarine warfare by looking after the lifeboats and providing Captain D. B. McAlpine and his crew with schnapps and cigarettes until neutral U.S. freighter *American Shipper* arrived. On 14 September south of Rockall Bank he attacked the merchant ship *Fanad Head* with his deck gun. After Captain G. Pinkerton and his crew had abandoned the ship, Lemp had several of his men use their rubber dinghy to board the vessel to set charges that would sink her and also to look for fresh food supplies. However, before abandoning ship, the *Fanad Head* had got off distress signals and the aircraft carrier HMS *Ark Royal* responded, launching three Blackburn Skua dive bombers. The *U-30* submerged to avoid the airborne attack, but its position underwater was betrayed by an inflatable dinghy that remained tied to the U-boat. However, the bombs dropped by the planes skipped on the water and exploded, damaging two planes to such a degree that they crashed into the sea. Adolph Schmidt, one of the boarding party from the submarine, witnessed all of this from the deck of the *Fanad Head* and swam out to the crashed airplanes and rescued the two pilots, one of whom was badly burned, and got them back to the *U-30*, in what historian Marc Milner calls "one of the most bizarre episodes of the war."[18] Schmidt was himself wounded when the third airplane from the *Ark Royal* strafed the submarine. Nevertheless, Lemp got Schmidt and the two British pilots into the U-boat and submerged just as three British destroyers began a depth charge attack. Lemp took his U-boat to a record 472 feet deep (143.8 meters), but the bombs and depth charges damaged the vessel, the most serious being leaks in the ship, cracked valves, and shattered instruments. Under cover of darkness the submarine escaped on the surface. Lemp then broke radio silence to request permission from naval command to bring the wounded Schmidt and the two British pilots into then-neutral Iceland for medical treatment, which he did on 19 September. Lemp extracted the oath of secrecy from Schmidt, before putting him ashore, that he would not reveal that the *U-30* had sunk a passenger ship on 3 September. The crew was also sworn to secrecy. Lemp was unquestionably something of a naval hero, having sunk three ships, brought down two airplanes (in a manner of speaking), survived a potentially disastrous depth charge attack, looked after his wounded crew and prisoners, and returned his injured boat to Wilhelmshaven with only one of his two diesel engines working.[19] But he also posed a problem for the high command nevertheless.

CHAPTER 4

ABANDON SHIP!

*We were eating our dinner, having an animated conversation, when we heard
an awful crash and realized what had happened. The lights were extinguished, water
was coming up the floor, chairs were overturned, dishes were breaking, we got
up and tried to walk to the steps which we finally found.*

—ALMA M. BLOOM[1]

"Well, I didn't think they'd do it," said Mary Louise Kelly, a high school mathematics teacher in Saranac Lake, New York, to her sister Lucretia Estelle, when she heard the loud explosion. A torpedo from the *U-30* entered the *Athenia* on the port side, exploding just behind the engine room, destroying the galley, many cabins on D Deck, and the trunk of No. 5 hatch. The ship was violently shaken, the lights went out, she listed sharply to port and then recovered partially and began to settle by the stern. The *Athenia* quickly slowed to a stop—she was adrift, dead in the water, "like some dead giant," as one passenger thought.[2]

In *Athenia*'s wheelhouse Third Officer Colin Porteous, the officer of the watch, immediately pulled the lever that closed the watertight doors throughout the ship, thereby attempting to create a series of watertight compartments throughout the length of the ship. Porteous then sent the emergency stop signal on the ship's engine room telegraph and, through the bridge speaking tube to the radio room, gave an order to Chief Radio Officer David Don to send out an SOS signal. Finally, he gave the sustained blast on the ship's steam whistle which was the recognized emergency signal. Porteous later told a passenger that he could not understand why he had not seen the torpedo track in the water, because he had been looking in the direction from which it must have come. Captain James Cook, Chief Officer Barnet Copland, and several other ship's officers were at dinner when the torpedo struck. First Officer J. J. Emery attempted to calm the diners and helped them make their way to their cabins to find their life preservers. Chief Officer Copland made his way out to the boat deck and gave orders to get the lifeboats swung out over the side of the ship. Once on deck the chief officer saw a cloud of black smoke astern of the port beam and the outline of a submarine about a half mile away and moving parallel to the ship. He could not make out the number because of the smoke. Quartermaster Angus Graham also saw the submarine when he came on deck. It seemed about one hundred yards off the ship and from the strong smell he thought it might have fired a gas shell. Captain Cook left his dinner, quickly climbed up to the bridge, and immediately checked that the watertight doors had been closed. He spoke next to the radio officer and told him to send out the SOS both in the clear and in the naval code and to signal the ship's position. He then sent for the chief engineer to get a report on the damage to the ship and to start the emergency dynamo working so that lights could be restored on the ship. By this time the *Athenia* had taken on a 6- or 7-degree list to port and was settling at the stern. Captain Cook pointed out to Third Officer Porteous a cloud of black smoke some seven hundred or eight hundred yards off the port quarter. Finally, he ordered the remaining crew on the bridge to assist in the launching of lifeboats.[3]

Chief Engineer J. Carnegie got his lifejacket and a flashlight and went below to make his inspection. He proceeded down the staircase through the engineer's alleyway on the port side of the ship to the engine room. When he reached C Deck he found that the deck had been buckled and torn apart by the force of the explosion. Shining his flashlight into the dark he could see that pipes from the area of D Deck, more or less at the waterline, had been blown a considerable distance upward and that a substantial amount of water had entered the ship and already risen to within two feet of C Deck. By this time the third-class staterooms on D Deck at the stern of the ship would have been underwater also. Chief Engineer Carnegie managed to open the door to the engine room in the hope of finding some of his men, but the engine room was completely flooded and no men or bodies were in sight. The bulkhead between the engine room and the fire room was destroyed, the fuel oil tanks ruptured, and the stairways from the third-class and tourist dining rooms to the upper decks were shattered. The blow to the ship and to many of the crew in the engine room had been mortal. The explosion in the engine room and its flooding had destroyed the power plant in the ship. Although emergency lighting was started, there was no power to get pumps working to counteract the flooding. The watertight doors had been closed, but the explosion had so opened the seams in the ship that the integrity of the watertight compartments had been breached. The flooding could be slowed down, but it could not be stopped. Thus time had been purchased, which was of critical importance in getting all of the lifeboats launched and the passengers on board, but the ship could not be saved. The chief engineer returned to the bridge with a grim report and the news that he found more damage at the shaft of No. 5 hold with a number of dead and injured people near by.[4]

In addition to the engine room and the third-class staterooms on D Deck, the ship's galleys were also destroyed by the torpedo explosion. George Williams, a cook from Glasgow, said that the galley floor where he was working seemed to split right open. Some were killed outright by the concussion. Furthermore, the cooking ranges overturned, sending hot food, and especially hot soup and boiling cooking oil, flying in all directions. Cooks and stewards in the galley were scalded by the boiling soup or thrown against the cooking ranges and were horribly burned. Thomas McGregor, a twenty-two-year-old cook from Motherwell, Scotland, was badly scalded by steam when the explosion took place in the galley. Bedroom steward Claude Barrie, who had been a soldier in the Great War, thought he smelled cordite, as a mate cried out, "The swine has hit us." George Hail, a twenty-eight-year-old first-class steward from Bridgeton, Scotland, who had survived the sinking of a ship some years before, was working in a pantry. He was struck on the head by debris and knocked to the floor. Hail got to his feet and made his way on deck, not sure whether the people lying on the deck were dead or alive. The galleys also flooded quickly, making the recovery of the injured and unconscious difficult. "Frankly, I didn't think I'd see Bridgeton again," he said later.[5]

The explosion destroyed the electrical generators, so the whole ship was plunged into darkness until the emergency lights could be turned on, and the flooding of the engine room caused the ship to take a sharp list to the port side. When the torpedo struck a substantial number of the ship's passengers and many of the crew were at their evening meal. Boatswain W. Harvey was eating dinner in the forward mess room when he heard the explosion and felt the ship give a "shiver." He had been torpedoed three times in the First World War and recognized immediately what had happened. The result in the three passenger dining rooms on C Deck was noise and confusion as dishes and glassware crashed to the floor and chairs overturned, sending people sprawling on the floor. Pax Walker-Fryette felt the ship heel over and all the china, cutlery, and people slid to one side of the room. When she got up she felt something wet along her leg and realized that she had been cut in the knee. Douglas Stewart and his wife were sprawled amid all of the broken crockery and debris, "waiting for the end," as he put it, until the ship gradually righted itself. Until flashlights were found, only lit matches provided any light to find the way out onto the deck. Judith Evelyn called out "Andrew" to her fiancé Andrew Allan, and they found each other in the darkness of the cabin-class dining room. With the aid of matches and cigarette lighters they climbed up the stairway to A Deck and their lifeboat station. Evelyn noted the lack of confusion among her fellow passengers and sensed in herself a feeling of energy to meet the crisis.[6] Arthur T. Mikelsen was sitting at dinner with his cabin mates when he felt the ship "quivering" and then an explosion that sounded "the same as would a giant fire cracker being put in a huge tin container." Mrs. Sara Bloom Grossman of New York thought the explosion sounded like "a blown up paper bag being burst," while she and her daughter Olive were finishing their meal in the third-class dining room. They climbed up to the boat deck to lifeboat No. 10. In what he said was his best "Boy Scout voice," Montgomery Evans called out confidently that everyone should take their time and "everything would be all right." Evans selected a souvenir spoon from a table, got to his stateroom where he put on his coat, and picked up some chocolate and cigarettes, although he later complained that he forgot the book manuscript that he had been working on for the past year.[7] Dorothy Dixon, a schoolteacher from Pasadena, California, was in the cabin-class dining room when the explosion shook the ship. She said she was "thrown to the floor and rolled across the room to the port side," losing her purse with her money, passport, and rail ticket home. Eventually she was able to get back to her room and find her lifejacket and make her way to No. 10 lifeboat. Judith Evelyn found her way to her cabin and got her lifejacket, but when she joined Andrew Allan and his father at their lifeboat station she realized that it was going to be cold in the boats. Over Allan's protests, she went back to her cabin again, put on her fur coat, and picked up several more, including one for Allan himself. She gave away the remaining coats to others on the promenade deck who were in need.[8]

Joseph B. L. MacDonald, a marine superintendent from Bronxville, New York, was eating dinner with his wife, Elnetta, in the cabin-class dining room at the table with the captain, the chief engineer, and others when the torpedo hit. When they got up on deck, MacDonald and his wife saw the conning tower of a submarine about one third of a mile off the port beam. They also saw clouds of black and white smoke and concluded the black smoke came from the submarine's diesel engines and the white smoke from its guns. After waiting a moment, MacDonald concluded that the submarine was not going to fire at the *Athenia* again and that it would be safe to escort his wife to their lifeboat station No. 6. He then went below to their cabin on B Deck to find lifejackets, looking at the destruction at the No. 5 cargo hold and the dead bodies amid the wreckage. Mrs. Elizabeth Lewis, a housewife from Los Angeles, California, her daughter Margaret, and her son Donald were finishing their meal in the cabin-class dining room when the torpedo hit. In the dark and the confusion Mrs. Lewis lost her daughter but clung to her son. They made their way to her stateroom where their neighbor, MacDonald, who had been looking for his lifejackets, carried nine-year-old Donald up to the lifeboat No. 6, while she went to get their lifejackets and find Margaret. She could not find her daughter and when she got back on deck she saw her son already in a lifeboat. In the end, all three of them got into different lifeboats.[9]

The torpedo hit closest to the third-class dining room, the furthest aft of the dining rooms on C Deck. Alma M. Bloom, a teacher from Cincinnati, Indiana, was eating dinner with her friends when the explosion overturned chairs and sent the dishes and tableware crashing. She remembered water coming across the floor and the stewards helping people out of the room and toward their cabins to get lifejackets. Patricia Hale remembered the explosion as the "slamming of a thousand ton door." "Something seemed to run, ripping, tearing, right under our chairs," she said, then darkness engulfed them, dishes crashed to the floor, and water surged up to their knees. Miss E. M. A. McCarthy had just left the third-class dining room and was almost on deck when the torpedo struck. She was thrown back into the companionway and onto the floor. Everything was dark and there was thick smoke and dust, but through it all she saw "a flash like lightning and heard a detonation she presumed was gunfire." The emergency signal went off and Miss McCarthy went directly to her lifeboat station.[10] Mrs. Mary Ann McGoorty was with her small daughter Margaret in the third-class dining room when "I heard a loud report and everything went dark." She was hit in the leg by some falling debris and was separated from her daughter. In the darkness she called out to her daughter and heard her voice, but she was pushed out of the dining room and up the stairs to the deck without ever seeing her daughter "Peggie" again. Barbara Rodman, a secretary from Garden City, New York, who was in the third-class dining room, thought the "smell of cordite and sulphur was almost overpowering" and they were likely to be asphyxiated. Parts of the ceiling collapsed next to her and splinters were flying. "I do not believe that any of us expected to see daylight," she remembered. Bernice Jansen was thrown on the floor together with the dishes and food. She remembered the "terrible smell of ammonia" and the confusion in the darkness.[11]

Mrs. Mary Levine, a housewife from Brooklyn, New York, was in the tourist-class dining room when the torpedo exploded. Through the darkness and commotion she got back to her stateroom with Helen Hannay, who had a cabin nearby and had been sitting with her at dinner, in order to find Mrs. Levine's sleeping baby. The baby was wrapped up in a blanket just as the stewardess, Miss Johnstone, appeared. Together they all went off to find their lifeboat station. Mrs. Levine persuaded Miss Johnstone to stay with her to help with the baby. Helen Hannay, one of the college girls from Houston, Texas, and her friend Martha Bonnett, a student from Chariton, Iowa, went back to their cabins to get coats and lifejackets and then returned to the boat deck to get in lifeboat No. 11. Their chaperone, Gladys Strain, said that all the girls got their lifejackets. When the torpedo hit the *Athenia* Mrs. Wilson Levering Smith grasped the arm of her twenty-four-year-old son Wilson Jr., who was with her in the dining room on C Deck. She could hear the water rushing in below her and smell the smoke and fumes. Aided by a ship's officer with a flashlight, they made their way hand-in-hand to her room on B Deck, where they got lifejackets and coats. They saw several bodies near the rear hatch and the broken mast of the ship. W. Ralph Singleton, who was just finishing his meal at the second sitting, was covered in dust and small particles of debris by the explosion. Rather than attempt to make his way through the darkened corridors, Singleton went up to the promenade deck and well forward to get to his room in the forward part of the ship where he found his lifejacket and made his way to lifeboat No. 1.[12] Literally within minutes, all three of the dining rooms on C Deck were emptied as people made their way to their staterooms to get lifejackets or directly to their lifeboat stations.

Many passengers on the *Athenia* were also in their cabins. Some had been seasick much of the day, others were dressing for dinner, and still others were asleep. Don Gifford, a young college student from Schenectady, New York, was asleep in his bunk on C Deck when the explosion threw him out of bed. Gifford made his way out into the passageway, which was littered with timbers and wreckage and filled with fumes. The stairway had been demolished, many cabins on the port side were destroyed, and a number of passengers killed. "I reached the deck by scrambling out of the hole where the stairway had been and went to my lifeboat post," he recalled. Mrs. Margaret Ford, a widow from East Dearborn, Michigan, had been very seasick and was in bed in her third-class cabin in the forward part of the ship when the torpedo hit. The ship was plunged into darkness and she heard things falling and women screaming. She rushed out into the passageway and helped women and children make their way up to the lifeboats. She was dressed only in her nightclothes, so she went back to her cabin to get a coat and then went to lifeboat No. 2. Also seasick and in bed was sixty-two-year-old Helen Edna Campbell of Winnipeg, Manitoba. The concussion from the explosion sent the ceiling of her cabin on A Deck crashing down and plunged the room into darkness. "Steady, don't faint," she told herself, but when she attempted to flee she found herself fumbling with the wardrobe door. After making her way into the companionway she returned to search for her lifebelt. This she could not find, but being dressed only in her silk underwear and slippers, she was fortunate to reach her wool dressing gown. Baby John Easton from Hamilton, Ontario, was being given a bath by his mother Lily when the torpedo struck. Water and smoke were filling the corridor when she went out of her cabin and a Scottish sailor told her to hand baby John to him and climb up the shattered stairway as best she could. When she got on deck she was given a lifejacket and her freshly bathed one-year-old baby returned to her, clad only in the sailor's coat.[13]

Barbara Cass-Beggs had been seasick and had gone to bed with little Rosemary when she heard the noise of the explosion and saw the light go out. She got out of bed, slipped on her coat, and started to dress Rosemary when David rushed into the cabin and told her, "Put on your life belts, leave everything and come up on deck." She gathered up Rosemary, clad only in her pajama tops, and headed up the two flights of stairs, forgetting her purse in the bunk.[14] Kate Ellen

Hinds, a housewife from Houston, Texas, was in her cabin changing for dinner. Darkness enveloped the room, splinters flew everywhere, and strong fumes filled the air. Water began streaming across the floor. She called out to her son who was in the next cabin. His cabin door had been blown off, but the debris filled the companionway and the stairs had been destroyed. Her son scrambled along the remnants of the stair railings and pulled her out of the water onto B Deck, from which they made their way to the lifeboats. Ruby Mitchell and Margaret Calder were both seasick and in bed in their cabin when the torpedo struck and the lights went out. Margaret screamed and started for the door, but Ruby searched under the bunk for the lifejackets. Mrs. Calder's sister, Christina Horgan, came down to the cabin to get the two girls. "We have to go upstairs immediately," she said. "There's something's gone wrong." So with the four lifejackets they made their way up the stairs to the deck. They could not see well because of the dark and there was a strange smell of gas, but Ruby felt there was something wrong about the stairs. "I'm stepping on people," she said. Chrissy Horgan told her not to think about it and to hurry on.[15]

Professor John H. Lawrence of the radiation laboratory at the University of California, Berkeley, had also gone to change for dinner in his stateroom on D Deck. The explosion left the room in darkness and filled with smoke and fumes. "Water was rushing in, and everything was in a shambles," Lawrence said; he went out into the corridor and attempted to save himself. "I proceeded to the stairway," he recounted, "which had been completely demolished but [I] grabbed the upper ledge and made my exit on to 'C' deck," which brought him to safety.[16] Young Ken and Nick Bjeko, Polish refugees, were thrown from their bunks when the torpedo hit. Water began filling the cabin when their older brother rushed in and led them to safety. George Calder had eaten dinner and returned to his cabin to look after his wife, who was in bed seasick. When the torpedo exploded in the ship the upper berth and the wardrobe in their cabin collapsed and the mirrors and glass objects shattered. Mrs. Calder jumped out of bed, gave her husband her flashlight, and put on her coat. They could hear women screaming and smell strong fumes. They put on their lifejackets and made their way out into the companionway and tourist lounge, which was "an absolute shambles." When they got near the aft hatchway they saw three men and a young girl dead. Once on deck they began looking for their young son, who they eventually found sitting in a lifeboat wearing his lifejacket. Mary Louise Kelly and her sister Lucretia Estelle, a mathematics teacher at Hunter College High School in New York, had just eaten dinner and were in their cabin when the explosion took place. They immediately put on warm clothing and lifejackets and with the aid of flashlights made their way up to the lifeboat station, where they gave their bathrobes to women in nightclothes.[17]

Father Joseph O'Connor had been seasick and stayed in his cabin rather than go to dinner. He heard the roar of the explosion and water immediately began streaming across the floor. Although his cabin door was jammed shut, he was able to break out the panels and get into the companionway and eventually up the shattered stairway. When he got on deck, Father O'Connor found quite a bit of confusion, but people remained orderly nevertheless. He gave general absolution to everyone on the ship and heard confession from a number of people. Young Rev. Gerald Hutchinson had just left the second sitting for dinner and was walking along a corridor when the explosion shook the ship. The ship lurched sideways and he nearly lost his balance. He remembered gun smoke and dust filling the air. A friend who had been peeling an orange was surprised to have it popped out of his hands and into the air by the concussion. When he finally made his way on deck he found a certain amount of chaos as people searched for family members and attempted to find their lifeboat stations. Hutchinson and three of his companions looked to see what they could do to be helpful. David Blair, of Vancouver, attempted to get down to his wife in her cabin, but the companionway was wrecked and flooded with water. "It was impossible to do anything," he said. "Everything was blown away." In despair, he concluded she was dead and went back up on deck to save himself. However, once on deck, "I found her there unable to remember anything of what had happened except that some man in the alleyway had dragged her through the water to safety just after the blast."[18]

Not all of those who were in their staterooms were so fortunate. Fifteen-year-old Jane Hannah, who had been visiting in Scotland with her mother, Helen, was actually on deck with a seasick friend when the *Athenia* was struck. However, Jane's mother was seasick in their cabin on D Deck, below the third-class dining room, and young Jane ran to find her. She started down the stairway to D Deck but she said, "I couldn't go any further because it was already flooded with water and oil." Amid the offensive smell of what she described as "gas," the crew were working to rescue passengers and they told her to leave and go to her lifeboat. Mrs. Hannah was among those missing. When the ship was hit James Goodson was coming up from D Deck to the tourist-class dining room. He heard the explosion, felt the ship shudder, and realized that this was a calamity. When the emergency lights came on he returned to the companionway he had just left and witnessed what he called "Dante's Inferno." The wooden stairway was smashed and D Deck below was flooded. People were clinging to bits of wreckage trying to stay afloat. "I started by reaching for the outstretched arms and pulling the weeping, shaking, frightened women to safety; but I soon saw that the most urgent danger was to those who were floundering in the water, or clinging to the wreckage lower down. Many were screaming that they couldn't swim and were close to drowning." Young Goodson got into the water and worked to rescue the children first, who he said put their small arms around his neck and hung on as he swam and worked his way back to the broken stairs and handed them up to waiting crewmembers—stewards and stewardesses—who passed them up to the boat deck.

"Bloody guid, mon!" said one Scottish crewman who could not swim, "Keep 'em coming." Goodson got all of those who were alive and then helped other members of the crew look for passengers in flooded staterooms. As they struggled through the water in the disorientating companionway of the listing ship, Goodson found no more living passengers. Indeed, he found the dead body of the young boy who shortly before had sung the old sentimental songs so beautifully.[19]

Father O'Connor could hear cries for help coming from a stairwell. With the aid of a flashlight, he and several others made their way down a shattered stairway to find what he called, "the most tragic and pitiful sight of all." There pinned beneath the collapsed stairwell was a woman holding a baby. The infant was quickly passed up to the deck, but the woman was clearly dying. One of her legs had been cut off and she had lost a lot of blood and was crushed by the wreckage. Father O'Connor gave her the last rites and she died as the seawater rose around her. She had to be left were she was as the ship settled. Mrs. Rachel Lamont and her ten-year-old son, Alexander, were in their cabin preparing for bed when the torpedo hit. The concussion of the explosion sent the heavy oscillating fan off a cabinet, crashing onto Mrs. Lamont's head and stunning her. Alexander called to his mother, but only when she was splashed with the water pouring into the cabin did she respond. She cried out, "Alex, are you there?" and in the darkness he stumbled over her and pulled her up. They were able to squeeze their way out of their cabin and amid the broken timbers, clouds of dust, and floating luggage, make their way to the stairwell. They climbed past the dying woman and several dead bodies and up the shattered staircase. The woman's severed leg was floating on a piece of luggage. "I will never forget that sight," Lamont said years later.[20]

Those people who were on deck probably had a better idea of what had happened when the *Athenia* was struck, although that clearly did not make things less difficult for them. Fourteen-year-old Montrealer Donald A. Wilcox and his mother had been visiting family in England. While waiting to go to dinner they had walked around the ship for some fresh air. His mother walked up on the promenade deck while Donald went out to the very forepeak of the *Athenia* at the front of the ship. This is the classic position in which to feel the wind and the forward surge of any seagoing vessel. He was watching the knifelike stem of the ship slice through the water, throwing up a dramatic bow wave, when the explosion of the torpedo made the bow of the ship jump a foot or so out of the water and Donald almost lost his balance. He and his mother each made their way to their staterooms, put on their lifejackets, and went to their lifeboat. James Boyle, a bus driver from Detroit, Michigan, his wife, Mary Ann, and their ten-year-old daughter, Jeaninne, were sitting on the hatch cover in the third-class promenade deck, also in the bow of the ship. The explosion heeled the ship over but they kept their balance. They also saw the huge cloud of black smoke around the stern of the ship and across the water. They immediately went to find their lifejackets and their lifeboat station. Seventeen-year-old Harry Bridge, a student from Abilene, Texas, was traveling with his mother and sister. He was sitting on C Deck forward when he saw the explosion, which caused a huge "fountain of water and oil [to] leap up from the side of the ship, which immediately heeled over at an acute angle." He was thrown to the deck, and when he got up he saw what he called a "smoke screen" a quarter of a mile away.[21] Harry's mother, Edith, was reading announcements in front of the purser's office when the explosion plunged the ship into darkness. She held on to the man standing next to her as the ship rocked and they were covered in a gritty dust that she thought was cordite. Her hat and pocketbook were lost and her wristwatch and glasses broken, but she made her way out on to the deck, where she too saw the smoke on the water from the submarine. She met her daughter Constance in a companionway, who brought the lifejackets from their stateroom, and then found Harry and they all made their way to their lifeboat station. Dr. Lulu Sweigard, an instructor in the Department of Physical Education at New York University, was walking on deck when the torpedo hit. She was knocked off her feet by the concussion. "I tried to rise but the boat had listed sharply over to the port side," she recalled. Edith Lustig, a Jewish refugee from Germany, was on deck and thrown overboard by the explosion and never seen again.[22]

Thomas Quine, a chiropractor from Fullerton, California, was on A Deck looking in the direction of the submarine he concluded, although he did not see it. He did see hatch covers blown in the air and several people killed when the torpedo hit. When he heard a second explosion he looked toward the sea and saw a cloud of smoke; "like smoke from a gun, and faintly visible the bow and stern of a submarine," he said. Quine then went off to find his wife, Annie. The explosion of the No. 5 hatch covers was also witnessed at close hand by Dr. Watson Bidwell, an instructor at the University of Denver. He was sitting in the tourist lounge on A Deck, just a few feet away when the hatch cover was blown up. When he went outside he saw dead bodies at his feet; he also saw two "geysers" of water between one hundred and two hundred yards away from the ship and was certain they were being fired at from the submarine. Passing more dead bodies, Bidwell went in search of his wife, Anne, shouting her name in the dark corridor. "Here I am Doc," she called out and she remembered him telling her, "we are still being shelled." Mrs. Mathilda Johnson from Duluth, Minnesota, sitting in the lounge on A Deck thought the explosion was like "an earthquake in the ocean."[23] Also in the tourist lounge on A Deck were John and Isabella Coullie of Chicago, Illinois. John jumped to his feet when he heard the explosion and his wife fell into his arms as the ship heeled over. When they went out on deck they saw several dead people and a number of women, some in nightclothes, covered in soot with blood streaming down their faces. There was the powerful smell of gunpowder, and Coullie told his wife, "I think we are being shelled; let's get out of here." They went to the port side of the ship and from there, Coullie said, "I saw a submarine clear above the water about a quarter of a mile off as near as I could judge." They got their lifejackets from their stateroom and eventually found a lifeboat. "Two bodies were shot across in front of me, blackened," reported Thomas McCubbin, a Montclair, New Jersey, sales representative who had been standing on a section of the upper deck that was collapsed by the blast. He saw black smoke and cinders come out of the air funnels on deck, and then went off to find his lifejacket in his stateroom. One of the ship's bellboys, seventeen-year-old Felix Caulfield from Garngad, Scotland, picked up a young girl from the deck and started to carry her to a lifeboat, when he realized that she was dead—her neck broken. Joseph M. Insch, a machinist from Yonkers, New York, and his wife, Elsie, were reading newspapers in the tourist smoking room on the promenade deck when the torpedo struck. Joseph took his wife by the arm and they made their way onto the deck looking for their thirteen-year-old daughter, also named Elsie, who had been playing deck tennis. When the second explosion occurred they saw one man killed in a deckchair and another on a stairway. There also appeared to be an explosion above them, what many thought to be on the mast. When their daughter found them, they attempted to get their lifejackets. However, they gave up their search for lifejackets when a steward with a flashlight showed them a hole in the companionway where the barbershop had been and returned to their lifeboat station. Russell Park and his father had gone to the ship's library after dinner, and Russell had just checked out a book on trains when he was jolted out of his chair by the explosion. He and his father made their way in the dark to their lifeboat station. His father then went to get his mother who, being seasick, had remained in her cabin. Russell never saw his father again.[24]

Mrs. Jessie Morrison was traveling back to Detroit, Michigan, with her eleven-year-old son John. They were standing on the third-class deck near the No. 5 hatch when the explosion occurred. Although they kept their footing then, they were thrown under a bench by the second explosion. They then went straight to their cabin to get their lifejackets, but not before they saw sticking straight out of the sea what looked like a long stick and what they concluded must have been a submarine periscope.[25] Mrs. Mary Ellen Tinney, a housewife from Yonkers, New York, was returning home with her two sons, Harry aged eleven and William aged seven. Mrs. Tinney and William were seated on the tourist deck when the explosion killed instantly a man and a woman sitting near them. She was thrown against the ship's rail, but grabbed William's hand and started across to the other side of the ship when the second explosion erupted and seemed to send the mast crashing down nearby. She too saw something sticking straight out of the water, something that could have been part of a mast, she said, and from which there came a "dull red glow, which was followed by a thick black smoke which spread like a large cloud low over the water." She and William found Harry and they went to their lifeboat station.[26] The most professional description of the effect of the explosion at hatch No. 5 came from a marine engineer who was standing nearby. "The explosion of gasses came right up the trunk of the hatch," noted Charles Van Newkirk, a marine engineer from Allegheny, Pennsylvania, who had been paid off in Britain and was returning to the United States to join a new ship. "The effect of the explosion was like a heavy door slamming," he said. "The hatch went up in the air and the people who were reclining on the hatch went up in the air also and then went down the hatch." People were panic stricken at first but went immediately to their lifeboat stations. Ida Mowry from Providence, Rhode Island, had just come up from dinner and was sitting with her two daughters in deckchairs on the tourist promenade deck when the torpedo exploded. It seemed to her that the ship would sink immediately and she saw near the No. 5 hatch the bodies of several members of the crew and passengers. She was sure that the second explosion was a shell fired from the submarine and her daughters saw smoke from a ship in the distance. They could not get to their cabin, so they went straight to their lifeboat. Mrs. Georgina Hayworth, of Hamilton, Ontario, and her two daughters, Margaret aged ten and Jacqueline aged six, had come up on deck to watch the sunset over the port side of the ship. The concussion of the exploding torpedo shook the slats out of their deckchairs and pieces of metal flew all around them. One piece of shrapnel struck young Margaret Hayworth in the forehead, causing a serious gash. Eleven-year-old Hay "Scotty" Gillespie from Russell, Manitoba, had been seasick and was on deck wrapped in a blanket when a man standing nearby, wearing a deerstalker cap, called out that he saw a puff of smoke on the sea surface. Gillespie turned and saw the smoke himself, just as the torpedo hit the ship. He was joined shortly by his mother and younger brother who came up from the dining room. They were turned back from attempting to get their lifejackets from their cabin and went straight to their lifeboat station.[27]

"There's a submarine," a cabin boy cried to Mrs. Mary B. Dick, a housewife from Boston. She had just come from dinner and was out on deck at the stern of the ship. She saw a periscope in the water herself and had started running when the torpedo hit and, as she put it, "everything went dark." Norman Hanna of Bangor, Northern Ireland, on his way to make a new life in Canada, had been seasick for much of the day but came up on deck for some fresh air about seven o'clock. He was eating an apple and reclining on the aft hatch cover when a woman screamed, "Look!" When he turned to the port side of the ship he saw a submarine and a white streak in the water leading to the ship. He was thrown to the deck by the explosion and feared that the ship would overturn. A bright flash followed and a shell exploded on the tourist deck, sending a splinter that "whizzed by my face." Thomas E. Finley Jr., a teacher at Loomis Chaffee School in Windsor, Connecticut, was sitting with his wife, Mildred, on the tourist-class promenade deck overlooking the stern of the ship when the explosion threw a cloud of black smoke and debris into the air. He and his wife hurried down a stairway toward their staterooms when a second explosion caused such a shock that they were sent sprawling onto the deck below. They got their lifejackets and went to their lifeboat station.[28]

Dr. Edward T. Wilkes of Long Island City, New York, was returning home with his family when the torpedo struck. Dr. Wilkes was standing on the third-class promenade at the stern of the boat and was thrown off balance by the explosion. He called out for his two sons, Jonathan and Daniel. He then went to find his wife, Matilda, who being seasick had remained in her cabin on D Deck, below the dining rooms. "I had only gone down five steps or so from the deck level in the dark, when a torch shone on black murky water and forms of people could be seen swimming or floating towards the staircase." He could not go any further, so he returned to the deck to look for his boys but eventually went to a lifeboat station. Jonathan, Dr. Wilkes was told, was last seen being led to a lifeboat, but was eventually listed as missing. Daniel, who had been in the stateroom with his mother, Matilda, when the explosion flooded the staterooms on D Deck, managed to squeeze out through the cabin door, which as a result of debris and fallen timbers could only be partially opened. Daniel eventually made it up from D Deck to a lifeboat, but his mother was lost. Mrs. Doris MacLeod was taking her three children back home to Washington, D.C. She and her seventeen-year-old daughter, Betty, were sitting in the third-class lounge on B Deck while fourteen-year-old John was outside on deck. Fifteen-year-old Dorothy was seasick and remained in her cabin. When the lights went out with the explosion Mrs. MacLeod and Betty got separated but quickly found each other. The two then went down to their stateroom to find Dorothy, "who had got out of bed and was screaming for me." The three now returned to the deck to where they found John. Mrs. MacLeod also saw "a flash of flame surrounded by smoke," some distance away from the ship. She concluded they needed their lifejackets. "Betty and I went down below again to fetch lifebelts, leaving Dorothy and John at the top of the stair," she later remembered. "When we got back on deck I tried to keep my children together but John said he had been ordered to another lifeboat station so I had to let him go." She and her daughters went to lifeboat No. 10. All of them successfully got off the *Athenia* in lifeboats.[29] The shock and panic and fear of the explosions and flooding on board the *Athenia* now had to be overcome by the practical, but complicated, procedure of launching the ship's lifeboats and getting into them.

CHAPTER 5

TO THE LIFEBOATS

It was WOMEN AND CHILDREN FIRST.

—Donald A. Wilcox[1]

The lifeboat is the most important device for preserving the lives of passengers and crew of crippled oceangoing vessels. Even so, the lifeboat and its complicated launching apparatus remain almost inevitably unable to perform perfectly the tasks demanded of them in those very circumstances that require their services. Typically, the lifeboat was a double-ended wooden boat between 25 and 30 feet in length and with a recommended capacity of between sixty and seventy passengers, although capable of actually holding rather more. There were side benches all along both sides of the boat and five or more thwarts that went across the boat for people to sit on while rowing. Along the outside of the boat there were grab lines—rope loops that reached down to the waterline that could be held by people in the water and also used by people to clamber into the boat. In case the boat tipped over, there were often handholds along the bottom which gave people something to grip. Although steel was sometimes used, lifeboats were generally wooden clinker-built—that is to say they were made of wooden lapstrakes, a form of construction that was less vulnerable to drying out while the boat baked in the sun on the side of the ship—and therefore were less likely to leak when put in the water. Even if the boats did leak or were swamped with water they were equipped with watertight compartments that would keep them afloat while fully loaded. It was expected that lifeboats would be powered, or at least maneuvred, by oars, ideally combinations of four, six, or eight, and steered with either a rudder or a steering oar, or sweep. Often the boats were also equipped with a simple sail rig, which it was presumed could be put up and handled safely by the untrained passengers in the boat.

Lifeboats are launched from the side of a ship by devices called davits. The *Athenia* was equipped with a modern version called Welin Quadrant davits. These were in effect two small cranes, placed at each end of the lifeboat, which both lifted the boat off its cradle, or resting place, and swung it out over the side of the ship. The crane mechanism was moved by a crank and worm gear on the bottom of each davit. The hoisting and lowering power was managed through double block and tackle systems, controlled by a line called a fall, one at the bow and one at the stern of each boat. In the textbook procedure the boat would be hoisted off its cradle by the fall and the davits would then be cranked out, swinging the boat over the side of the ship. The passengers assigned to the boat would then get in and sit down on the side seats. At each end of the boat the bitter end of the fall, given a number of turns around the "gypsy" (a drum with flanged edges), would provide enough friction to hold the boat. Several members of the crew holding the bitter end of each fall could then slowly ease the fall and allow gravity to lower the boat, weighing several tons fully loaded, into the water in a controlled manner. Once the boat was in the water, the blocks were unshackled, and the boat was free to move away from the ship. Unfortunately, in circumstances drastic enough to require that a ship be abandoned, many of these step-by-step actions to launch a lifeboat cannot be practically performed. All of these systematic procedures can be upset by a violent storm or a collision at sea, not to mention the explosions and possible fire caused by a ship being torpedoed, at which time the vessel may be heeling several degrees to one side or the seamen expected to manipulate the boats may have been killed or injured or the passengers panicked and uncontrollable. Furthermore, in the case of this sailing of the *Athenia* on the eve of the international crisis, a number of the experienced members of the crew had left to join the Royal Navy, which further reduced the efficiency of the remaining crew getting the lifeboats launched and manned.

The *Athenia* had twenty-six lifeboats, thirteen on each side of the ship. Beginning in the bow with Nos. 1 and 2, the odd-numbered boats were on the starboard side and the even-numbered boats on the port side. The boats were also double stacked, the lower boats being given the additional letter A; thus there were both 1 and 1A, as well as 2 and 2A, all the way up to Nos. 14A and 15A. The exceptions were boats 3 and 4 which were single stacked and placed close to the bridge on the promenade deck, or boat deck. The lower boats were slightly larger, 30 feet 3 inches long and 9 feet 9.5 inches across (9.14 and 2.98 meters), while the upper boats were 28 feet 2 inches long with a beam of 8 feet 2.5 inches (8.58 and 2.50 meters). These boats had benches along both sides and four thwarts. Other exceptions were boats 5 and 6, which were powered by gasoline engines as well as oars and also served as ship's utility boats. The larger lifeboats were rated to hold 86 souls and the smaller boats 56. The Donaldson Line concluded that they had spaces for 1,828 people in the boats—410 more than the 1,418 passengers and crew the *Athenia* was carrying. Nevertheless with between 56 and 86 people in the boats they seemed crowded and unmanageable, giving rise to the conclusion by some survivors that the lifeboats had been intended for far fewer people. The *Athenia* was also equipped with 21 life rafts that could carry 462 more people; 18 ring buoys, essentially for throwing; and 1,600 lifejackets, a barely sufficient number.[2] It is not clear how many of the rafts and ring buoys were used.

Lifeboats 1, 1A, 2, and 2A were at the bow of the ship on the third-class open promenade deck on either side of the foremast. Second Officer K. G. Crockett was in charge of these boats. Chief Officer Barnet Copland was specifically in charge of the seven lifeboats on the port side of the cabin-class promenade deck, or boat deck. These were Nos. 4, 6, 6A, 8, 8A, 10, and 10A. However, Chief Officer Copland also had overall responsibility for launching all of the lifeboats, which during the crisis took him to various parts of the ship. First Officer J. J. Emery had responsibility for the seven boats on the opposite side of the boat deck: Nos. 3, 5, 5A, 7, 7A, 9, and 9A. The boatswain, William Harvey, looked after the lifeboats on the tourist-class promenade deck, Nos. 11, 11A, 12, and 12A. The remaining lifeboats at the stern of the ship on the third-class promenade, or poop deck, were Nos. 14, 14A, 15, and 15A, and they were the responsibility of Third Officer Colin Porteous. All of these lifeboats had been inspected by the Board of Trade surveyor just before the ship sailed from Glasgow; and in the aftermath of the declaration of war on Sunday morning Captain Cook had ordered that the boats be made ready for possible use by having the canvas covers removed, the plugs inserted, and additional supplies placed in them.[3] Would all of these precautions be adequate if an emergency arose? This would be the test.

When the torpedo struck and the emergency whistle blew, Second Officer Crockett went directly to the four lifeboats on the forward deck of the ship and assembled his crew to get these boats launched. Margaret Ford, a housewife from Dearborn, Michigan, went to lifeboat muster station 2 and had great praise for the deck steward who tried to be cheerful and keep peoples' spirits up with words of encouragement and by singing songs like "Pack Up Your Troubles in Your Old Kit Bag." Boats 1, 1A, 2, and 2A were swung out on their davits and lowered to the deck level, filled with passengers and crew, and further lowered into the water. Boat No. 2 was the responsibility of tourist lounge steward J. Grant, who had about fifty people in his boat, including five or six crewmembers. Mrs. Mary Dick of Boston claimed to be the second person into the boat. Boat No. 2A had seventy-five people on board, mostly women and children. Later on Second Officer Crockett took command of this boat and kept it riding comfortably during the night, firing off flares from time to time. W. Ralph Singleton got into one of the forward lifeboats and commented on how skilfully the crew operated the boat and the fact that it was dry and it shipped no water throughout the night.[4] All four of these boats got away very quickly, perhaps before eight o'clock, and stood off about a half mile from the *Athenia*.

First Officer Emery went to the seven lifeboats on the starboard side of the promenade deck. He had to direct a large number of passengers who had gathered at the muster stations. Boats 3, 5, and 7 were lowered into the water without passengers. Rope ladders were put over the side and passengers began climbing down into the boats. However, the weight of people on the ladders was too great and one of the side ropes broke, leaving people dangling. Ruth Rabenold, who was returning home to New York after two years of study at Oxford, was climbing down the ladder into boat No. 3, but she saw several women ahead of her miss the boat and fall into the water. Emery got most of those on the ladder into the boats by providing another line on which people could slide into the boats. Barbara Rodman was the first to successfully make the switch. Judith Evelyn found herself partway down the broken ladder and was hauled back on board with some trouble. Emery then secured the broken ladder with a piece of rope and enabled people to resume using it to descend into the boats. Miss J. E. Harvie went to muster station 5 and helped a number of elderly women and women with children get into these boats. One of the elderly women was Helen Edna Campbell. A sailor hoisted her up onto the railing and told her to swing her leg over the side and climb down the ladder. When she got to the bottom of the ladder she found it wet and dangerously slippery. "When the boat swings in you jump backward," someone shouted, "and I'll catch you." She found herself more or less tossed into the boat, hurting her ribs in the process. Another woman on the ladder fell into the sea and because she was rather stout the men in the boat had a very difficult time pulling her in, breaking her arm as they did so. There were several of the ship's crew in Campbell's boat but none of them were sailors; fortunately there was a fisherman who took charge of the boat, got them clear of the ship, and started people bailing water. Boats 5A, 9, and 9A were launched more or less without incident, although they scraped and bumped along the side of the listing ship. Seaman Dillon took charge of boat No. 5A, which was loaded from the promenade deck with about sixty-four people all wearing lifejackets. The boat was cut away from the falls with a hatchet, and as it pulled away from the ship two stewards climbed down the lifelines into the water and were hauled into the boat.[5]

Boat No. 7A was the last of these boats to be launched and it got away at about nine o'clock. This was done with some difficulty because by that time the *Athenia* had developed a list of about 12 degrees to port. Mrs. Elizabeth Campbell of Upper Darby, Pennsylvania, managed to get into this lifeboat, having earlier put her ten-year-old daughter on another boat. Margaret McPherson of White Plains, New York, went to the No. 5 lifeboat with her ten-year-old daughter, Fione, but eight-year-old Margaret was missing. She called Margaret's name but without success; in desperation Mrs. McPherson and her older daughter got into the last boat. Eleven-year-old Russell Park had been brought to his lifeboat station by his father who told him to wait there until his mother was located. Neither his mother nor father had come back to the boat deck when an officer told young Russell to get into the last boat.[6] Georgina Hayworth got her injured daughter Margaret and six-year-old Jacqueline to their lifeboat station. Jacqueline held on to her mother's skirt while Mrs. Hayworth tended Margaret. However, when Margaret and Mrs. Hayworth were placed in the lifeboat, Jacqueline lost her grip and fell backward into the crowd of people behind her. Mrs. Hayworth called to a sailor to pass her second daughter over to her, but another child was placed in the lowering lifeboat. Jacqueline was picked up and put in a different boat. Jeanette Jordan and Florence Hargrave, with coats over their pajamas, found that their assigned lifeboat was filled, but they went up to the boat deck and got into No. 7A. Miss Hargrave claimed that there was no member of the *Athenia*'s crew on board. Thomas McCubbin had not been able to get into his assigned boat either, but found a place in the last lifeboat. Mrs. Wilson Levering Smith and her son got into the boat, and while there were a fair number of men in the boat to do the rowing and the boat was relatively dry, she did note that there was only one crewmember and he was the assistant bartender rather than an able bodied seaman.[7]

The seven lifeboats on the opposite side of the promenade deck, the port side, were the responsibility of Chief Officer Copland. However, his larger duties demanded his presence all over the ship. The assistant purser and several seamen were able to step in and assist both the loading of these boats and their launching. Boats 4, 6, 6A, 8, and 8A were lowered without difficulty and got away safely. Rev. Dr. G. P. Woollcombe left the dining room and got his coat and hat from his cabin and then went to lifeboat No. 4. After about fifty women and children were loaded into the boat, Woollcombe was asked to get in as well. A steward took over the boat and they were lowered unsteadily to the water. He remembered that the light was quickly fading. Patricia Hale and her friend Margaret had made their way to their cabin to change into the warm clothes and lifejackets they had wisely laid out and then reported to lifeboat No. 4. She recalled that once the boat had been lowered into the water the tackle at one end jammed and had to be cut away. No axe could be found, so this had to be done laboriously with someone's pocketknife. Miss Hale could hear people in the water calling for help, but the immediate urgency was to move the boat away from the ship. Young Jane Hannah gave up looking for her mother and went to her boat station, but the lifeboat had already been launched. Mercifully, she was able to find a space in No. 6A with a friend.[8]

Able Bodied Seaman W. J. Macintosh, who took charge of boat No. 8, thought that they were clear of the ship within ten minutes of the emergency signal. Mrs. Mary Steinberg of the Bronx fell into the water and lost her handbag with her passport and money, but was dragged into No. 8. Frank Connolly, his wife Sally, and his three boys, Francis, Raymond, and Thomas, all got in boat No. 8 as well. Connolly and the several other men did the rowing, because there were only two crewmembers on board and most of the passengers were women and children. Seaman Macintosh kept his boat close to the ship to rescue anyone who fell into the water, and he managed to assist several women off the ladders on the side of the ship, but after a number of boats were successfully launched he pulled further away. Barbara Bailey, who had some Civil Defense training, understood the importance of avoiding panic, waited until her dining room had cleared and then went to her stateroom, found her coat and lifejacket, and made her way to the boat deck where she was told to get into No. 8A, which was already in the water and appeared loaded with people. Bailey asked a man standing by her on deck to rip her skirt in order to free her legs and she clambered down the side of the ship holding on to a steel cable. As she got near the water it looked as though the boat was drifting away from the ship, and while she was deciding what to do next a voice said, "Come on, you're doing fine." Two hands grabbed her ankles and pulled her into the boat in a heap. "We were seventy living and one dead," she remembered.[9]

Getting into the lifeboat itself could be perilous. Dr. Lulu E. Sweigard, a physical education instructor at New York University with a newly minted PhD, was confronted with the problem of having to climb down a fire hose to get into her lifeboat. The hose was too large to get her hands completely around it, "but the strong grip I have in my hands and my training in rope climbing did not fail me." She landed "without a bump," but others were not so skilled. Three women behind her fell into the sea, too weak to grip the hose, unskilled in using their legs for support, and too frightened to follow instructions shouted to them. They had to be pulled into the lifeboat. This prospect awaited John and Isabella Coullie. John asked "Bella" if she thought she could make it, and they started down. However, when a wave pushed the boat away from the side of the ship the man in the boat lost his grip on the hose and Bella fell into the sea between the boat and the ship. "I thought she would be crushed to bits," he later said, and he urged her to hang on to the grab lines along the side of the lifeboat. He then jumped into the sea also and attempted to help her climb into the boat, but this was made extremely difficult not only because of the surging of the boat in the waves but also as a result of the oil pouring from the ruptured fuel bunkers that made everything slippery and impossible to grip. Eventually John climbed into the boat himself and tugged at his wife's foot while another man pulled on her lifejacket straps so that the two of them managed to drag her into the lifeboat. Both of them were exhausted, covered in oil, and choking on the oil and seawater they had swallowed.[10]

People were surprisingly calm and orderly, and while many people were clearly frightened there was little panic or hysteria. Many of the male passengers worked to assist the crewmembers to manipulate the boats in the davits, lent their strength and weight to working the falls, and also rowed once the boats were in the water. Various crewmembers called out, "Women and children first," and for the most part men willingly stood aside, although in some instances this meant that boats did not have enough men in them to effectively row the boats. Copland and his crew had some problems with the foreign passengers at muster station 10 because of the language barrier. After their women and children got into the boats, the male refugees surged forward to get in also. With some force-fulness the "women and children first" loading procedure was made clear. In some instances women refused to get into the lifeboats without their husbands or sons. Indeed in many cases the policy of "women and children first" had the result of splitting up families by putting them in different boats that were res-cued by different ships, thereby creating an enormous amount of anxiety and confusion. Barbara and David Cass-Beggs were confronted with this agonizing dilemma. Not certain that the ship would stay afloat until a lifeboat that could take them both would be available, but unwilling to be separated, they made the painful decision to put their three-year-old daughter Rosemary into what they thought was the hospital boat. With the assumption that a child would always be looked after, little Rosemary was passed over the rail to a sailor and into the boat, wearing her pajamas and wrapped in a blanket.[11]

Passenger Joseph B. L. MacDonald, who had enjoyed a career at sea, even-tually took charge of boat No. 10. When he and his wife Elnetta arrived at his muster station the boat had already been lowered to the promenade deck and he helped mothers and children get in. When the boat was in the water and it was seen that some men were needed, MacDonald and his wife climbed down the ladder. Once in the boat, he gave directions to several male passengers for handling the lines and assisted several more people to get on board from the side ladder into the boat, including several ship's stewards. Among them was nurse Campbell, who took charge of both bailing out water and firing off flares. MacDonald then got the boat about three hundred yards away from the ship and streamed a sea anchor to keep the boat from drifting too far away. Also in the boat were Doris MacLeod and her daughters Betty Jean and Dorothy Mae. She gave great credit to MacDonald and said that he "was very good at his job and everybody obeyed him."[12]

Boat No. 10A had been thrown on its side by the explosion of the torpedo, although it did not seem to be seriously damaged by the concussion. With the help of Boatswain's Mate Macdonald and other crewmembers, the boat was righted and hoisted up by the davits and loaded people, but then problems developed. The boat was not properly released, requiring that all of the passengers get out and the boat be repositioned. A second time the passengers climbed into the boat and then climbed out again. As Bernice Jansen described it, "They cranked and cranked but the boats didn't come out and so the men lifted them up while the others cranked." On the third try, loaded with slightly fewer passengers, the boat was successfully lowered into the water. The remaining passengers and members of the crew then scrambled down the lifelines and the falls into the boat. As the lifeboat surged in the waves, Jansen missed the gunwale and fell into the sea. "Deck chairs and parts of the boat were washing against me and the oil from the boat [ship] poured out where I was tredding [sic] water," she recalled. "My scalp was badly cut but fortunately I didn't know it." She thought she was in the water for about twenty minutes and feared being drawn under the lifeboat before seizing one of the grablines, after which she was pulled into the boat by two men. The boat was cast off and while the oars were being dug out from underneath the crowd of people, the boat drifted along the side of the ship underneath another lifeboat that was being lowered. Shouts and cries stopped the second boat and with the help of the newly extracted oars they gradually got under way.[13]

Boatswain William Harvey looked after the four lifeboats on the tourist-class promenade deck. Boats 11 and 12 were swung out and loaded with passengers and then lowered into the sea without any problems. Quartermaster Angus Graham helped with boat No. 11. College student Don Gifford watched people struggling down the side ladders and it seemed to him that women and children were being thrown into the boats. Therefore he jumped into the water off the port rail and climbed into boat No. 12. Later in the evening Captain Cook had First Officer Emery put in charge of boat No. 12, by which time he was able to reassure the passengers that several ships were on the way to rescue them. No. 12A was filled with between thirty and forty children ages ten to fourteen and eight mothers with infants. This boat was got clear of the ship without difficulty and streamed a sea anchor during the night.[14]

The increasing list of the ship to the port side presented a problem for launching boat No. 11A on the starboard side. When the loaded boat was about six or seven feet from the sea the stern fall "took charge," that is, slipped out of control and allowed the stern of the boat to drop faster and further than the bow. Rev. Gerald Hutchinson and several others attempted to help Quartermaster Graham, but they all got terrible rope burns on their hands in the process. Graham shouted immediately for the bow fall to be slacked away quickly, which was done and the boat was brought level in the water. Joseph Insch said that in addition to the officer there were six male passengers attempting to handle the falls. He and his wife, Elsie, got in at the last minute, together with their daughter and another little girl, although the boat was already very crowded. Helen Hannay and her friend Martha Bonnett had found a place in No. 11A. When the fall slipped, people tumbled into the stern of the boat, like "rag dolls," James Goodson remembered. Several people were thrown out of the boat into the sea, many were bruised or injured, and one broke an arm. The two girls both held on, although Hannay injured her shoulder and was hit in the eye, and the boat was filled with seawater and fuel oil. Mrs. H. DeWitt Smith of Plainfield, New Jersey, was also in the boat and held on when it careened down, but her nineteen-year-old daughter, Jeannette, fell into the sea and was picked up by another boat.[15] Witnessed by many people on the *Athenia*, this incident was a frightening sight. Years later, Scotty Gillespie vividly remembered seeing the lifeboat dangling at a precarious angle.

DeWitt Smith, who had put his wife, Ellen, and daughter, Jeannette, in No. 11A, heard their screams as the boat went on its end, but by the time Smith got back to the rail and looked over the side the fall was being cut and the boat made level. After deciding that there was nothing more he could do to be helpful on the *Athenia*, Smith took off his shoes and trousers and climbed down a rope into the water and swam about one hundred yards to another boat. That boat was already crowded with between eighty and ninety people, Smith reckoned. He clung to the grab line on the side of the boat until, as he put it, "I was invited to come aboard, an invitation which I gladly accepted." Chief Officer Copland ordered Quartermaster Graham to take charge of the boat No. 11A, although he had suffered rope burns on his hands and legs attempting to stop the stern fall from taking charge. Graham found that the boat was taking on water and ordered that the crew start bailing. It was presumed that the boat suffered some damage when it landed in the water and was leaking as a result. Even with steady bailing about two feet of water remained in the boat through the night. Ruby Mitchell was also supposed to get into No. 11A, but Mrs. Calder had not been allowed to come up to that lifeboat station. She told the sailor, "Well, that's my daughter, and my sister, and the little girl that's travelling with me. I've got to go to them." So Ruby, Margaret Calder, and Cristina Horgan were allowed to join Mrs. Calder in another boat. Ruby remembered that they eventually had to slide down ropes to get into their lifeboat.[16]

———————————

Third Officer Porteous left the bridge and took charge of the four lifeboats at the stern of the ship on the third-class promenade deck. Boats 14, 14A, and 15 were launched quite smoothly. Hugh S. Swindley, a man at least in his sixties who was sailing to Toronto, had been thrown to the deck of the third-class promenade when the torpedo hit. Ironically, he had been shipwrecked twice before, when the Orient liner *Oratava* went down in 1897 and when a schooner he was sailing on sank off the Australian coast in 1906 or 1907. Swindley made his way up the companionway ladder and helped the crew launch several of the boats. No one was injured in the launching of these boats, he said. They also slid one of the life rafts over the stern of the ship—a "heavy piece of 'furniture,'" Swindley called it.

Mrs. Edith Bridge got her daughter, Constance Edith, into boat No. 14, but when she started down the ladder to the boat it pulled away from the ship. The woman below her on the ladder fell into the water and was pulled into the lifeboat, but Mrs. Bridge climbed back onto the ship and left on a later boat with her son Harry. Assistant Steward R. Grant managed No. 14A with the help of six members of the crew, and they got the boat under way in between fifteen and twenty-five minutes. The boat was filled with 103 women and children and only 2 male passengers. Later in the evening Chief Officer Copland was put in No. 14A with its precious cargo. The boat road easily during the night, but it was low in the water and Copland had the canvas boat cover spread over the occupants as the wind and waves rose. Copland also burned several flares in the course of the night.[17]

Boat No. 15A, on the starboard side, had trouble launching, in part due to the listing of the ship. The stern fall jammed on the "gypsy barrel," the flanged drum around which the fall was wrapped several times to provide enough friction to allow several crewmembers to lower safely a boat weighing several tons. In this case, the bow fall had been paid out, leaving the boat dangling at a 45-degree angle about eight feet above the water. Third Officer Porteous gave orders that the after fall be cut and the bow fall let go, allowing the boat to drop the rest of the way into the water, now held along the side of the ship only with the bow line. Agnes Stuppel of Hollywood, California, watched all of this from the deck with considerable misgiving, but eventually climbed down a rope lifeline into the boat About ninety passengers, mostly women, then got into the boat from a side ladder and four lifelines. There was quite a bit of water and oil in the boat. Lucretia Estelle Kelly said that she was "totally immersed," but the boat righted itself despite the damage to it. Cadet J. T. Donald, who was put in charge, found the plug, which had apparently been knocked out of place when the boat struck the water, and had it installed. However, because of the damage the boat suffered, the boat leaked badly. Even with pails obtained from another boat and steady bailing all night there remained about eighteen inches of water in the bottom of No. 15A. Swindley also climbed down the lines into the boat and struggled to get the oars out from under the crowd of passengers. Eventually he abandoned rowing and used his new handmade English boots to bail for the rest of the night. Nevertheless after the sea anchor was put out, the boat road easily during the night.[18]

After the last three boats were launched on the starboard side, there remained only boat No. 5, the motorboat, standing by to take off the remaining officers and several passengers who had refused to leave earlier. It was just after nine o'clock, or about one hour and fifteen or twenty minutes after the torpedo attack. James Goodson had been working steadily to help the crew get people out of the damaged part of the ship and then assisting passengers into the lifeboats. When the last lifeboat left he felt depressed and at loose ends. He went down to the purser's office to see if he could retrieve his money, but of course could not get into the safe. He came back on deck, but decided not to wait for the motor lifeboat to return to the *Athenia*. He saw a lifeboat about one hundred yards away and made up his mind to swim for it. Goodson climbed over the side of the ship and using a dangling rope went hand over hand until he eventually lost his grip and plunged into the sea. It took a long time to get up to the surface, he swallowed seawater—the North Atlantic waves were rougher and colder than he had expected—and the lifeboat, which he could only see intermittently, now looked much farther away. Goodson was a good swimmer, but he wished that he had a lifejacket. Despite the fact that men were attempting to row the lifeboat, eventually Goodson caught up with it. However, when he attempted to climb into the boat several people tried to push him back out. A sailor ordered them to stop and with the help of several young women he was pulled on board. "I collapsed in a wet heap on the bottom of the boat and gasped my thanks to my rescuers. Amid peals of young female laughter I heard: 'Hey! You're an American!' 'So are you!' I mumbled in reply." He was wrapped in a blanket by several scantily clad college girls, including Caroline Stuart and Anne Baker. This was a rescue much beyond expectation.[19]

The ship now had a list of between 10 to 12 degrees to port and was noticeably down at the stern. First Radio Officer David Don had been sending SOS signals steadily since the ship was struck, "SSSS SSSS SSSS ATHENIA GFDM torpedoed position 5644 1405." This was the international code for a submarine attack, the *Athenia's* call letters, and her latitude and longitude. By 8:45 p.m. these messages had been picked up by the Malin Head radio station in County Donegal on the northern tip of Ireland and relayed to ships at sea and to the Admiralty in Britain. Radio Officer Don was able to report that the Norwegian freighter *Knute Nelson*, which had been seen by the submarine *U-30* earlier in the day, had responded and was returning to pick up survivors. It was estimated that it would be within sight shortly after midnight. Don told the *Knute Nelson* that he would be abandoning ship shortly and that he would screw down the telegraph key to make a constant signal to serve as a directional radio beacon in the night to assist the freighter in finding the *Athenia*. Between 9:22 and 9:26 p.m. the first radio officer was also able to report that the Swedish steam yacht *Southern Cross* and the American freighter *City of Flint* had responded and were heading for the *Athenia* with all possible speed. The Admiralty received the distress signal at 10:30 p.m., and before midnight the order was given to detach two destroyers, HMS *Escort* and *Electra*, and just after midnight HMS *Fame*, from duties escorting the battle cruiser HMS *Renown*, which was proceeding to the home fleet base at Scapa Flow in the Orkney Islands in Scotland. The destroyers then made a course for the *Athenia* at 56° 42′ N, and 14° 05′ W, at a speed of twenty-five knots.[20]

Before the officers abandoned ship an inspection had to be made to see that there was nothing more that could be done to save the vessel and that no one was left behind. Chief Officer Copland was told by the second steward that all living passengers had been "cleared out" of the ship. Third Officer Porteous reported that the hand-operated between deck watertight bulkhead doors could not be completely closed. The buckling of the ship, caused first by the force of the exploding torpedo and then by the stress put on the ship by the flooding of the stern part of the vessel, had sprung the door fittings and the bulkhead rivets and seams. Copland attempted to make his way to No. 5 hatchway, where the full force of the explosion had been visible and where several people had been killed. However, the between decks passages on the port side were both twisted and flooded and he was unable to get there. He tried to open the control valves for the sanitary discharge, but could not move them. Along the starboard work alleyway he found several bodies and checked to see if they were actually dead. With the aid of a flashlight Copland was able to determine that the water was now nearly up to the midship line on C Deck, having flowed through the third-class dining room. He also checked pantries, galleys, and dining rooms farther forward and found no more water and no more bodies. He could then report to the captain that while he had counted about fifty dead bodies, all living people were off the ship except the ship's officers and a handful of others. Captain Cook inquired specifically about Mrs. Rose Griffin, the unconscious patient in the ship's hospital, and was assured that all were gone.[21]

Nothing more could be done; it was time to leave. The captain, keeping in mind that during the last war the Germans had sometimes taken the sinking ship's senior officers prisoner, changed out of his uniform and into civilian clothes. He then hailed lifeboat No. 5, the motorboat, and the second wireless operator and the boat was brought alongside the ship. The several remaining passengers, including Dr. Edward T. Wilkes and Father Joseph V. O'Connor, got on board boat No. 5. Father O'Connor would leave behind his portable altar, chalice, and sacred vessels. The remaining officers got into No. 5 between eleven o'clock and midnight. The captain took with him the ship's papers and log, and he distributed several of the officers and crew to other boats that lacked any experienced sailors to handle the lifeboats. Third Officer Porteous took charge of the boat and carried out the assignment to try to redistribute passengers from the overloaded boats, carefully transferring them to those boats with fewer people in them. The chief officer was put into boat No. 14A, the first officer into No. 12, the second officer into No. 2A, and the boatswain into one of the early boats.[22] The *Athenia* was then seemingly left to her fate.

CHAPTER 6

THOSE IN PERIL ON THE SEA

*The rowing was desperate for a long time, then the oars rested as we were swept
to what seemed to us a terrific height by the swell. Then down we sank—to rise again.
All of us violently ill—even the crew. The boat filled rapidly with water.
I stood in water to my knees. All night water was bailed out.*

—Dorothy Bulkley[1]

The moon cast a pale light across the sea. From time to time the endless six-foot waves would crest, catch the eerie light with a certain sparkle, and hiss ominously for just a moment. The emergency lights on the *Athenia* burned long into the night also, illuminating the irony of their situation to those in the lifeboats. And every once in a while a flare would go up from one of the lifeboats, as if to say "we are here too." From time to time also clouds would pass before the moon, bringing light rainsqualls, just to remind them again that they were cold and wet and separated from anyone on a very broad ocean. "We were a bunch of huddled forms," one survivor recalled, "tossed about on the swells."[2] For the children, some crying, some fallen asleep, and the rest who were cold, wet, drenched with fuel oil, seasick, and anxious, there was only the endless up-and-down twisting motion of the boats riding the Atlantic swells.

Getting into the lifeboats was no resolution of the crisis. The precariousness of the situation was nicely stated by Charles Wharton Stork: "Ah! So we're safe, if you can call it safe to be in an open rowboat far from land in darkness with a sea that runs to waves five feet above our gunwales." Nevertheless for Eva Blair getting away from the *Athenia* in the lifeboat was a liberation. "The realization dawned upon me unexpectedly," she said. "*God had spared my life!*"[3] Judith Evelyn's recollections were filled with more practical problems. Once they were all in the boat on the water, it proved impossible to release the shackles holding the blocks and the falls to the boat. Axes were produced to cut the falls so the boat could be freed from the ship. As her lifeboat began to move away from the *Athenia* someone, "in true storybook fashion," as she put it, roused everyone to begin singing. Just at that moment, however, they nearly ran into another lifeboat in the darkness, which stopped the singing for good. Dorothy Bulkley found her boat in even more dangerous circumstances. Before they were released and able to push way from the ship another boat, 11A, was being lowered right on top of them. Shouts and screams seemed to stop the boat for a moment, dangling just above them. The falls were cut with axes and knives, Sara Grossman remembered, and the boat finally freed. Herbert Spiegelberg, who was also in Bulkley's lifeboat, later told his Swarthmore College students and colleagues that they had just been able to dig the oars out from beneath the people jammed into his boat and push off from the side of the *Athenia* when the stern of 11A splashed down into the water. It was so dark that he could not see how many fell into the sea, but the screams of those in that boat led him to believe that there were many. When the bow fall of 11A was slacked and the boat leveled, people had to be pulled out of the water and back into the boat. Several people were injured, including Mrs. Elsie Insch who was hit in the face and badly scarred by one of the blocks. The boat was now filled with badly shaken people, not to mention seawater and fuel oil pouring from the ruptured bunkers in the ship. The flares in the boat also ignited, causing another panic because people feared that being covered in oil they might themselves catch fire. The flares had to be put out before they caused any injury or damage. The boat splashing into the water from six to twelve feet probably sprung some of the planks and may well have dislodged the plug as well. In any case, the boat leaked badly for the rest of the night, despite constant bailing.[4]

Many boats leaked for one reason or another. Alma Bloom said that the men in her boat were busy bailing until the plug was found and put in place. May Ingram, who sat covered with a blanket, recounted that her boat leaked and that people bailed with their shoes until a pail was found. This enabled them to lower the amount of water in the boat, but it was never completely emptied. She said the boatswain's mate in charge of their boat had them put up the mast in order to make sail, but what was presumed to be the sail turned out to be a tarpaulin. People in Jeanette Jordan's boat bailed with their shoes until a pail was found, after which a small man who had been "desperately ill" bailed throughout the night. Hugh Swindley bailed all night. Barbara Rodman's boat had to be bailed constantly, and several people in it were injured also. They also picked up some people in the water, including a woman whose arm was broken. "I stood in water to my knees," Dorothy Bulkley said, but when she got cold and bent down to get out of the wind she was in water up to her waist. There were also children in her boat who were "half submerged." Thomas Quine said that his boat leaked at first, but after six hours it stopped. He concluded that the dry seams had swelled up sufficiently to stop the leaking. In addition to leaking, there was a danger that the boats would take seawater over the sides and occasionally they did. Most of the boats were loaded to capacity or more, with the result that they were riding low in the water. The waves, which were running about six feet when the boats were put in the water, increased over night to about ten feet, so there was some real danger. "The seas were mountains," Helen Edna Campbell remembered.[5] Nevertheless there were some boats that did not leak, did not ship water, and were perfectly dry all night.

Another real problem was the difficulty in attempting to maneuver the lifeboats. Many survivors complained that there was no rudder in their boat, or that the rudder was broken, or that the tiller was missing. Theoretically a steering oar, or sweep, could have been used, but there was a problem with oars also inasmuch as they seemed to have been in very short supply. Charles Van Newkirk, a seaman who was traveling on the *Athenia*, reported that on his boat there were only five oars and a rudder, but no tiller and no pail. In fact, the oars and other gear were stored on the bottom of the boats, under the thwarts. But in the dark, when the boats were filled with as many as ninety frightened people, many of them women and children and a number of people who did not understand English, it proved very difficult to extract the oars, find the oarlocks and set them in place, and find people capable of rowing. Both Professor Spiegelberg and Hugh Swindley described the difficulty of getting the oars out from the bottom of their filled lifeboats and getting the boat under way.[6]

Rowing these huge, heavy boats was a real problem. Helen Hannay said there were not enough men in her boat to row, so they just drifted. There were not any men in Agnes Stuppel's boat, she said, until some swimmers were hauled into the boat from the sea and they rowed. Having also been pulled out of the sea into his boat, young James Goodson gave his sweater to one of the college girls and offered to row. He was placed between two refugees, one of whom spoke Yiddish and could understand Goodson's German and the other who talked to Goodson in broken English. Their objective was to keep the boat headed into the wind. Ida Mowry said there were six men in her boat, two elderly gentlemen, two stewards, and two sailors; the two sailors rowed while the others bailed. Gustav Anderson worked one of the four oars in his boat, attempting to keep the craft headed into the wind. But after an hour he "collapsed from exhaustion." Joseph Insch and a boy of seventeen each took an oar, while eight women struggled with the two other oars. Together they managed to get their boat about five hundred yards away from the *Athenia*. Professor Charles Wharton Stork teamed up with a young man in boat No. 7. They had not been able to find the oarlocks, so the young man held the oar while Stork rowed. Stork concluded that all they could do with the oars was to steady the boat. He also gave credit to young Wilson L. Smith Jr., who worked one of the other oars. F. Elwood MacPherson rowed, but his boat was so crowded that he had to row standing up. Montgomery Evans attempted to row sitting on a thwart, but whenever he tried to brace his feet on the floorboards he was repeatedly warned that he was about to step on the baby of motion picture director Ernst Lubitsch. As a result he was so unbalanced that he concluded that the young women in the boat were doing much better at the task. Mrs. Jessie Gillespie rowed, aided by her two sons, aged eleven and ten. One of the Texas college girls, Maxine Robinson, only sixteen years old, said she rowed for four hours. "My hands are all blistered from rowing," she pointed out later. Hugh Swindley remembered seeing one man in his boat rowing steadily while desperately seasick. In Judith Evelyn's boat there were two oars on one side and four on the other. Attempts to extract additional oars from underneath the people huddled in the bottom of the boat met with "screams of terror"; as a result it was almost impossible to row the boat.[7]

All of these matters might have been taken care of by *Athenia* crewmembers, but of course many of them had been killed or injured by the explosion of the torpedo in the engine room. Some survivors complained that there was no crewmember in their boat, or the person commanding the boat was a steward or bartender rather than an experienced seaman. Certainly the passengers, both women and men, did most of the rowing. Eventually Louis Molgat, from Ste. Rose du Lac, Manitoba, who had served in the French navy during the First World War, took charge of his boat, together with a Danish passenger. Edith Bridge said there was one ship's "officer" in her boat, but that he was injured and unconscious. There were four crewmembers in his boat, Joseph Insch said, but two of them had broken arms. One crewmember who rowed and bailed was nurse Campbell, who helped Joseph B. L. MacDonald in boat No. 10. Indeed several nurses were singled out for their help in the boats. Fourteen-year-old Donald Wilcox rowed in his boat. There were several members of the crew who worked to fend off his boat from the *Athenia* until all the passengers were on board. In the meantime passengers, including a number of women, were at the oars. As the boat got under way, the crewmembers took over some of the oars. Wilcox remembered there being five oars on each side and three rowers on each oar, and Second Officer K. G. Crockett instructing them on how to row effectively in the six-foot swells. The lifeboat was so big and so heavy in the water that to Wilcox, attempting "to take a normal stroke of the oar felt as if it had been placed against the side of a house, as the fully loaded lifeboat didn't move an inch!" In fact the initial object was merely to get the boats away from the *Athenia* and then stream a sea anchor so that the boats would not drift too far apart. The Donaldson Line report concluded that there were responsible employees in every boat, but it is clear from the point of view of some survivors not all of them showed leadership or even assertiveness. Sir Richard Lake, the former lieutenant governor of Saskatchewan, remembered the "quiet courage" of the people in lifeboat No. 6, despite everyone being seasick. "Nothing but words of cheer and encouragement could be heard," he said. Sir Richard, although seventy-nine years old, and Lady Dorothy both willingly helped to row their lifeboat.[8]

Many passengers thought that the crew of the *Athenia* did excellent work in the crisis and they were very grateful to them. James Boyle wanted to "give all credit" to the officers and crew for "their handling of the passengers and life-boats." Professor Damon Boynton also thought the efforts of the officers and crew were "exceptionally fine in view of the total unexpectedness of the disaster." There were no signs of panic that Sara Grossman could see and she thought everything was handled efficiently. May Ingram had great praise for the seaman who handled her lifeboat. "He swore like a good sailor, urged people to row and row better, and we all got along quite well," she said; and Ralph Singleton felt his lifeboat was handled very skillfully in the open sea. Doris MacLeod said the sailor who was in charge of her boat was very good and everyone did what he said. Matilda Johnson thought the crew "worked hard and efficiently" or in Barbara Rodman's words, with "amazing efficiency." Dr. John Lawrence gave special praise for Chief Officer Copland, for whom he had great respect. Elnetta MacDonald gave great credit to nurse Campbell and Mary Levine to Stewardess Johnstone.[9] Clearly attitudes toward the *Athenia* and her crew varied with personal experience.

For the women and children and older men in the lifeboats, it was a very traumatic experience. As the waves increased during the night to between six and ten feet, many boats shipped some water. If people were not wet enough, the boats were also hit by brief rainsqualls. Edith Bridge remembered that after it started to rain efforts were made to use the boat cover for some protection, but by the time the cover was dug out the rain stopped. No one was really dressed for these conditions. "Some people were practically without clothing, others wore light summer dresses with no coat, a few of us had light coats," Dr. Lulu Sweigard remembered. "The chill crept deeper and deeper into our bones," she said. Bernice Jansen did not remember much of her experience in the boat. As she was wet and exhausted from falling in the sea, someone put a coat over her. James Goodson, soaked from his swim to the boat, attempted to warm up by sharing a blanket with two scantily clad college girls, but rowing actually proved a more practical way to get his blood circulating. The college girls tried to lift everyone's spirits by singing school songs. Goodson thought they were "simply grand." George Calder got his wife and seven-year-old son on board the lifeboat and helped with rowing the boat for about six hours. He remembered that he was "physically and emotionally exhausted." Jeannette Jordan thought everyone in her boat was exhausted. Although the children slept and several adults were hysterical, most of them sat silent and motionless with their chins on their life-jackets. "All were wretchedly seasick," she said. Three-year-old Rosemary Cass-Beggs remembered sitting in the bow of the boat, calling out for her mother until Mrs. McMillan Wallace came forward and picked her up, covering her up with a blanket. She was puzzled by the strange sensation of being sick without having a stomachache. "She never cried," Mrs. Wallace said; Rosemary sang herself a song and went to sleep. Ruby Mitchell, dressed only in her silk pajamas, was cold, wet, and covered in oil, but she was comforted by a woman who took the young girl on her lap and sheltered her in her coat. "Ruby, you've got to stay awake," the woman urged, and the tired little girl replied, "Yes I will, I will."[10]

Although the night was not stormy, the six- to ten-foot waves created a lot of motion for the lifeboats. Judith Evelyn commented that not only was almost everyone seasick, but that when the boat lurched and twisted in the swells many of the women also screamed in fright. The children in her boat, some dressed only in their nightclothes, whimpered and cried all night. Moreover there was a baby right at her feet and every time she attempted to move it the mother, lying sick on the bottom of the boat, clutched the child to her. "I can still feel that baby's fingers every so often on my ankles," Evelyn remembered. Dorothy Bulkley sat next to a woman who had a broken shoulder and her daughter who had a broken arm. Dorothy Dean sat near two "wonderful" Jewish refugee children from Austria who spent the night bailing and "not once did they complain." Ellen Hutchinson, who had fallen on the ship and injured her back, said she had been thrown into her lifeboat. She spent the night on the bottom of the boat with two people on top of her. She was almost unconscious by the time they were rescued. Berta Rapp, a twenty-two-year-old Jewish refugee from Austria, did pass out in the boat and did not regain consciousness again until after she was rescued. Later on in the middle of the night the motor lifeboat went from boat to boat attempting to shift passengers from overloaded boats to those that had more space. Hugh Swindley helped a woman and her child shift to another boat, and he said a number of people left his boat at the same time.[11] The people in the lifeboats were also given assurances that rescue ships had been reached by radio and that they would appear shortly. Those ship's officers who had remained on the *Athenia* to look after the launching of lifeboats were also placed in various of the boats without an experienced person in charge.

The fact of war was not lost on those in the lifeboats either. After the first torpedo strike against the *Athenia*, the German submarine *U-30* fired a second round of torpedoes, although one torpedo stuck temporarily in the submarine and the second ran wild on an erratic course without hitting the *Athenia*. The *U-30* also remained in the area for some time. The survivors in the lifeboats could not be sure of what was happening, but they were aware of the submarine's presence. Elizabeth Alton's daughter had pointed out to her mother the smoke on the horizon, and when they were some distance away from the *Athenia* they were aware of something passing beneath them. "It caused the boat to vibrate," Mrs. Alton said, "and we smelt a distinct odour of oil." Edith Bridge heard a "swish in the water" and felt a vibration in her lifeboat also. Dorothy Dean and her mother, Amy, heard what they called a rumbling sound and felt something scrape along the bottom of their boat. Eva Blair remembered a "dull thud" along the bottom of her boat and they feared that they had struck a mine. However, they concluded that it had been a torpedo and that people in another boat had been thrown from their seats by the turbulence in the water. At what he thought was 2 a.m. Douglas Stewart also heard a humming sound and felt something scraping along the bottom of the lifeboat. Somewhat later he was sure the submarine surfaced. Don Gifford thought there had been an explosion underwater about an hour and a half after the *Athenia* was first hit. This shook the boat slightly, but did not threaten to overturn it. Barbara Rodman feared that the explosion she felt would shatter her lifeboat.[12]

Many people reported that there had been another explosion, heard or felt, while they were in the boats. Several people saw what must have been the *U-30*'s periscope also. Ten-year-old Alexander Lamont saw what he described as "black and rusty looking with a black pipe sticking above the rusty black metal" moving rapidly through the water toward the lifeboat. "I yelled, 'There is something coming! Behind us!'" The *Athenia* sailor steering the lifeboat called out, "It's the bloody U-boat." Florence Davis remembered what she described as "a stick above the surface of the water." Hessie Hislop saw "a long thin pole, probably a periscope," about eight hundred yards away, and it seemed to her that there was a second explosion somewhere under the lifeboat. The thirteen-year-old daughter of Joseph Insch saw "a pipe sticking up through the water and moving along quite rapidly."[13] When Ruth Rabenold saw "a metal rod" sticking out of the sea she concluded that the explosion on the *Athenia* had indeed been caused by a submarine. Frances Shoen said that the periscope passed only a few yards from her boat and was visible for some time. Norman Hanna saw a periscope about ten feet away from his boat, after they got some distance from the *Athenia*, and he said a cable on the submarine caught the bottom of the lifeboat and almost upset it. Charles O. Bowen of Vancouver later told newspaper reporters, "the submarine came up under us and tried to upset No. 1 and No. 4 lifeboats," and he also claimed that it fired at the *Athenia*. Several weeks later when questions arose as to whether the *Athenia* could have been sunk by a submarine, Caroline Stuart of Plainfield, New Jersey, wrote to the State Department to say that she had seen a submarine periscope and she knew what one was. She asserted, "my father built submarines for Russia in the Russo-Japanese War and so I have always known what a periscope was."[14] Clearly the *U-30* was maneuvering to inspect the ship, but whether the sensations observed in the lifeboats were caused by the submarine passing beneath them or by the last torpedo is impossible to determine.

Some time after midnight people in the lifeboats began to see lights on the horizon. It was the Norwegian freighter *Knute Nelson*, which had been sailing from Oslo bound for the Panama Canal and had earlier on Sunday seen the *U-30*. The ship picked up the SOS radio messages from the *Athenia* at about 8:45 in the evening and signaled back, "THE OLD MAN DOESN'T BELIEVE YOU'VE BEEN

TORPEDOED—BUT HE'S COMING TO YOUR ASSISTANCE ANYWAY." Captain Carl J. Andersson calculated that he was about forty-five miles south of the *Athenia* and he altered course and turned his ship around to respond. The *Knute Nelson* was a 435-foot (132.58-meter) freighter, built in Odense, Denmark, in 1926 for the Fred. Olsen & Company steamship line operating out of Oslo. All hands went to work to get the lifeboats and ladders put out and the ship made ready. But they were still a long way away and moving at only fourteen knots.[15]

"Ye don't think we can be saved?" an elderly Scottish woman asked Professor Stork. "We're practically saved already," he replied with cheery confidence. "I say it and I don't dare not think it," he reflected to himself rather less boldly. Nevertheless, the twinkling lights of the *Knute Nelson* looked like those of a fairy castle to Barbara Bailey. Elwood MacPherson was standing in his boat at an oar when they started rowing toward the *Knute Nelson* at about 12:30 a.m. However, it was not until nearly 2:30 in the morning that they got close to the ship and then slipped right past it. By great effort, "with hard rowing on bended oars," they got their boat turned around and brought along the lee side of the freighter. The ship was in ballast, riding very high, so that the deck towered at least fifteen to twenty feet above the surface of the water. Boatswain's chairs were lowered over the side to the lifeboats to hoist up the women and children. The younger passengers climbed up a rope ladder and finally MacPherson and the three crewmembers followed. Safe at last, but for the first time he could not breathe and thought he would collapse. Despite the rope burns on his hands, Reverend Hutchinson decided to climb up the rope ladder, although the sight of the person ahead of him struggling to hold on was unnerving. Young Donald Wilcox remembered the lifeboat rising and falling in the water alongside the ship and being told to wait until the boat surged upward before reaching out to the cargo net that he was to scramble up. It was difficult to get a grip on the netting and everyone scraped their hands and knees, he said. However, as they got close to the deck the strong arms of the crewmembers lifted them on board.[16]

Other boats gathered alongside, waiting. Eva Blair was hoisted up in a boatswain's chair, but "with the first upward heave, my body was dangling in midair!" Fearing that she would fall to her death between the ship and the lifeboat, she was convinced that "only super-human strength enabled me to hang on to the main rope." Something very nearly like that happened to Lady Dorothy, the wife of Sir Richard Lake. While being hoisted up from the lifeboat in a boatswain's chair her hands slipped from the rope and she fell backward. Fortunately her legs caught in the ropes on either side of the wooden seat and she was suspended upside down along the side of the ship, her skirts falling over her head. A crewmember clambered over the side and got a firm hold on her ankles while she was carefully eased up onto the deck. With incredible aplomb, Lady Dorothy straightened herself up, smoothed her skirts, and said, "Whew! That was a close one! If I had fallen into the boat, I would have killed them!!" By the time Barbara Bailey's boat came alongside, the *Knute Nelson*'s accommodation ladder had been lowered, but the platform was still about six feet above the lifeboat. She was more or less thrown by three men to a Norwegian sailor on the platform and then made her way up the steps.[17]

Captain Andersson and his crew worked to accommodate over four hundred passengers and crew of the *Athenia*. The staterooms and salons for officers and crew were given over to the survivors and the shelter deck was made as accommodating as possible. The survivors were hoisted on board, their lifejackets cut off, and they were given something to eat or drink. Eva Blair was led directly to the galley where she was given some beef tea. Barbara Bailey was given some gin, which she in turn brought to an *Athenia* crewman who had been scalded in the explosion and was near death, she thought. Elwood MacPherson gave his raincoat to a wet, shivering Jewish mother and his clan MacPherson blanket to her two children. Blankets were provided to many who were dressed only in their nightclothes or underwear. Dr. Altschul and his wife slept on the floor of the captain's cabin using lifejackets as cushions. Captain Andersson was sometimes described as elderly and rather gruff. James Goodson saw the somewhat amazed and compassionate Norwegian captain telling the several college girls to "Go down! Down! Any door! Any room! Warm! You must have warm!" Their solution was to climb into the warm beds of the Norwegian sailors. Warmth and a place to collapse was what most people needed. Survivors squeezed into all the available spaces on the ship, from the captain's bathtub to various cargo holds. Many would have joined Margaret Ford's grateful statement of "how very fine the captain, officers, and crew of the *Knute Nelson* were to us." Night gave way to dawn about 6:00 a.m. while many of the survivors dozed fitfully, still not able to either relax or find comfort. Tea and hardtack and soup were served from the ship's limited stores, and mugs were "re-cycled" as quickly as they were emptied without worrying about washing. Dry clothing was given to people, but coats were also made out of canvas sacks and slippers out of odd bits of cloth. Dr. Edward Wilkes, who had lost his wife and as far as he knew both of his sons, was the only physician on the ship who could speak English and went around patiently applying first aid to people with cuts, bruises, and burns. With the assistance of one of the *Athenia*'s stewardesses, Dr. Wilkes shaved the scalp of Bernice Jensen and gave her eight stitches for a cut she sustained when she slipped into the sea while descending to her lifeboat. Benzene was used to clean off the fuel oil that had covered her when she was in the water. Ten people were badly injured, with burns, fractures, and deep wounds being the worst. Captain Cook, the chief engineer, and the second engineer came on board the *Knute Nelson* also and attempted to assess what had happened. Four hundred thirty survivors were brought on board the *Knute Nelson*.[18]

While the appearance of the *Knute Nelson* within a few hours of the orders to abandon the *Athenia* was almost a miracle, a terrible tragedy occurred during the rescue that significantly expanded the number of deaths in the overall calamity. Sometime after 2:00 a.m. on Monday morning, while it was still dark, there were as many as six boats clustered along the starboard side of the ship. Lifeboat No. 4 came alongside and lines were seized, although sailors on the *Knute Nelson* waved them off. With the seas now reaching ten feet, the lifeboat was difficult to manage and drifted toward the stern of the freighter into the wash of the huge propeller. Because the *Knute Nelson* was empty and riding very high in the water the propeller broke the surface when it turned. Douglas and William Stewart, who were pulling on the same oar, realized that the lifeboat was going to be drawn right into the propeller. They pushed the blade of their oar against the hull of the *Knute Nelson*, and although "the oar bent in an arch till we thought it would break, . . . it held, and we cleared the propeller blades by a mere foot and a half." Patricia Hale and Margaret Patch were also rowing as hard as they could in lifeboat No. 4. "For one awful moment the stern seemed about to come right down on us," Hale remembered.[19] Quartermaster Dillon also brought lifeboat No. 5A alongside the *Knute Nelson*, well back toward the stern. A line had been passed to 5A to keep the boat from drifting away. However, when the engine of the *Knute Nelson* was turned on and the vessel moved forward, the line parted and 5A drifted under the stern counter of the ship. Efforts to fend the boat off the side of the ship with oars were unsuccessful. Dillon's boat was drawn right to the huge propeller, which sheared through the bottom of the boat at the keel, slicing through the planking and shattering the craft. Andrew Allan, who saw the man sitting on the thwart in front of him cut in half by the propeller, turned and plunged into the sea. "Got to get away from the blades," he told himself. It seemed an eternity until he reached the surface of what he remembered as a "churning red sea" and could breathe again.[20] Judith Evelyn, in the opposite end of the boat sitting next to Reverend Allan, Andrew's father, was unaware of what was happening and suddenly found herself in the sea with saltwater in her mouth and nose. Allan's father was never seen again. The wreckage of the boat capsized, turning some seventy people into the water.

James Goodson in one of the other six boats alongside the *Knute Nelson* saw the whole tragedy unfold and called to the helmsman in his boat to steer for those in the water. The strongest swimmers made for the ladders along the side of the ship or for Goodson's boat and were pulled in. George McMillan, assistant pantryman on the *Athenia*, saw several Norwegian sailors rescue a number of people from the sea, even by climbing down onto the rudder of the *Knute Nelson* to do so, but many people just slipped underwater in the darkness. Thomas G. Fielder, of Orono, Maine, and his cabin mate John Bernard were thrown into the water but managed to grab hold of some floating wreckage and were joined by several others. Fielder's water-filled wristwatch stopped at 2:50 a.m. They drifted away from the *Knute Nelson* for some time and were picked up by lifeboat No. 8. Quartermaster Dillon shouted to those in the water to "hang on to the boat." Two of the Texas college girls, Louise and Catherine Mackay, were able to cling to the wreckage. Allan and a steward turned a section of the boat upside down in order to trap air underneath and then climbed up on this frail craft. Although buoyed up by her lifejacket, Judith Evelyn in her heavy, wet fur coat slid underwater several times before she called out "Andrew," for the second time that evening. Miraculously he answered "Judith," as he had in the darkened dining room, and she was pulled up across from him on the upturned boat. All the while they drifted away from the *Knute Nelson* into the dark.[21]

Coming up out of the night, shortly behind the *Knute Nelson*, was the yacht *Southern Cross*, owned by the Swedish millionaire industrialist Axel Wenner-Gren and his American wife, the former Marguerite Gautier. His great fortune was derived largely from the success of the Electrolux vacuum cleaner manufacturing company, but also from his interests in SAAB and the Bofors gun patents in Sweden. Wenner-Gren became increasingly regarded with suspicion by the Allies during the war. His links with Herman Goering and the Duke of Windsor were compromising. However, none of these considerations diminished the generosity of Wenner-Gren and his crew in rescuing the *Athenia* survivors. The *Southern Cross*, previously owned by Howard Hughes, was one of the largest and most luxurious private yachts in the world. The yacht had been built in Glasgow in 1930, displaced 1,851 tons, and its waterline length was 266 feet (81 meters), but its dramatic counter stern and clipper bow, together with a substantial bowsprit, made its overall length even greater, 320.5 feet (97.6 meters). Painted a brilliant white and with gleaming brass trim and varnished woodwork, the *Southern Cross* was a striking vessel. She carried a complement of five officers and thirty-four uniformed crewmembers. The *Southern Cross* had left Norway on 31 August and was bound for the Bahamas when she picked up the distress signal from the *Athenia* at about nine o'clock.

Seaman R. Grant brought his boat, 14A, alongside the *Southern Cross* about 2:30 in the morning, followed shortly by 15A, commanded by Cadet J. T. Donald. With a powerful spotlight on his vessel, and assisted by flares fired periodically from the lifeboats, Captain Karl A. Sjodahl and Chief Officer Hjalmar Rothman of the *Southern Cross* assessed the dispersal of the lifeboats and positioned the yacht so as to pick up boats that could not reach the *Knute Nelson* or had drifted past her. John Coullie remembered rowing toward a spotlight shining on a lifeboat being picked up. A flare was lit in his boat and the spotlight was directed to them. The *Southern Cross* came alongside, "and we were pulled up one by one and the lifeboat was left to drift away." An exhausted Gustav Anderson heard someone in his boat ask what they should do if the rescue vessel were a German ship. Anderson was "glad to be rescued by anyone," but he also recognized the large blue-and-white Swedish flag draped over the side of the boat.[22] The fact that the sides of the yacht were lower than those of the *Knute Nelson* was reassuring to Patricia Hale, exhausted from rowing; the problem of getting up from the lifeboat was eased further by the rope nooses that were fitted under survivors' arms to hoist them up. Babies and small children were carried up by the Swedish sailors, some by their clothing held in the sailors' teeth. When a relieved Dorothy Dean reached the deck Mrs. Wenner-Gren cried out, "She must be English, my God she's smiling"; but some women also collapsed when they finally got on deck. DeWitt Smith climbed aboard the *Southern Cross* just as the sun was coming up. He had been in boat 11A, which had been damaged while being launched from the *Athenia* and had leaked badly all night. The bailing stopped as the survivors reached the *Southern Cross* and Smith observed that the boat sank as the last passengers got out.[23] Survivors were taken on board until between six-thirty and seven o'clock in the morning of 4 September.

The *Southern Cross* too had a disaster with one lifeboat. At about five in the morning, while it was still dark, Able Seaman W. J. Macintosh found his boat, No. 8, on the weather side of the *Southern Cross*. He was unable to bring the boat around the bow of the yacht to the lee side where the survivors were being taken on board, so he reversed course and attempted to steer the boat around the stern. It was important that the boat be kept clear of the *Southern Cross*, especially as it passed around the yacht's overhanging counter that extended several feet beyond the waterline. However, many of those at the oars in the boat did not understand English and were in fact anxious to get as close to the yacht as possible—one person actually seized a line hanging from the *Southern Cross* and attempted to climb up it. Therefore despite Macintosh's efforts to push the boat away with an oar, the boat, being tossed by what were now ten-foot waves, slid irreversibly under the projecting stern of the *Southern Cross*. In an instant the boat, surging upward on the crest of a wave, hit the counter of the yacht on a descending roll and was capsized, turning Macintosh and all of the passengers into the sea. The Gillespie family were caught when the boat went over, but fortunately they could swim. Scotty Gillespie was tangled in ropes and hit by the gunwale, although he managed to free himself and climb onto the exposed bottom of the boat. James Gillespie was trapped for a moment under the boat and was hit on the head, but he made his way out and was pulled into another lifeboat. Mrs. Gillespie, who said she "thought this was the end of it," pulled herself onto a raft that was floating nearby. One of the members of the crew pulled people onto the upturned boat. Sailors from the *Southern Cross* quickly got into one of the empty *Athenia* lifeboats alongside and pushed off into the sea to rescue people struggling in the water. Thomas Fielder, thrown into the sea now for the second time, swam to a swamped lifeboat along with several others and was rescued by sailors from the *Southern Cross*. His cabin mate, John Bernard, however, slipped away this time. Nicola, the infant daughter of the film director Ernst Lubitsch, was kept above water by her nurse Carlina Strohmayer until they were both rescued. Some of the sailors plunged into the sea also. Montgomery Evans saw one of the sailors in the water holding a child by its clothing, "like a cat with a kitten."[24] What must have been at least fifty or sixty people were saved, but it is estimated that about six were lost.

Ruby Mitchell saw the disaster with the lifeboat just in front of them, but their own boat was brought alongside the yacht and made fast. She remembered being thrown upward from the lifeboat by one sailor and being caught by another on the deck of the *Southern Cross*. She was then taken inside the yacht to warm up and given some hot soup. Then she was made to get out of her wet pajamas and provided with a shirt by one of the crew. This shirt she wore for the rest of her adventure across the Atlantic.[25]

As with the *Knute Nelson*, not all of the remaining lifeboats were physically able to get to the *Southern Cross*. Helen Hannay said that they were too exhausted to row to the *Southern Cross* and drifted past her in the night. Joseph Insch said his boat rowed toward the yacht and got within thirty yards but could get no closer. They hailed the yacht, but of course the crew were working to get people in lifeboats alongside up onto the deck. Even the wreck of the ill-fated 5A was caught in the *Southern Cross*'s searchlight but drifted by, upturned and with Quartermaster Dillon, Judith Evelyn, Andrew Allan, and several others clinging to it, but there was no help for them.[26]

Once on board the *Athenia* survivors were graciously treated by the owners and crew of the *Southern Cross*. Rev. Dr. G. P. Woollcombe was taken directly to an officer's cabin, given a "tot" of gin, and put to bed, where he promptly fell asleep. Dorothy Dean and her mother found space in the salon under a grand piano, where they were served soup and cheese sandwiches. Montgomery Evans was given sandwiches by a Japanese steward, offered brandy, and then led to a wood-paneled library, which reminded him, rather painfully, of the book collection he had been transporting back to the United States that was now doomed in the cargo hold of the *Athenia*. Evans dozed on the floor until roused to be given bouillon and coffee. "We were in a dreadful state," John Coullie wrote, "but they gave us some hot soup and blankets so we just lay on the floor exhausted after nine hours in the lifeboat." People were crowded everywhere on the yacht, in every cabin, along the decks, and on the stairways. Babies and children were put in one room. A frantic Mrs. Gillespie was told that two young boys who had been pulled out of the water were sleeping below decks; they turned out to be her sons, Scotty and James. Axel Wenner-Gren attempted to provide clothing to those survivors who had been dressed only in their nightclothes or who had discarded some apparel while in the water. Dr. Louis Burns of Philadelphia gave first aid to those who were injured, including several of the Swedish sailors who had injured themselves rescuing survivors from the upturned lifeboat.[27] Once on board the *Southern Cross* many anxious and distraught survivors, in a state of shock really, worried about the fate of missing members of their families.

Altogether 376 survivors were brought on board the Swedish yacht. Everyone was grateful to get out of the lifeboats, not to mention to have escaped the stricken *Athenia*. Although the *Southern Cross* was an exceptionally large steam yacht, it did not really have facilities for all of these people. The arrival of other rescue vessels—three Royal Navy destroyers and the American freighter *City of Flint*—allowed the survivors to be transferred. Those who went to the destroyers were brought to Scotland and those who chose to go to the *City of Flint* were taken across the Atlantic to Halifax. The tremendous efforts of Mr. and Mrs. Wenner-Gren and the crew of the *Southern Cross*, a private yacht, were particularly appreciated. George Calder wrote in his deposition to the Department of State in December, "I feel strongly that enough credit has not been given to the owner, Mr. Wenner-Gren, of the 'Southern Cross', and its officers and crew, for all their unselfishness and untiring efforts for our comfort." In his deposition, also in December, H. DeWitt Smith said that he had written to Rear Adm. Emory B. Land, chairman of the U.S. Maritime Commission, "in praise of the officers and crew of the 'Southern Cross.'"[28]

During the course of the night of 3 September, three 1,375-ton Royal Navy *Escapade*-class destroyers were detached from screening HMS *Renown* while proceeding to Scapa Flow in the Orkney Islands, north of Scotland. On HMS *Electra* the starboard watch had just been piped to "cruising stations" when signal lamps flashed the orders to make all speed to assist the *Athenia*'s distress call. *Electra* had been built by R. & W. Hawthorne Leslie and Company of Newcastle upon Tyne in 1934, was 329 feet (100 meters) in length, was capable of speeds of between thirty-six and thirty-eight knots, and carried a main battery of four 4.7-inch guns. Her captain was Lieutenant Commander S. A. "Sammy" Buss, who led the ship with distinction in the war, escorting HMS *Hood* and *Prince of Wales* in the search for the *Bismarck* and rescuing the three survivors of the *Hood*, and escorting HMS *Prince of Wales* and *Repulse* to Singapore in December of 1941, only to be lost in the Battle of the Java Sea on 27 February 1942. *Electra* was joined on the night of 3–4 September by HMS *Escort*, commanded by Lieutenant Commander J. Bostock, who was later awarded the Distinguished Service Cross. *Escort* was built by Scotts Shipbuilding & Engineering Company in Greenock, launched on 29 March 1934, later torpedoed in the western Mediterranean, and sunk while being towed to Gibraltar on 11 July 1940. Later HMS *Fame* arrived and provided protection against submarines. Led by Commander P. N. Walter, *Fame* had been built by Vickers-Armstrong in Newcastle and launched on 28 June 1934. Sometime after seven in the morning *Fame* picked up distress signals from the SS *Blairlogie*, a freighter some 140 miles farther south and left to provide assistance. Steaming at about twenty-five knots for some 240 nautical miles, the *Electra* went to "Action Stations" at 4:00 a.m. Cargo nets and ladders were made ready. By first light the shape of the *Athenia* could be made out on the horizon and by 4:35 a.m. lifeboats, wreckage, and people in lifebelts could be seen.[29]

HMS *Electra* first undertook an antisubmarine patrol around the *Athenia* and the lifeboats, and HMS *Escort*, using her searchlights, began looking for *Athenia* lifeboats. Barbara Rodman remembered drifting for hours after having been so close to *Knute Nelson* that they feared they might be hit by it, and then "suddenly a warship appeared out of the darkness and the *Escort* pulled alongside our boat and rescued us." Mary Dick thought she was brought on board *Escort* as early as four in the morning. Margaret McPherson and her daughter Fione were taken by the sailors to the torpedo room. There she was reunited with her second daughter who had been looked after by a playmate's father. To Professor Charles Wharton Stork this was "the most terrifying experience of the night." The waves by this time were between eight to ten feet in height and the up-and-down motions were exaggerated when the lifeboat came alongside the ship. Even then it was at least ten feet to the deck of the destroyer. Sixty-two-year-old Helen Edna Campbell saw the "tall, grim, dark, wall of the destroyer" and thought she might faint, and when the first woman up the ladder fell back into the boat and broke her leg, she was certain she could never make it. But a sailor said to her, "Here you, put your hands on that ladder and hang your weight on them." He shouted, "Don't you dare let go," as she was hoisted up to the deck.[30] Ropes and rope ladders were put over the side for the men to climb. Later women were hoisted up by a noose that was placed around them, and children were carried in the arms of the sailors. The officers urged everyone to be careful and take their time, and the boats were emptied in about fifteen minutes, but there were some accidents.

The most dramatic rescue by *Escort* was without doubt that of the shattered and overturned boat of Quartermaster Dillon, 5A, that had been smashed by the *Knute Nelson*'s propeller. Twenty or so people had managed to cling to the keel and the ridges of the strakes that made up the hull of the boat, but they were constantly swept by waves that washed them back into the sea. The boat drifted past the *Southern Cross* and fell momentarily into the beam of its searchlight and was then swallowed up by the night again. One by one people slid off the boat and disappeared. Judith Evelyn and a man next to her helped for the second time pull a woman with long black hair back to the boat. The woman said "thank you," and Evelyn, hovering on despair, wondered to herself, "for what?" As the gray dawn began to break an object gradually took shape near them and a searchlight again caught them in its beam. Evelyn could just make out "H-66" on the side and realized that this was a naval vessel. *Escort* came alongside the over-turned boat, put ladders over the side, and lowered one of its own boats to get sailors onto the water's surface. Helped by Andrew Allan, but weighted down by her water-logged fur coat, Evelyn managed to get to the ladder. She was so weak that she could not lift her arms or take a step and was in danger of falling back into the water when sailors grabbed her lifejacket and hoisted her onto the deck. Allan followed, wrapping ropes around his hand so that he would not let go. But few were left. In addition to Evelyn and Allan, only Quartermaster Dillon, one steward, two stewardesses, and perhaps three passengers were all who remained to be saved on the wreckage of boat No. 5A. "I clung on to the overturned life-boat for about three hours before being rescued," recalled Catherine Mackay. Lieutenant Commander Bostock of the *Escort* reported they had picked up about two hundred survivors, although a number of corpses were seen in the water and three people died after being brought on board.[31]

On the decks of HMS *Escort* survivors stood about exhausted, artificial respiration was given to several people, and Dr. Lawrence provided first aid to people from the *Athenia* and *Escort* alike. The elderly man that Judith Evelyn and Andrew Allan had kept alive on the lifeboat died on board the destroyer. Sailors cut off Evelyn's lifejacket and took her in out of the cold to help her out of her wet clothes. Her hands were so stiff that she could not manage the buttons, so a sailor just ripped off her dress; when she was covered by a blanket, the rest of her undergarments were taken off as well. A sailor then picked her up and carried her to the officers' quarters where she had something to drink and tried to sleep. However, other women and infants were also brought into the room, and while still icy cold herself Evelyn attempted to warm a baby. The officers' steward worked tirelessly to provide them with food and tea, to find some new clothes, and to dry their wet garments. When at last they were able, Evelyn and Allan tried to come to grips with the fact that Andrew's father had been lost. Helen Edna Campbell was shown to a couch were she sat with an American girl. The two just cried and, although they were still seasick, they then fell asleep. Thomas Finley Jr. was the last to be rescued by the *Escort* at about 7:30 in the morning. When he got on board he found his wife, who had been picked up from another boat earlier in the morning. For the crew he had nothing but praise. "The crew gave clothing and turned over their sleeping quarters to the survivors with complete generosity," he said. Alma Bloom felt the same. She was brought tea and blankets and looked after for twenty-four hours. "Never have I seen such consideration, thoughtfulness, and kindness as every member of the crew displayed," she grate-fully acknowledged. "Thank God for the British Navy!," Campbell later wrote.[32]

HMS *Fame* arrived at about 7:00 a.m. and took over the antisubmarine patrol, allowing HMS *Electra* to begin approaching the lifeboats as some light began to appear in the sky. *Electra* continued to pick up people until perhaps as late as 10:00 a.m. It seemed "rather problematical" to Herbert Spiegelberg how a rescue could be made with the seas running as high as they were. It looked certain that the lifeboats would be smashed against the side of the destroyer. However, just as they came alongside, cushioned fenders made of oakum were put over the side against which the boat could rub harmlessly. A perilous rope ladder was then put down. This too looked dubious until two sailors jumped over the side of the ship on each side of the ladder, holding onto the railing with one hand and resting one foot on the ladder. As the lifeboat rose on the crest of a wave, they reached down into the boat and picked up a passenger by the arms and lifted that person onto the ladder, where other sailors on deck could take hold and pull the survivor the rest of the way. Women, children, and men all worked their way up from the boat and onto the *Electra*, "without one single hitch." As Spiegelberg said, it was "not always a very dignified sight, but still an admirable performance." Late in the morning Chief Officer Copland finally brought boat No. 14A up to the *Electra*. Although it had not leaked, it was riding very low in the water with only three strakes of its planking providing freeboard. This boat carried 105 passengers, most of them children, and very few men who could row. Copland had kept the boat heading into the wind and riding rather comfortably with a sea anchor, and he had tried to protect the passengers by covering them as best he could with the canvas boat cover; but with the rising wind and waves it was critical to get them on the destroyer. These young survivors were among the 238 hoisted aboard by the *Electra*'s sailors.[33]

All these people were particularly cold, hungry, and exhausted, having been in the lifeboats for between eight and twelve hours. Spiegelberg was grateful for the "charming if austere hospitality" of the destroyer and praised the sailors for the food and warmth they provided. He thought that the sailors' hammocks were the perfect way to restore one's balance after hours in a tossing lifeboat. Mrs. Ellen Hutchinson, who was almost unconscious in the boat, had little recollection of getting on the *Electra*, but she said that words "can not describe how good the men on the destroyer were to me and to everybody." Mrs. Kate Hinds also had praise for the *Electra*, "whose men fed, washed and gave up their hammocks for us and showed us every courtesy"; and Elnetta MacDonald said the sailors were "the finest boys I have ever known." Perhaps the most knowledgeable tribute to the British sailors came from the American marine engineer returning to the United States on the *Athenia*: "As a seaman, I cannot find language sufficient to give due praise to the men of His Majesty's Navy. They took the best possible care of all survivors who could possibly be picked up by them."[34]

Before Chief Officer Copland could eat or take his rest, he consulted with the *Athenia*'s doctor, who was on the *Electra*. They concluded that despite specific instructions the previous night on the *Athenia*—that Mrs. Rose Griffin be sought out in the infirmary and placed in a lifeboat—it now transpired that this had not been done. Mrs. Griffin had hit her head in a fall on Saturday and had been unconscious in the *Athenia* infirmary when the ship was torpedoed. Copland and two of his crewmen, Boatswain William Harvey and Able Bodied Seaman McLeod, returned to the *Athenia* sometime around ten o'clock on Monday morning. *Electra* provided her motor whaleboat and four sailors, led by Midshipman Cecil Bryden Chilton. The ship was then some distance away, had a 30-degree list to port, was down at the stern, and was riding low in the water, but they brought the whaleboat alongside. Copland and his crew went on board and made their way to the infirmary, where water now covered the floor. There indeed they found Mrs. Griffin in bed, still unconscious, and carried her back to the lifeboat. Chief Officer Copland then made a quick fifteen-minute inspection of the *Athenia* in the light of day to see if it might still be possible to save the ship. His conclusion, however, was that the amount of water in the ship and the concentration of flooding in the stern half of the ship indicated that "it would not last much longer." Copland and his crewmen returned to the *Electra* with Mrs. Griffin. The chief officer reported to Lieutenant Commander S. A. Buss on the bridge of the *Electra* that he found the *Athenia* beyond saving. It was about eleven o'clock on Monday morning, 4 September 1939. Just then, while the officers were talking, they could see the *Athenia* heel over on her port beam. Her bow rose almost straight up out of the water, showing her bright bottom paint with water streaming off. Almost in slow motion, the *Athenia* then settled stern first into the sea.[35]

CHAPTER 7

ON DRY LAND

IMPORTANT

H.M.S. ESCORT and H.M.S. ELECTRA proceeding Clyde. All survivors
ATHENIA picked up. H.M.S. ESCORT approximately 300, H.M.S. ELECTRA
approximately 200. About 100 all believed to be American citizens on Swedish
Yacht SOUTHERN CROSS proceeding Christiansund (corrupt group).
Further unknown numbers in Norwegian Ships SKUTE [sic] NELSON. Expected time
of arrival 0645 tomorrow Tuesday. Request ambulances for 10 injured.

—H.M.S. ESCORT TO A. C. NORTHWEST APPROACHES[1]

By midday Monday, 4 September, the Admiralty was informed that their two destroyers, HMS *Escort* and HMS *Electra*, had rescued about 500 *Athenia* survivors and would bring them ashore in Glasgow the following morning. Actually, the destroyers had picked up 640 souls. Other survivors, the Admiralty was told in rather garbled language, had been rescued by the Norwegian freighter *Knute Nelson* and the Swedish yacht *Southern Cross*. In fact 236 of those survivors who were on the *Southern Cross* were transferred to the American freighter *City of Flint*, to be taken directly across the Atlantic to Halifax; 140 were also transferred to the *Escort*, making a total of 402 survivors on board that destroyer to be returned to Glasgow, Scotland. The *Electra* carried 238. The *Knute Nelson* had picked up 430 survivors and made a course for Galway, Ireland. It had been a remarkable rescue operation, but it was far from over.

During the afternoon the two destroyers left the area where the *Athenia* had gone down and headed east for the North Channel and the Clyde estuary to bring their survivors to safety. The night was not uneventful, as the ships carried out an attack on a presumed U-boat. Ship's alarm bells were sounded and depth charges were dropped, although no submarines seemed to actually have been there. While warned by the sailors, many of the survivors were frightened by the dramatic actions taken by the ships. In the early morning, when the destroyers were attempting to make their way up the Clyde estuary, such thick fog was encountered that it was impractical to make the Admiralty Oil Wharf at Old Kilpatrick, closer to Glasgow, where they were expected. Instead the ships put in along the Sugar Quay at Albert Harbour in Greenock, several miles down-river from Glasgow. At about seven o'clock in the morning the survivors began coming down the gangway into the dockyard in their bedraggled state—some still dressed in the nightclothes in which they left the *Athenia*, some partially clad and draped in blankets, some wearing clothing given to them by the sailors. Many of these people were still in a state of shock, some injured with bad burns or broken limbs, many bruised, and numerous children without their parents or siblings, weeping and quite distressed. "My right leg was torn and bruised and bound up and I was barefoot," Helen Edna Campbell recalled, and inasmuch as she had not combed her hair or washed for forty-eight hours she was shocked when she saw herself in a mirror. Each person was registered as they left their ship in the first attempt to determine who was saved and who was lost. But there had been no preparations for them there at the quay and no shelter or facilities either. Dockworkers unloading the freighters tied up at the pier had first cheered when the ship made its mooring, then they shared their food with the survivors as they got off the ship. But when one of the workmen went into town to get cigarettes and mentioned that the survivors of the *Athenia* were huddled in the dockyard and suffering, this was the first news of the survivors to reach Greenock. Word spread rapidly and within a matter of minutes the wives of the shipyard and dock workers, perhaps more familiar with maritime disasters than most, streamed through the Albert Harbour gates in a magnificent spontaneous gesture, carrying coats, mackintoshes, blankets, dresses, and undergarments.[2]

At about 8:15 the local member of Parliament for Greenock, Robert Gibson, was informed of all this by telephone. He in turn called Provost Davey and the town clerk and arranged for a local clothing store to bring down to the docks clothing of all kinds—suits, dresses, shoes, and undergarments, items in all sizes and for men, women, and children. A reporter for the *Daily Telegraph*, who had come to the pier to get the story, found his mackintosh given away by a dockworker's wife to a shivering ship's steward dressed only in trousers and an undershirt. "You'll be no minding," she assured the reporter. Peter Wright, who ran a car hire firm, arranged for tea and buns to be delivered and a baker's van arrived with cakes, scones, and buns. Even more importantly, eight badly injured people were taken to the Greenock Royal Infirmary and nineteen were taken the Western Infirmary and the Victoria Infirmary in Glasgow, suffering from everything from broken limbs and burns to shock. Among them was Mrs. Rose Griffin of Toronto who, although rescued unconscious from the *Athenia* by Chief Officer Copland and his crew, died in the hospital of her injuries. By late morning as many as twenty-four buses that originally had been organized to pick up the survivors at Old Kilpatrick arrived at the Albert Harbour in Greenock and loaded passengers to take them to the Adelphia Hotel, the Central Hotel, and the Hotel Beresford in Glasgow. Crowds of people came out onto the streets to cheer as the buses drove into Glasgow. Commenting on the generosity and sympathy shown by these local people, Judith Evelyn said, "Of all the English people I have ever met, I thought they most typified what we call the backbone of the British Empire."[3]

In the early afternoon the buses reached the Glasgow hotels where the survivors were greeted by photographers and newspaper reporters, and motion pictures were taken. The Donaldson Line had asked the three hotels to be ready to offer the survivors a breakfast. However, a lavish lunch was provided when they arrived, although some were too exhausted at this point to actually eat. Doctors and nurses looked after those with injuries. Rooms were assigned and the hotels enabled people to send telegrams to friends and family to let them know that they had survived. Shaving kits and toothbrushes and combs, together with ten shillings for spending money, were given to people who at that point probably needed sleep as much as anything. Clothing was provided to those in need. Young Russell Park was taken to a department store and fitted out with a completely new set of clothes. Helen Edna Campbell was given a dress, a coat (way too large), a hat, and some ill-fitting shoes. "I looked even worse than when I got off the destroyer, and felt like a refugee," which of course she was. "But I was grateful to be covered," she said. Within a matter of days, many of these survivors were moved to other hotels in Glasgow, or were encouraged to stay with nearby friends or family, in order to make room for those people who had been brought into Galway on the *Knute Nelson*.[4] To manage all of this the lord provost of Glasgow, Patrick J. Dollan, assumed immediate responsibility and announced the creation of a disaster fund to provide for the expenses of hotels, food, and clothing, and to give each survivor some spending money. After meeting with the lord provost and then his board of directors, Norman Donaldson, the president of the Donaldson Atlantic Line, wrote to Dollan to say that the firm was "extremely grateful for the able way in which you handled the situation in connection with the 'Athenia' survivors . . . taking care of the whole position including feeding, clothing, housing, etc." He said the kindness and generosity of the city was appreciated especially by the Americans and he had "pleasure in enclosing [a] cheque" for £1,000 for the fund. Donaldson later said to Dollan that he did not know "how we could have carried through without your help and that of your staff." The Corporation of Glasgow also voted £500 for the fund, the Clyde Trust £500, the Fairfield Shipbuilding Company that had built the *Athenia* £250; and private individuals across Glasgow also stepped forward and contributed. Eventually £5,062 was raised for the Lord Provost's *Athenia* Disaster Fund.[5]

Lord Provost Dollan cabled President Franklin Roosevelt in Washington, D.C., and the U.S. embassy in London, "Glasgow will look after American citizens and other survivors of ATHENIA disaster." The president replied, saying, "I wish you to know how deeply I and the American people appreciate the efficient, generous, and humane manner in which Glasgow and its citizens came to the help of our fellow countrymen and women in their need. I express to you my heartfelt thanks and assure you that Glasgow's gesture will not be forgotten." The flamboyant New York mayor, Fiorello H. La Guardia, who had met Dollan earlier in 1939 when the lord provost visited the United States, also cabled his thanks to the lord provost; and over the next weeks many private individuals wrote to express their gratitude for the kindnesses shown to them by Glasgow.[6]

Glasgow went to great lengths to help the *Athenia* survivors, both Americans and Canadians, cope with both their losses and with the forced waiting for some form of transportation back to North America. For those in Glasgow, trips were arranged for entertainment. Jeanette Jordan wrote to her family in Madison, Wisconsin, about tours to Loch Lomond and to the Robert Burns country that had been arranged for the survivors. Afternoon tea was provided daily. A memorable highlight for all was a performance given by Sir Harry Lauder, the celebrated music hall singer from the Great War era, who had been long retired but was willing to entertain the *Athenia* victims. James Goodson described him as "a short and stocky figure with his kilt and Glengarry bonnet, and long gnarled black stick" who told wonderful stories and sang many of his old songs—"Roamin' in the Gloamin'," "On the Bonny, Bonny Banks of Loch Lomond," and many other favorites. "He left us all in tears, feeling a whole lot better," Goodson concluded.[7]

The American ambassador in Britain was Joseph P. Kennedy, the Boston millionaire businessman and Roosevelt supporter who had previously served the New Deal administration as chairman of the Securities and Exchange Commission and the Maritime Commission. On Sunday, 3 September, Kennedy had spent a harrowing day attending the House of Commons to hear the prime minister announce the war with Germany, after which he conferred by telephone with first Chamberlain and then President Roosevelt. With some emotion the ambassador explained the implications of the day's events to Secretary of State Cordell Hull and the president over the transatlantic telephone. "It's the end of the world," he told the Roosevelt, "the end of everything." That night Kennedy had not been long asleep when the duty officer at the embassy phoned him at 2:30 a.m. to transfer a call from the Foreign Office. As the ambassador remembered, "The clipped accents of an unknown clerk spelled out a message that he said had just been received—'S.S. Athenia, Donaldson Line, torpedoed 200 miles off Malin Head, 1,400 passengers aboard, S.O.S. received, ship sinking fast.'" This bulletin was immediately cabled to the secretary of state, followed by further telegrams giving the Department of State additional increments of news as it became available. In fact painfully little was known in those early hours, other than the report that the ship was sinking, that there were about 1,400 people on board, and that a substantial number of them were American citizens. The

Donaldson Line reported that 145 American citizens had boarded the ship in Glasgow, 65 in Belfast, and 101 in Liverpool, but it would actually take days to get an accurate list of names and definitive lists of who were saved and who were lost. During the course of Monday, 4 September, it became apparent that several ships had answered the *Athenia*'s distress calls, and with the arrival of the navy destroyers on Tuesday the Admiralty and the Foreign Office had more information that could be passed on to Ambassador Kennedy. It was understood that some people had been killed by the explosion of the torpedo, but it was assumed, incorrectly, that all other passengers had got safely into the lifeboats.[8] It also became clear that the survivors, having abandoned the *Athenia* with only the clothes they were wearing and most of them without either money or documents, would need an enormous amount of assistance when they reached land.

American embassies in Europe had urged U.S. citizens to return home as the war crisis developed. Now that American citizens had been killed or were suffering distress while attempting to return home the government assumed some responsibility for them. Ambassador Kennedy talked on the transatlantic telephone with Under Secretary of State Sumner Welles on Tuesday morning and outlined to him the situation, particularly the destitute condition of the survivors. Welles asked if there was anything the American Red Cross could do, and Kennedy urged him to obtain Red Cross support for clothing and medical and hospital care. In fact a meeting was in progress next door, Welles said, to work out the details of an assistance program with the American Red Cross. Secretary of State Hull cabled back on Thursday to say that the Red Cross had made $10,000 available for medical care, clothing, and temporary assistance of *Athenia* survivors in Glasgow. These funds were to be disbursed at the ambassador's discretion, although the money was not to be spent on transportation. The department would lend money to Americans for transportation home. However, a retired American industrialist living in Switzerland and friend of the ambassador, Herman Klotz, sent Kennedy $20,250 on 8 September for relief for the victims of the *Athenia*. The consulate general in Glasgow also had some emergency funds that were available for assistance. Most of these monies were spent on temporary accommodation, while waiting for eventual transportation back to the United States, and to replace clothing. By 17 October the embassy reported that a total of $5,717.31 had been spent, $185.38 on medical expenses, $2,929.11 on clothing, and $2,602.82 on temporary accommodations. On 18 October Consul General Leslie A. Davis sent a check for £1,140 to the Glasgow director of public assistance together with his thanks to the Corporation of Glasgow, "for the kindness shown to American survivors of the *Athenia*."[9]

The Canadian government was also alerted to the sinking of the *Athenia*, which had been headed toward Quebec City and Montreal with returning Canadians. The Canadian high commissioner in London, Vincent Massey, cabled the Department of External Affairs in Ottawa on Monday, 4 September, to say that the Canadian Trade Commissioner in Glasgow had reported, "CANADIAN ATHENIA PASSENGERS RESCUED AND LANDED GLASGOW [and] WILL DOUBTLESS REQUIRE OUR SERVICES PERHAPS FINANCIAL ASSISTANCE." Massey also promised a list of the names of people on the ship. The message was received in the late afternoon and by seven and nine o'clock in the evening cables went back to Massey authorizing him to provide financial assistance through his own office and that of the trade commissioner in Glasgow. Monies provided were to be considered a loan where possible; however, that provision was later changed to an outright grant. Massey also urged External Affairs to arrange for a large amount of money to be appropriated, perhaps through the Canadian Red Cross, so as not to compare badly with the $10,000 made available by the American Red Cross for their citizens. The Canadian Red Cross cabled £2,000 by the end of the week, and Canadians survivors were urged to get in contact with G. B. Johnson, the Canadian trade commissioner in the city. Vincent Massey later wrote to the lord provost on behalf of the Canadian people to express "our grateful thanks" to the people of Glasgow and to enclose a check for £1,315 from the Canadian government to help meet the expenses incurred.[10]

Much of Ambassador Kennedy's energies in the days after the sinking were devoted to attempting to put together an accurate list of Americans sailing on the ship—who had survived and who had been lost—and investigating what had happened and who was responsible for the destruction of the ship. Telegrams and telephone calls poured into the embassy from the State Department, from congressmen, and from private citizens asking about the fate of specific individuals. In fact because the *Athenia*'s passengers had been picked up from three cities—Glasgow, Belfast, and Liverpool—before the ship started its voyage, it proved very difficult for the Donaldson Line to put together an accurate list of the passengers. As for who survived and who was lost, that determination was made difficult by the fact that not only were survivors brought back to Glasgow in Scotland and Galway in Ireland, but a number were on the SS *City of Flint* proceeding across the Atlantic where it landed in Halifax, Nova Scotia, on 13 September. Several people were also interviewed on the radio, and information about the fate of the *Athenia* reached some by that means. Barbara Rodman's parents and her brother went to the NBC studios in New York on the evening of 5 September to hear her describe her experiences in a broadcast from Glasgow.[11] In the meantime, Kennedy began his own efforts to find out what had happened. Both the consul general in London and the consul general in Glasgow began taking sworn statements from all of the American survivors as to where they were when the explosion happened, what they saw on board the *Athenia*, and how they managed to survive. This was an enormous undertaking, but it yielded very definite opinions that the ship was torpedoed by a submarine that pursued a very persistent effort to sink the ship, possibly firing a deck gun, and maneuvering submerged through the water among the lifeboats after the ship was stricken.

Lord Provost Dollan invited Ambassador Kennedy to come to Glasgow to see the work that was being done for the American survivors. However, with both embassy and consular staffs overburdened by dealing with all of the Americans in Britain attempting to leave, the ambassador sent his twenty-two-year-old son, John F. Kennedy, up to Glasgow on the night train to represent him and to assure the survivors that the American government was concerned about them and would see that they got home to the United States. Young "Jack" Kennedy had been given leave from Harvard to join his parents in the spring of 1939 and he had spent the summer traveling extensively in Europe, visiting many of the places that were at the very center of the war crisis, and returning to London just as the war broke out. Kennedy arrived in Glasgow on Thursday morning and was met by Lord Provost Dollan and U.S. Consul General Leslie A. Davis. He saw for himself the pain and suffering the survivors had endured. Kennedy made a special visit to the injured in hospital, where one of the University of Texas girls, Helen Hannay, was introduced to him as someone who had worked to assist several young mothers get their children up from the lower decks. He also went to the several hotels in Glasgow to assure the American survivors that the government would arrange for a U.S. passenger ship to bring them home, where he was given a sometimes stormy reception. The thought of a single, undefended American ship taking them back across the Atlantic was not reassuring to these survivors who had been through the traumatic experience of being torpedoed, seeing dead people amid the wreckage, and enduring the perils of escaping into the night in lifeboats. Kennedy attempted to ease their anxiety by saying that the ship would be distinguished by having a large American flag painted on the sides of the vessel, that it would be fully illuminated at night, and that America's neutral status would protect the ship under international law. As for international law, one person shouted, "You can't trust the God damned German Navy. You can't trust the God damned German Government." Several people demanded that the ship returning them be protected by a U.S. Navy escort. Thomas McCubbin, from Montclair, New Jersey, insisted that "a convoy is imperative. Ninety destroyers have just been commissioned by the United States Navy and surely they can spare us a few." Someone else claimed that "two years ago the whole Pacific fleet was sent out for one woman [Amelia Earhart]." One of the young women stated, "We defiantly refuse to go until we have a convoy. You have seen what they will do to us." Gladys Strain, the organizer for the Texas college girls, declared, "We can't go through that again," and many other women agreed.[12]

Kennedy told the American survivors that he would explain their concerns to his father, the ambassador, and that he did. On his return to London he drafted a memorandum pointing out the "shock" that the survivors had suffered and the fear that they would be "exposed" to danger "unnecessarily" if they sailed home unescorted. The ambassador reported to Secretary of State Hull that his son had been impressed that the survivors were "in a terrible state of nerves and that to put them on a ship going back to America for seven days without a convoy or some kind of protection would land them back in New York in such a state that the publicity and criticism of the Government would be unbelievable."[13] But this was not to be. Young Kennedy also urged that the repatriation arrangements be made through the Port of Glasgow, and that the American government extend its thanks to the men of the British destroyers, the city of Glasgow, and Lord Provost Dollan. The newspapers called young Kennedy an "Ambassador of mercy," and because of his very youthful looks presumed that he was about nineteen years old. It was this "boyish charm and natural kindness" that allowed him to ease a very stressful situation. He graciously complimented both the Americans and their Scottish hosts. "I have never seen people more grateful for all that has been done for them by Glasgow than those to whom I have spoken today," and he went on to say that the extremely "generous gesture" by the people of Glasgow "will be fully appreciated by my countrymen." He later commented to his Harvard friend Torbert MacDonald that he was "full of praise" for the survivors, who in view of all of the difficulties had "behaved very well" without demanding their rights.[14]

The lord provost also took young John F. Kennedy to a special meeting of the Glasgow Corporation. There Kennedy had an opportunity to express to the corporation how well the survivors had been looked after. "Everybody is being well taken care of, and everybody I spoke to wanted me to tell my father and the American Government how grateful they were," he said. After he returned to London, Kennedy sent his thanks to the lord provost and assured him that he had told the ambassador "how much you had all done for the 'Athenia' survivors and he wanted me to tell you how grateful we all are." Lord Provost Dollan was delighted at Kennedy's mention that the ambassador wanted to visit Glasgow as soon as possible. Consul General Davis wrote to the ambassador that Jack Kennedy's visit had been "most welcome," which pleased the senior Kennedy who in turn praised Davis for his "energetic efforts, as well as those of your staff."[15]

Some time on late Monday afternoon the Norwegian freighter *Knute Nelson* turned south for Galway, under orders from her owners to bring her cargo of *Athenia* survivors into a neutral port. Ireland, although a member of the British Commonwealth, declared its neutrality on Saturday, 2 September, thus making Galway convenient for reasons of both distance and politics. The *Knute Nelson* radioed to Harbor Master Captain T. Tierney, that they were making for Galway with hundreds of refugees. Captain Tierney quickly informed all the local authorities to be prepared to deal with disaster relief. The mayor, Joseph F. Costello, the town clerk, C. O. Cleireachain, and the Catholic bishop of Galway, Most Reverend Dr. Michael Browne, formed a committee on Monday evening to make preparations with Galway County Council, the Board of Health, the Galway Central Hospital, the local hotels, and the local bus company. Lady Mayoress, Mrs. Costello, also organized a committee of thirty-eight local women to lead the volunteers, including the Girl Guides, who would be essential in looking after the specific needs of people. The Irish cabinet met in Dublin late on Monday and made £500 available to the mayor to provide food, clothing, and medical care to the survivors. Instructions were sent to units of the Irish Army and the Gárdá Síochána, the Irish police force, to cooperate with local authorities in providing care and facilities; and the local schools were to be made available to house people. Sean T. O'Cealleigh, acting for the minister of education, made available the Preparatory College at Taylor's Hill, Coláiste Éinde, to be used for refugees, as well as the Galway Grammar School. The Irish Red Cross also started a subscription to raise money to assist the relief effort.[16]

Shortly before midnight on Monday a pilot boat with Captain Meskill went out to Black Head to meet the *Knute Nelson* and steer the ship into Galway Roads to anchor. Some time in the middle of the night a tender from Galway City, *Cathair Na Gaillimhe*, under Captain William Goggin, anchored in the roadstead to wait for the freighter. The tender carried a local priest Father Conway, Dr. S. O'Beirne, and Dr. R. Sandys, and below decks were a number of nurses. Units of the 1st Infantry (Irish-speaking) Battalion, under Commandant Padraig O'Duinnin, were on board to carry the stretcher cases off the ship, and members of Gárdá Síochána were standing by. While it was still dark a launch took out to the tender several more doctors, some journalists, Mayor Costello, Commandant O'Duinnin, Gárdá chief superintendent T. O'Coileain, and U.S. minister to Ireland, John C. Cudahy, who had come into Galway overnight. Dawn broke on a cold, raw day, with low clouds and white caps on the water. The *Knute Nelson* gradually made her way to the roadstead, dropping anchor just after ten in the morning, Tuesday, 5 September.[17]

"As we drew along side the *Knute Nelson* a tremendous cheer went up from the survivors who lined the decks," wrote the *Connacht Tribune* correspondent, Sean Kenny. "Many of them broke down completely and wept openly," and more touching scenes were to come. Minister Cudahy was the first up the ladder to greet the survivors and to confer with Captain Cook, but he was followed closely by Father Conway and the doctors. Under the direction of the doctors, the Irish soldiers brought the stretcher cases and injured onto the tender first. There were ten seriously injured stretcher cases removed from the ship; among them were several elderly people, two *Athenia* crewmen who had been hurt in the explosion, and three children. Then the walking survivors made their way down the stairway, many only partially clad or wrapped in blankets and some wearing makeshift footgear made of gunnysacks and bits of cloth, a number of whom suffered from broken bones, burns, and bruises. Many people seemed still in a state of shock, particularly the children who were crying or calling for their parents. Even so, when asked how she was doing, one young woman called down blithely from the *Knute Nelson* to a reporter on the tender, "I have lost everything except my sense of humour." Gratitude toward Captain Andersson and his crew was also felt by most survivors. When all the survivors were on board the tender and the *Knute Nelson* began to weigh anchor to return to sea, one of them called out, "Three cheers for the Captain of the *Knute Nelson*," which was followed by still another shouting, "Three cheers for his crew."[18] Very grateful farewells were said to the Norwegian crew who had worked so hard to provide as much comfort as possible to the survivors.

When the tender came into Galway at just about noon, hundreds of people lined the quay and gave the survivors a heartfelt cheer. "The whole city of Galway turned out to welcome us," Father O'Connor said. But many were shocked and wept at the sight of the distressed survivors dressed in their borrowed sweaters and dungarees, or cloaked in blankets. They were a bedraggled lot and the children were most pathetic. "I remember we were all very shocked, you know, because there were a lot of women and children on that ship," Linda Grave Johnson recalled. "It really was appalling." The Gárdá assisted getting people off the tender, the injured first. White-uniformed nurses from the Galway Central Hospital and the Army Medical Corps waited on the pier to assist all those with injuries. Once ashore, each person was given a hot cup of Bovril, good Irish bread and butter, and tea. As in Glasgow, each of the survivors registered with the authorities, both for purposes of entry and to sort out the tangle of who was saved and who was lost. The Gárdá assisted people through this registration process. A witness to all of this, Sean Kenny declared, "It was a sight that will imprint itself on my memory for all time." Eventually people were taken by bus to the Royal Hotel, where the survivors were given something more to eat and were directed to other hotels, homes, and facilities where they could stay for the next several days. Toilet articles—combs, toothbrushes, shaving equipment—were provided, and in many instances new clothing was given. Galway, then quite a small city, opened its doors to the survivors. "The people of Galway have the greatest sympathy for these victims of the first casualty of the sea," said Bishop Browne, "and are anxious to give them the Christian reception which should be afforded to human beings in such circumstances." Countless stories were told of shopkeepers refusing to take money for goods, not to mention the offer of free drinks for any survivor who made it to a pub.[19]

When learning that their rescue ship was heading for Galway, Anni Altschul, clearly in something of a state of shock, kept repeating to her husband, "You know, I have a cousin in Ireland, Edith lives there." Her first cousin, a hat maker, had left Vienna when the Nazis took over Austria, going first to Spain and then Ireland. Dr. Altschul tried to explain patiently that there were several million people in Ireland, but that when they landed they would make inquiries and see if the cousin could be located. After having been taken ashore on the tender, registered with the Gárdá, and brought to get tea and food, Anni simply shouted out loudly, "Edith!" and there among the women in the Galway reception committee was, as she put it, "my cousin in Ireland." "After a long, long kiss, Edith asked, 'What are you doing here?'" Edith had become the manager of a hat factory in Galway, but had lost all contact with the Altschuls and had no idea that they had left Prague. She looked after them with "a truly motherly instinct." The president of the University of Saskatchewan, Dr. James S. Thomson, Dr. Altschul's new employer, cabled him, congratulating him on surviving.[20]

With the arrival of the *Knute Nelson* in Galway and the second accurate registration procedure, the painful process of attempting to reunite families could begin. On the *Athenia*, Dr. Edward T. Wilkes, of New York, had lost touch with his wife and two sons. In Galway Dr. Wilkes received a telegram that his son Daniel was safe in Glasgow, although his son Jonathan had not turned up on any lists, and he feared that his wife, Matilda, who had been in her stateroom, was probably lost. A. C. Ackroyd, from Dublin, had put his wife and two children in one of the lifeboats and had not seen them since, but his wife telephoned from Glasgow to say that they were all safe. James Boyle, a Detroit bus driver, who watched his wife and son get into a "women and children" only lifeboat, read in a newspaper that they had made it to Glasgow. James Goodson, who had been sailing back to Canada, learned that his name had been called out in the Royal Hotel. His uncle in Kent knew he had been on the *Athenia* and telephoned friends working for Shell Oil in Ireland, and the Shell manager, Jack Warren, sought him out to offer him a place to stay. In Canada the father of young Donald Wilcox learned that his son was safe in Galway when he saw a picture of him in the *Montreal Gazette* standing at the railing of the *Knute Nelson*. David and Barbara Cass-Beggs, who had eventually got into a lifeboat together, had been rescued by the *Knute Nelson* but were distraught not to find their daughter, Rosemary, on the ship. With the assistance of an Anglican clergyman in Galway they were put on a train for Dublin in order to make their way to Glasgow to see if their baby was among those brought in by the two destroyers. Bernice Jansen was sent to the Galway Central Hospital where her cuts and bruises were treated. Because of her head injuries and the fact that she had been so groggy while on the freighter, she was x-rayed although found to have no fractures. Gradually her pain diminished and on 13 September her eight stitches were taken out. Her outlook began to improve also. Although the whole experience had been terrible, "I haven't been depressed since the first day," she reported home. She was having some new clothes made and that cheered her up. "The people here are wonderful!" Visitors came to the hospital every day, and "we have lots of fun here with everybody."[21]

The U.S. Legation in Dublin had been informed of the pending arrival of the *Athenia* survivors on the *Knute Nelson* through its consular agent in Galway, Robert A. Tennant, who telephoned the consul general in Dublin, Henry H. Balch, on Monday. The Legation, headed by the heir to the Milwaukee meat-packing fortune and former ambassador to Poland, John C. Cudahy, sprang into action. The consul general cabled the State Department that the *Knute Nelson* was expected to reach Galway on Tuesday morning, and he asked if there would be emergency funds to provide relief for citizens in need. Minister Cudahy and his second secretary, John H. MacVeagh, and Mrs. MacVeagh left for Galway on the overnight train, arriving at five o'clock in the morning. The diplomats joined Mayor Joseph Costello on the tender and went out to meet the *Knute Nelson* at about 10:30 in the morning.[22]

Minister Cudahy climbed on board the *Knute Nelson* and met with Captain Cook and several officers, crew, and passengers from the *Athenia* on the morning of 5 September, and he was able to form a very definite opinion about what had happened. When he returned to Galway and cabled his conclusions to Secretary of State Hull, he asserted that "beyond question that ship was submarined." Cudahy returned to Dublin by Thursday, while MacVeagh, and eventually Consul General Balch, took affidavits from the American survivors in Galway to put together a detailed file of sworn testimony on what had happened, what had been seen, and what had been experienced.[23] It was expected that from this testimony a clear picture would emerge of who or what caused the sinking.

Ireland declared its neutrality in the war. Many Irish officials were circumspect about what might have caused the sinking of the ship and asserting who was responsible. The actual eyewitness accounts were often confusing and contradictory, and even those who claimed to have seen the submarine could not provide identifying numbers or markings. The matter was further clouded by the German government's immediate denial of responsibility for sinking the ship and its accusation that it had been sunk on the orders of the new first lord of the Admiralty, Winston S. Churchill, in an attempt to bring the United States into the war. In these circumstances, relations must have been rather strained, inasmuch as Irish Commandant O'Duinnin reported that the American officials were "noticeably arrogant and bumptious," and they skillfully "rejected any fact or statement likely to suggest that the disaster might be cause by any other means [than a submarine attack]." Although Gárdá chief superintendent O'Coileain took the American officials and the minister to the hospital where they could interview survivors, his own report noted that the Americans "were more concerned with gathering evidence solely in support of the theory of an attack by a submarine than with the care of [their] nationals." For the Irish newspapers, however, there were no doubts. "ATHENIA PASSENGERS SAW A SUBMARINE," the *Irish Times* declared boldly. However, even Minister Cudahy admitted to President Roosevelt that "there has never been any evidence that the *Athenia* was sunk by a German submarine."[24]

As in Glasgow, one of the major concerns for the Legation staff was the well-being of the Americans caught in the *Athenia* sinking. Minister Cudahy conferred with both the mayor and the bishop of Galway about matters of relief and accommodations for the *Athenia* victims. Secretary of State Cordell Hull cabled Cudahy that the American Red Cross had made $10,000 available for medical expenses, clothing, and temporary maintenance of the survivors. Another $5,000 was authorized by the State Department as a fund against which the *Athenia* victims could borrow money for transportation back to the United States. Consul General Balch went out to Galway on Thursday, 7 September, to take over from Cudahy and MacVeagh the responsibility of looking after the Americans. Balch met with the Galway Committee and told them that the Cunard White Star Company had agreed to pay for the subsistence expenses of the survivors and would transfer them to Glasgow by way of Belfast, where their return to America would be arranged. Clothing and incidentals became the only major expense upon which the Red Cross funds would be spent. Balch set up an office in the Great Southern Hotel where he could meet with the Americans and make arrangements for their monetary needs and also take down their statements about what had happened in the crisis on the *Athenia*. By 3 October Balch reported that a mere $28.55 had been spent for medical services and $2,357.10 had been needed for clothing. However, he estimated that maintenance and further medical bills would likely amount to $4,100.[25]

The Canadian Trade Commissioner in Dublin, James Cormack, drove by car to Galway on Wednesday, 6 September, arriving at the Great Southern Hotel at about ten o'clock in the evening. He was able to talk with several officials, including members of the Gárdá Síochána, and a number of survivors staying at the hotel. The next morning he met with the representative of the Cunard White Star line, who acted as the agent for the Donaldson Atlantic Line in Galway, in order to determine the number of Canadians who were among the survivors from the *Knute Nelson*. It became clear that although all of the people who came ashore were registered, it would be difficult to specifically identify the Canadians because many people with Canadian addresses also identified themselves as British, Scottish, or Irish. Furthermore a number of people had already left Galway to stay with Irish families and friends. Thus he sent on a list that he admitted was inaccurate but was the best he could do in the circumstances. He did call a meeting at the Great Southern Hotel for all the Canadians in the town and about one hundred were able to come. There he conveyed the sympathy of the Canadian government and explained what provisions and arrangements had been made for them thus far. All of this was well received by the survivors. Commissioner Cormack expressed his gratitude to the Irish government and the local authorities in Galway for all their efforts. When the Canadian government attempted to reimburse the Irish government for their expenses the check was graciously returned by Minister of Local Government and Public Health P. J. Ruttledge, with the assurance that the Irish government "would like to feel that the Canadian passengers on the Athenia, in common with those of other countries, who landed safely on Irish soil, were afforded by the Irish people the assistance so much required in the hour of need and suffering."[26]

Just as government officials, embassies, and high commissions were informed of the sinking of the *Athenia* and the fact that the ship's survivors would be brought into Glasgow and Galway, private individuals learned of the tragedy from the newspapers. Families with loved ones or friends on board, or suspected of being on board, were frantic with anxiety. Many telephoned, wired, or wrote to their government or their diplomats to get some information. Professor Charles Wharton Stork cabled his family in Philadelphia the simple message: "Safe, Glasgow." To the best of their ability the officials attempted to compile an accurate list of the passengers and who was accounted for among the survivors in Glasgow and Galway. The circumstances of last-minute bookings, picking up passengers from three different ports, and rescuing survivors by several ships and returning them to dry land in different countries made the compilation of an accurate list extremely time-consuming and difficult. Both the U.S. and Canadian governments, together with the Donaldson company, did the best they could. Names were released to the newspapers as soon as the information was available. The Department of State and the Ministry of External Affairs sent out telegrams to those who had inquired directly. The U.S. government did attempt to inform families at home about loved ones as quickly as it could. "STATE DEPARTMENT ATHENIA SURVIVAL LIST INCLUDES JEANETTE JORDAN OF MADISON ONE OF AMERICAN SURVIVORS ARRIVING GLASGOW TODAY," a department official cabled her sister, Marion E. Potter, as early as Tuesday, 5 September. Ernst Lubitsch, the Hollywood film director, was staggered when he learned that his infant daughter had been on the ship. Sam Katz, a vice president of Metro-Goldwyn-Mayer, had heard her name mentioned in a radio broadcast and went immediately to tell Lubitsch. The extensive international resources of MGM sprung into action and as a result of endless telephone calls, news came from Lord Beaverbrook, the London press baron, that young Nicola had been picked up by the *Southern Cross*.[27]

A list of the names of Canadian passengers was also requested. Indeed very quickly specific requests were sent from Ottawa for information about the fate of people such as Sir Richard, the former lieutenant governor of Saskatchewan, and Lady Lake. Fearing that her husband and three sons had been lost on the *Athenia*, Mrs. Louis Molgat of Ste. Rose du Lac, Manitoba, cabled the lord provost of Glasgow for news on 7 September and was told the same day that all four had landed in Galway. Her eight-year-old son at home with her assured her that if his father and older brothers were lost he would look after her. Gradually survivors were identified and a list was compiled and circulated. Although mysteries lingered, and for one reason or another new people were discovered throughout the week, it was not until 17 September, two weeks after the sinking, that the State Department issued a list of Americans missing.[28]

One group who had extraordinary resources for obtaining information through their own channels comprised several of the families of the party of the University of Texas girls. They had learned of the sinking late Sunday evening and began trying to get more information immediately. Tate Simpson, an executive for General Electric in Schenectady, New York, and the brother of Rowena Simpson, wired their father, A. D. Simpson, in Houston, Texas, in the middle of the night to say that he had not been able to get any reliable information but was optimistic because the ship had been still relatively close to land when attacked. A. D. Simpson cabled his friends at the National City Bank offices in London and the English brokerage firm of Silverston & Company. By 11:00 a.m. on Monday morning William B. Burton-Baldry, a partner in the brokerage firm, wrote back that he had called the embassy and that Rowena Simpson was safe and would stay with his family and that the National City Bank was searching for Genevieve Morrow, Anne Baker, Betsy Brown, Margaret Batts, Dorothy Fouts, and Marguerite Wiggins. Tate could wire his father, "OUR PRAYERS HAVE BEEN ANSWERED," together with the sensitive query, "HOW IS MOTHER?" Burton-Baldry assured Simpson that everything would be done for the girls, and on Tuesday cabled that he had information that "ROWENA AND GENEVIEVE MORROW LANDED GALWAY," and later in the day he reported that Helen Hannay was safe but in the hospital in Glasgow. Rowena Simpson was able to cable her father on Tuesday that she was safe and well in Bailies Hotel in Galway. On Tuesday morning also the National City Bank sent word that Anne Baker, Betsy Brown, and Dorothy Fouts were on the *City of Flint* and would be sailing to Halifax, while Burton-Baldry reported he was sending his secretary to meet Rowena Simpson and Genevieve Morrow and take them to his country home outside London. Burton-Baldry later wrote to Simpson that he had been able to use contacts that were not available to embassies and government officials to get the results. Meanwhile Texas congressmen Albert Thomas and Lindley

Berkworth had cabled and written the secretary of state seeking information about the Texas girls.[29]

On Saturday, 9 September, arrangements were made by the steamship company for most of the *Athenia* survivors to take the train from Galway to Dublin and then from Dublin to Belfast and Larne, where they boarded the ferry to the Scottish port of Stranraer and a return to Glasgow. Some of the *Athenia* people were still in the hospital, some had dispersed out of Galway to stay with friends or family in Ireland, and some had left Galway for London. However, by the end of the week most of the very grateful survivors had left.

The secretary of state sent instructions to the American Legation in Dublin on Thursday to convey to the Irish government that the U.S. government "is deeply appreciative of the hospitable assistance given to the American survivors of the SS *Athenia* by the authorities and people of Eire." The *Galway Observer* published Minister Cudahy's generous statement: "I cannot praise too highly the efficient handling of the situation by the Galway people and the Irish Government and their splendid human spirit." The Irish taoiseach, Eamon deValera, sent notes to both Bishop Browne and Mayor Costello informing them of his pleasure at the remarks of the American minister and of the American gratitude and extending his own thanks on behalf of the Irish government for their good work.[30] The Canadian high commissioner in London wrote to the Irish government also: "The Government of Canada is deeply appreciative of this generous action and wishes to extend to the Government and people of Ireland their sincere gratitude." Both the people of Galway and the government had responded quickly and generously. The *Athenia* crisis was one of the few incidents in the war where the people, the government, and the newspapers in neutral Ireland could participate openly. Cables were also sent by the secretary of state to the American legations in Oslo and Stockholm, asking that the U.S. ministers to those countries convey thanks to the master and owners of the *Knute Nelson* and the owner and crew of the *Southern Cross* for their "material assistance in saving the lives of American citizens." The British Foreign Office sent similar letters of thanks to the Norwegian and Swedish governments through their ambassadors.[31]

Both the Admiralty and the Foreign Office wanted representations to be made to Axel Wenner-Gren for so spontaneously using his private yacht, the *Southern Cross*, to assist the *Athenia* survivors. The British ambassador to Sweden, Sir Edmund Monson, Bt., wrote to Wenner-Gren on behalf of the British government "to thank you personally for the signal services rendered by your yacht." President Roosevelt also corresponded directly with Axel Wenner-Gren. The Swedish businessman knew Roosevelt slightly, had stayed at the White House in 1936, and sent the president a radio-telegram on Wednesday, 6 September, while he was still at sea and proceeding to the Bahamas. Wenner-Gren related his satisfaction at being able to provide assistance to the *Athenia* survivors, but he went on to suggest that because of the contradictory statements of the people he had picked up it was not possible to say definitely what had sunk the ship. "It is hard to imagine in view of the probable consequences that Germany intentionally would have sunk the steamer," he cabled to President Roosevelt. "There are also other plausible explanations to the catastrophe." Wenner-Gren also suggested to the president that he had contacts among the leaders of both Germany and Britain and as a result could inform the president of the background to the current international crisis and with the knowledge of these facts, "I feel that you might turn them to good account." The Germans were at the time attempting to open back channels that would facilitate neutral leaders, like President Roosevelt, to use their good offices to begin talks that would lead to an armistice and an end to the war before it broadened into a general European conflict. However, considerable suspicion existed in both Britain and the United States about Wenner-Gren's possible pro-Nazi sympathies at the time, and Roosevelt refused to be drawn into extending the good offices of the United States in mediating between the belligerents in the war. Roosevelt simply acknowledged the receipt of the telegram and cabled back, "I rejoice that you were able to pick up survivors of the ATHENIA disaster and I thank you for your part in saving American lives."[32]

CHAPTER 8

THE *CITY OF FLINT*

One of the pleasantest crossings any of us had.

—CALEB DAVIS[1]

By midmorning Monday, 4 September, after all of the *Athenia* survivors in lifeboats had been picked up, a fourth rescue ship arrived. The U.S. Maritime Commission freighter *City of Flint* had also received the distress signal sent out on Sunday evening and responded as well. The *City of Flint* was a 4,963-ton general cargo freighter built by the American International Shipbuilding Corporation at Hog Island, Pennsylvania, and launched in 1920. She had a complement of about ten officers and thirty crewmembers. She had sailed from New York in August under contract to the United States Lines and had unloaded and loaded cargo in Manchester, Liverpool, Dublin, and Glasgow and was homeward bound for New York when the SOS was picked up. However, the *City of Flint* was destined to play a distinctive role in the rescue of the *Athenia* victims and the early incidents of the war.

The ship's skipper was Capt. Joseph A. Gainard, a merchant sailor from Chelsea, Massachusetts. He had served in the U.S. Navy during the Great War and was an officer on the troopship USS *President Lincoln* when she was torpedoed while returning to the United States almost empty in May of 1918. After the war, Gainard left the Navy to work in the Merchant Marine service, where he rose in rank to that of master and where he had the distinction of having to deal with a mutiny in 1937. In March of 1939 Captain Gainard was given command of the *City of Flint* and began the first of several voyages to and from Europe. Late August found him in Manchester, Liverpool, and Dublin, where he was approached by a number of Americans, stranded as the war crisis unfolded, who asked if they could book passage back to the United States on the *City of Flint*. Gainard told them categorically no—the *City of Flint* was a freighter with no facilities for passengers. However, when Captain Gainard brought his ship into Glasgow on Thursday, 31 August, to pick up his last cargo, which included coils of rope, wool, and 30,000 cases of Scotch whiskey, he was given a message to telephone the Maritime Commission office in London. Gainard called Ambassador Joseph P. Kennedy, whom he knew well, instead, and talked to the ambassador's secretary. The ambassador had also been approached by a large number of

Americans and their families in the United States to help arrange passage back to the United States, including A. D. Simpson and Burke Baker of Houston, Texas, and their friend Jesse H. Jones, the chairman of the Reconstruction Finance Corporation. Kennedy had done as much as he could to get people booked on the remaining passenger liners heading for North America, like the *Athenia*; however, he had also used his influence as the former head of the U.S. Maritime Commission to make arrangements for up to thirty people to sail on the *City of Flint*. Neither Captain Gainard nor his crew were happy with this, but as Gainard himself put it, "After all, I suppose it was my duty to uphold the Ambassador to my country—particularly when he was Joseph P. Kennedy, and a New Englander, and a mighty fine individual in spite of his high office."[2]

Before he left the shipping agent's office Captain Gainard was introduced to one of the four Texas college girls who had been booked on his ship, Susan Harding of Fort Worth. The ambassador's secretary had not mentioned that any of the passengers were women. Miss Harding was undeterred by his attempts to discourage her from sailing on a freighter. Gainard concluded that he could discourage the college girls by inviting them on to the *City of Flint* so that they could have a good look around and see for themselves that the ship was not really suitable. "The girls went all over the ship, but instead of being upset with the things they saw, they seemed to grow more enthusiastic about us than they had been before they came aboard." He brought them into the wardroom "with my sternest face," to give them a good talking to, but the steward served them first coffee and then cakes, and the chief officer joined the conversation. Finally when the steward had served the third round of cakes, "I had gotten ashamed of the idea of trying to discourage them," the captain admitted, and he began thinking of how to make their trip as pleasant as possible. The conversation in the wardroom became increasingly cordial. "There was more laughter in that saloon that evening than the *City of Flint* had ever heard before." He concluded the girls were "absolutely irrepressible" and "nice" and he and the crew were going to enjoy having them. In fact the girls invited their friends who were booked to sail on the *Athenia*, which was moored across the pier from the *City of Flint*, to come and join them for coffee. Susan Harding cabled her relieved father, "SAILING FREIGHTER NEW YORK."[3]

When he got back to the ship Captain Gainard found that other passengers, Professor Harold H. Plough and Professor George Childs, both from Amherst College in Massachusetts, and several others, were already on board looking at the vessel. Gainard and his officers and men realized that taking on twenty-nine passengers was going to mean that they would all be put to some inconvenience, and it was clear that women on board would create special problems. The nine women passengers, including the five Texas college girls (a fifth was added), were placed in the captain's room (with a private bath), the chief officer's room, and

A view of the *Athenia* under way at sea, showing clearly the layout of the port side lifeboats. The ship was built on the Clyde in 1923 by the Fairfield Shipbuilding and Engineering Company to the specifications of a Cunard Class A vessel, and thus resembled a number of other passenger liners. PAUL STRATHDEE DONALDSON LINE COLLECTION

The attractive tourist-class dining room in the *Athenia*, showing the stairway toward which passengers groped their way in the dark after the ship had been hit by the torpedo
STEAMSHIP HISTORICAL SOCIETY

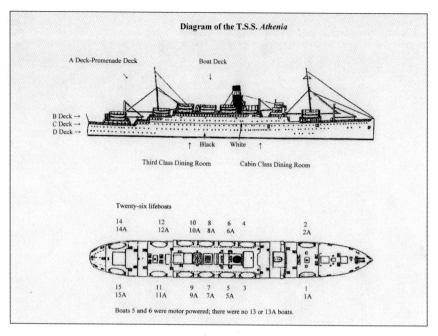

Diagram of the T.S.S. *Athenia*

A Deck-Promenade Deck   Boat Deck

B Deck →
C Deck →
D Deck →

↑ Black   White ↑

Third Class Dining Room   Cabin Class Dining Room

Twenty-six lifeboats

| 14 | 12 | 10 | 8 | 6 | 4 | | 2 |
| 14A | 12A | 10A | 8A | 6A | | | 2A |

| 15 | 11 | 9 | 7 | 5 | 3 | | 1 |
| 15A | 11A | 9A | 7A | 5A | | | 1A |

Boats 5 and 6 were motor powered; there were no 13 or 13A boats.

The lifeboat positions are shown by their numbers. *Author's collection*

In a photograph taken by Paul Vanderbilt in the summer of 1937, passengers on the *Athenia* are seen examining the davits of the port side lifeboats 12 and 12A on the promenade deck. Lifeboat 14 on the bridge deck can be seen in the upper left-hand corner. The lifeboat covers have been furled, revealing the grab lines along the sides of each boat. *Paul Vanderbilt, Library of Congress*

View of the stricken *Athenia* on the morning of 4 September 1939, well down in the stern and the bridge deck clearly awash. The ship sank at about 11:00 a.m. The falls for lowering the lifeboats can be seen dangling from the davits. Despite claims that the U-boat had fired its deck gun at the masts, they seem to be intact. MARINEQUEST

The *U-30* returning to port, probably in 1940. The submarine was a 206-foot Type VIIA U-boat; the fast-firing 3.5-inch deck gun can be seen forward of the conning tower. The *U-30* was built by A. G. Weser in Bremen in 1936. It survived the war, to be scuttled on 4 May 1945 as the conflict in Europe was coming to an end. MARINEQUEST

Chief Officer Barnet Mackenzie Copland, O.B.E., was a Scot who had a long career with the Donaldson Line. Copland had the misfortune of having a second ship, the *Esmond*, torpedoed by a U-boat commanded by Lemp on 9 May 1941.
W. W. NORTON

Captain James Cook, O.B.E, was from a Glasgow maritime family. He served in the Royal Navy during the Great War and joined the Donaldson Line in 1919, where he enjoyed a long career. *W. W. NORTON*

Fritz-Julius Lemp and Admiral Karl Dönitz on the deck of the *U-30* at the U-boat base at Wilhelmshaven in August 1940. Lemp is not in a dress uniform and has clearly just returned from sea duty. He is wearing the Iron Cross, which had just been presented to him by Dönitz. *Bundesarchiv, Barch, Bild 101II-MN-1365-27/Peter*

A view of the *Southern Cross* in 1935 anchored off Catalina Island, on the California coast, while still owned by Howard Hughes. Built in Glasgow in 1930, it was regarded as the largest private yacht in the world. Before the war was over Axel Wenner-Gren gave the *Southern Cross* to the Mexican navy, where it became the training ship *Zaragoza*. CORBISIMAGES

The *Knute Nelson* was a freighter built in Denmark in 1926 for the Norwegian steamship line, Fred. Olsen & Company. The ship was eventually sunk by torpedoes off the coast of Norway in September 1944. FRED. OLSEN & CO.

HMS *Electra*, shown here, was built at Newcastle-upon-Tyne in 1934. *Electra*, *Escort*, and *Fame* were all *Escapade*- or E-class destroyers and were roughly similar in looks. All three destroyers saw distinguished service in the war, both *Electra* and *Escort* being lost in action. CRONSTON FINE ARTS

The *City of Flint* was built in shipyards at Hog Island, Pennsylvania, in 1920, and in 1939 the ship was operated by the U.S. Maritime Commission. The *City of Flint* had the American flag painted on the sides in anticipation of U.S. neutrality in the war. The ship had taken on the *Athenia* survivors on 4 September and is here on its way to Halifax. The *City of Flint* was later torpedoed in the Atlantic while steaming in a convoy to North Africa in January 1943. NOVA SCOTIA ARCHIVES, JOHN F. ROGERS COLLECTION, 1995-370, NO. 51

Survivors line the rail of the *Knute Nelson* about to transfer to the tender to be brought into Galway. The young boy in the center of the picture, Donald A. Wilcox, was recognized by his father in Canada when this picture appeared in the *Montreal Gazette*. NATIONAL LIBRARY OF IRELAND, INDH 3395

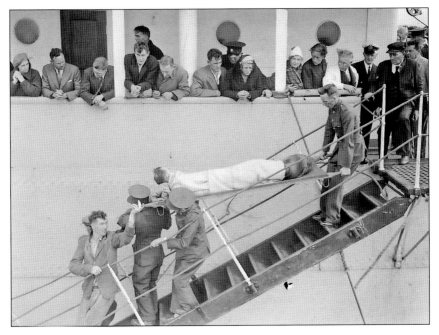

The badly injured survivors were the first to be transferred to the tender, assisted by Irish soldiers from the 1st Infantry (Irish-speaking) Battalion. NATIONAL LIBRARY OF IRELAND, INDH 3389

One of the cooks from the *Athenia*, who was badly scalded when the torpedo exploded below the galley, sending pots of boiling cooking oil flying IMPERIAL WAR MUSEUM, HU 51010/GETTYIMAGES

An infant, whose tiny foot is just visible, is wrapped in a blanket and carried off the *Knute Nelson* by an Irish soldier, followed by his mother. IMPERIAL WAR MUSEUM, HU 51012/GETTYIMAGES

Rowena Simpson and Genevieve Morrow from Houston and Betty Jane Stewart from Dallas, three of the University of Texas girls on the tender heading for Galway. Seated on the left was Robert F. Townsend, also from Houston. NATIONAL LIBRARY OF IRELAND, INDH 3392

The Galway tender *Cathair Na Gaillimhe* coming into port can be seen to be carrying many survivors, as well as officials from the city, Irish soldiers and nurses, and the U.S. minister to Ireland, John C. Cudahy. IMPERIAL WAR MUSEUM, HU 51007

A child, barefoot and wrapped in a blanket, is escorted ashore by an Irish soldier. *IMPERIAL WAR MUSEUM, HU 51015/GETTYIMAGES*

A young woman, in borrowed clothes and makeshift footwear, reaches land in some distress. *IMPERIAL WAR MUSEUM, HU 51011/GETTYIMAGES*

John F. Kennedy and the lord provost of Glasgow, Patrick J. Dollan, talking with survivors. The lord provost moved quickly to provide facilities for the survivors. *John F. Kennedy Library, PC 74*

The U.S. consul general, Leslie A. Davis, and John F. Kennedy, the son of Ambassador Joseph P. Kennedy, talked with survivors in Glasgow and attempted to assure them that they would be brought back to America safely. One of the survivors can be seen with a bandage around her head. Consul Davis was also linked to the *City of Flint* through his son, Caleb Davis, who had arranged for passage home on the freighter and worked to help create facilities for the *Athenia* survivors when they joined the ship. *APImages, 390909043*

Capt. Joseph A. Gainard dressed in a watch coat. Picking up *Athenia* survivors and having the *City of Flint* seized by the Germans were just the first of several adventures Captain Gainard experienced in the early months of the war. By the end of 1940 he had written his memoirs, *Yankee Skipper*, returned to service in the U.S. Navy, and been awarded the Navy Cross. HARPERCOLLINS

City of Flint lifeboat being lowered to help bring survivors over from the *Southern Cross*. Captain Gainard sent his biggest crewmen in the boat. As he put it, "There is something encouraging about a six-footer at an oar." HARPERCOLLINS

A lifeboat from the *Athenia* carrying survivors from the *Southern Cross* to the *City of Flint*. The sailors in uniform are part of the crew of the *Southern Cross*. In addition to the Jacob's ladder descending from the side of the *City of Flint*, it can be seen that the elderly woman on the left is also supported by a rope sling. IMPERIAL WAR MUSEUM, HU 51008

With lumber from the ship's stores, the crew and passengers built these crude bunks on the *City of Flint* for most of the 236 *Athenia* survivors taken on board. APIMAGES, 3909131314

The Coast Guard cutters *Bibb* and *Campbell* were sent by the American government to meet the *City of Flint* in the mid-Atlantic on 9 September and escort her to Halifax. Survivors with serious injuries and broken limbs were transferred to the cutter *Bibb* on the morning of 10 September, and fresh food and supplies were also delivered to the *City of Flint*. APImages, 3909131264

The *City of Flint* and *Athenia* survivors photographed from an airplane. Captain Gainard wrote that his passengers feared that they were being bombed by the airplane, although the people on deck are clearly waving to the plane. *Nova Scotia Archives, John F. Rogers Collection, 1995-370, no. 52*

Happy *Athenia* survivors line the rails of the *City of Flint* as the ship came into Halifax Harbor, where a warm reception awaited them. *Nova Scotia Archives, John F. Rogers Collection, 2004-047, no. 50*

Royal Canadian Mounted Police, among the many officials at the dock, assist *Athenia* survivors off the *City of Flint* in Halifax Harbor. *British Pathé Ltd./WPA Film Library*

The death of ten-year-old Margaret Hayworth on the *City of Flint* from injuries suffered when the *Athenia* was torpedoed brought home to Canadians the cruelty of the new war. *APImages 3909131330*

The passenger liner *Orizaba* was chartered by the U.S. government to take home *Athenia* survivors stranded in Glasgow and Galway and other Americans in Britain. *BRITISH PATHÉ LTD./ WPA FILM LIBRARY*

Children with new clothes and toys board the *Orizaba* on 19 September, bound for New York. *AUTHOR'S COLLECTION*

Survivors boarding
the *Orizaba*
in Glasgow
*BRITISH PATHÉ LTD./
WPA FILM LIBRARY*

Andrew Allan returned to Canada by way of the *Orizaba* and New York and is seen here
directing a radio play for the CBC in 1945. He subsequently had a distinguished career
in radio and television productions for the CBC. His father, Rev. William Allan, was lost
when the propeller of the *Knute Nelson* sliced through lifeboat 5A. *CBC ARCHIVES*

Judith Evelyn, who had been a promising actress in Canada and Britain before her experiences on the *Athenia*, went on to become very successful both on Broadway and in Hollywood. She is shown here in a scene from the Broadway play *Angel Street*, in which she played opposite Vincent Price and for which she won the Drama League's medal in 1942. In the 1950s and early 1960s she appeared regularly in both films and television drama. CULVER PICTURES

Portrait of Major James A. Goodson in late 1942. Goodson's original Royal Canadian Air Force wings can be seen over his right breast pocket and his U.S. wings on the left. Goodson served in the Royal Canadian Air Force, the Eagle Squadron of the Royal Air Force, and the U.S. Army Air Forces. Goodson became a highly decorated World War II Ace, destroying at least thirty German planes before being shot down himself.
Melanie Brooks

Young James A. Goodson with his mother, Mrs. Gertrude Goodson, about the time of the sinking of the *Athenia*
Melanie Brooks

Although baby Nicola was not a celebrity, her father Ernst Lubitsch was one of the most famous film directors of his time. Indeed, the baby's nurse, Carlina Strohmayer, became something of a celebrity for the care she gave the child during the *Athenia* crisis.
INTERNATIONAL MUSEUM OF PHOTOGRAPHY/CORBISIMAGES

Young Rosemary was reunited in Canada with her parents, David and Barbara Cass-Beggs, in late September 1939. David became a professor of engineering at the University of Toronto and later a power company executive, and Barbara developed expertise in folk music and music for children. Rosemary studied at Oxford and became a psychologist and a writer. ROSEMARY CASS-BEGGS BURSTALL initially in the chartroom. Additional sleeping quarters—bunks—would also have to be constructed. Wooden flooring was put down on the steel deck plates and the cots were set up in the shelter deck where the male passengers would sleep. Cots, sheets, pillows, blankets, and mattresses were ordered—six sets for each passenger in case they got wet. Electric lights were strung up to provide illumination. Bathroom facilities would be overtaxed. Additional life preservers had to be made. Although Maritime Commission ships were generously provisioned, the captain had his steward calculate what additional food supplies would be needed. Captain Gainard also asked Susan Harding to go into Glasgow and buy substantial quantities of Coca-Cola, cookies, and crackers, and she took the liberty of getting quite a bit of candy as well.[4] All of this planning and preparation was providential in view of the disaster that lay ahead.

These arrangements were being made against the backdrop of the international crisis and the outbreak of war in Europe that everyone had feared. The *Athenia* sailed from Princes Dock in Glasgow just after noon on Friday, 1 September. The Texas college girls gathered on the deck of the *City of Flint* to wave farewell to their friends as the passenger liner moved slowly down the Clyde. Captain Gainard was in a restaurant in Glasgow when he heard that Germany had invaded Poland. He went to the American consul general's office and telephoned the ship to have the American flag painted on the side of the vessel so that it could be identified at some distance at sea by a warship or a submarine. The chief officer replied that the men were already at work and that they would also paint the flag on the chartroom roof so that it could be seen from an airplane as well as from a ship. Finally ready for sea, the *City of Flint* sailed at eleven o'clock on the evening of Friday, 1 September. The new passengers gathered on deck, excited by the ship's departure, by all the activity on the Clyde, and by seeing the newly built Cunard liner, *Queen Elizabeth*, at its berth.[5]

Sunday, the second full day at sea, passed comfortably enough, although there was a little strain between some of the crew and the passengers. Nevertheless the passengers joined in working with the crew to get the sleeping quarters hosed down and cleaned up in order to be made comfortable. Amherst College student Caleb Davis, the son of the U.S. consul general in Glasgow, Leslie A. Davis, described helping to build some "deck chairs" and benches so that people could take their ease and sun themselves while listening to the radio coming from the chief engineer's cabin. He also exclaimed that the meals prepared by the steward, Joe Freer, were excellent; the best meals since leaving the United States, one person said. Altogether this voyage on the *City of Flint* promised to be "one of the pleasantest crossings any of us had." In the evening after dinner, card games were organized in the chief engineer's room for most of the passengers and several of the officers. About 9:00 p.m. the captain was handed a slip of paper by the radio operator. This was the distress signal from the *Athenia*. Captain Gainard was careful not to alarm his new guests that their friends might be in danger. He went immediately to the bridge to consult with his officers and to chart a course to where, given the wind and the currents, the *Athenia* and her lifeboats would be in about twelve hours' time. The *City of Flint* sent the radio message that it was making all speed and would expect to reach the lifeboats at about nine the next morning. Having himself spent a night in a lifeboat in the North Atlantic when the *President Lincoln* went down in 1918, Captain Gainard had no hesitation about steering the ship directly toward the *Athenia*'s radio signal at full speed. Caleb Davis thought the engines were working so hard that they sounded as though they "were about to disintegrate any moment." Because of the possible danger of submarines, the passengers were ordered to put on their lifejackets and to keep their passports in their pockets. All of the ship's deck lights were turned on and spotlights were directed toward the American flag to eliminate any ambiguity about the ship's nationality.[6]

When Captain Gainard left the card game he took with him to the bridge one of the two older women passengers, a schoolteacher who he recognized as being a dependable person. He realized that he was going to need the extraordinary help of both his crew and his passengers in order to be of assistance to an unknown number of survivors from the sinking *Athenia*. He also concluded that since the *Athenia* had been sailing to Canada there was no point in bringing the survivors back to Great Britain. The *City of Flint*, therefore, would proceed across the Atlantic, but it would need still more beds than those that had been improvised for the passengers. Gainard called on the ship's carpenter and one of the passengers, John Stirling, a former ship's carpenter from San Francisco, to organize the other male passengers, college students, schoolteachers, and professors, to begin building bunks with bits of lumber on the shelter deck—a space about 40 feet by 40 feet. Crew members joined in when they came off watch, and they all worked together through the night. "They were the best crew of volunteer workers you'd ever see," Captain Gainard said. "They couldn't do enough." Even the *Athenia* survivors, when they came on board, joined in the task. "I was one of the gang that went straight to work to build bunks for ourselves," Hugh Swindley wrote. Although it would take several days to complete, the results were a series of bunks in two tiers that would hold six to eight people in each tier. Heavy canvas was stretched over the rough boards and slats were put in place every two feet to define a single space. Two hundred fifty-five primitive, but workable, bunks were eventually put together. Blankets would be in short supply initially, but people would share, use their coats if they had them, and in some cases just cover themselves with bits of canvas or heavy paper.[7]

The steward, the two cooks, the mess boys, and some of the women passengers began making beef broth, sandwiches, and coffee to give sustenance to the survivors when they came aboard. Captain Gainard organized his passengers to "take the survivors in hand, the men one way, and the women . . . another route." They were to get the survivors into dry clothes, warmed up, and into the bunks as soon as possible. Dr. Richard L. Jenkins, a physician at the New York Training School for Boys who had been attending the scientific conference in Edinburgh, offered his services. Captain Gainard knew there would be injured and distressed people among the survivors and commented that "a real medical man was like a pot of gold at the end of the rainbow." He was right. The ship's hospital room was opened up and one of the college girls, Margaret Batts from Fort Worth, Texas, was assigned to work with Dr. Jenkins. The chief officer had the ship's four lifeboats made ready and swung out over the side and he picked a boat crew of the largest and strongest men from the ship. "There is something encouraging about a six-footer at an oar," Captain Gainard observed. When dawn broke several of the young women were stationed as lookouts. The *City of Flint* was in contact with the *Southern Cross* and several of the other rescue vessels during the night, but at 8:40 a.m. smoke from the *Southern Cross* was sighted and within minutes the freighter came alongside the steam yacht. On the *Southern Cross* Montgomery Evans said it seemed to take forever for the freighter to reach the yacht. Survivors now had to decide whether it would be safer to return to Scotland on the Royal Navy destroyers or to transfer to the *City of Flint* and sail for Halifax. Mrs. Isobel Calder decided that if she and her sister and daughter returned to Scotland they might never get back to Canada until the end of the war. Her young travel companion Ruby Mitchell remembered, "She figured she'd better just continue," so they prepared for the transfer. Large numbers of survivors could be seen on the decks of the *Southern Cross*, and empty lifeboats bobbed up and down in the swells nearby. Chief Officer B. L. Jubb took command of the ship's boat and had it lowered away. Dr. Jenkins with a first aid kit was the first one in the boat and he was joined by Jubb, Cadet Officer Carl Ellis, and seven crewmen.[8]

The most seaworthy of the *Athenia*'s boats had been saved and the first was rowed alongside the *City of Flint* by Swedish sailors from the yacht. It was filled with "miserable looking" women. Captain Gainard greeted the first person to come up the Jacob's ladder who ironically was German. She and those who followed her were welcomed by the captain and sent to get dried off and cleaned up—many people being covered in fuel oil as well as wet from seawater. Some people were only partially clad and cold and needed to be warmed up as well. Caleb Davis, who helped people get up from the lifeboats, carried stretchers, and lifted babies and children, described the scene: "they were a mess when they came aboard; all covered with oil, some of them practically undressed and shivering, too weak to stand up and sick all over the place as soon as they set foot on deck." The college girls were wonderful in comforting the women and children and taking them off to get warmed and be given something to eat. "Mothers and children [were] wailing and crying, but most of them were overcome with joy at the idea of being on an American ship," Davis noted. Montgomery Evans thought the freighter looked "rather dumpy" and the sides of the black hull enormously high, but he was glad to see the American flag painted on the side. "Staunch Britisher though I am," confessed Patricia Hale, "I have never been so thrilled and pleased as when I saw the Stars and Stripes painted large on the side of the *City of Flint*." Those people who were strong enough climbed up the side of the ship from the boats on a Jacob's ladder. A sling was devised for others too weak to climb and there were many helping hands, but this was slow and dangerous. One of the *City of Flint*'s crew concluded that it would be safer, faster, and less frightening to be brought up from the lifeboats with a cargo net hoisted by the one of the ship's winches. This worked so well with the stretcher cases and with the weak that it was eventually used to bring the remaining survivors on board. Through all of these efforts an anxious vigil was maintained for friends of the college girls who might be among the survivors on the *Southern Cross*. Even Captain Gainard recognized Anne Baker from Houston waving from one of the lifeboats as it came alongside, and Mary Underwood from Athens, Texas, followed shortly. By about four o'clock in the afternoon the boats from the *City of Flint* and the *Southern Cross* had made twenty trips ferrying people across to the freighter and the last of the *Athenia* survivors were taken off the Swedish yacht.[9]

The *City of Flint* now had 236 *Athenia* survivors, in addition to the twenty-nine passengers picked up in Glasgow. Captain Gainard observed dryly that a week before his freighter had facilities for no passengers at all. It was fortunate that the captain had ordered so many provisions in Glasgow when he learned he would have some passengers, but even that was not enough. Luckily, a Norwegian lumber ship *Alida Gortham*, passing the *City of Flint* while the *Athenia* survivors were being taken on board, offered whatever help it could give. Captain Gainard asked for blankets, clothing, and food, and they were quickly transferred. The Norwegian ship had lots of potatoes and evaporated and condensed milk, items that were particularly valuable with all of the babies and children on the *City of Flint*. Indeed the cooking and serving of meals became one of the first problems to be dealt with. A "Little Cabinet" was made up of the two professors, Plough and Child; Chief Officer Jubb; and the steward, Joe Freer, and they organized the meal schedule—there would be three meals a day and eight sittings. Cereal, porridge, scrambled eggs, bacon, and sausage were served for breakfast; soup with bread and jam for lunch; meat, two vegetables, and a small dessert for dinner; and children were served fruit or tomato juice in the afternoon. Young Scotty Gillespie ate so many oranges he was sure they were part of the ship's cargo and Rosemary Cass-Beggs thought the condensed milk tasted very strange. There were two mess rooms, one held thirty and the other ten. The crew's dining saloon was larger and was across from the galley. Alexander Hamilton Warner, from Nowata, Oklahoma, was put in charge of the mess rooms and managed the serving of food and washing of dishes. The ship's crew would eat first and the officers and college girls would eat last. Everyone had ten minutes to eat and would take out their own dishes, which would be washed immediately and given to another person. Even with this organization the cooking, eating, and dishwashing went on almost all day. Patricia Hale and her friend Margaret Patch volunteered to do dishes—given the water shortage it was a practical way to get their hands clean. The college students took food to those who were injured or too sick to get out of their bunks. They also saw to it that the children drank their fruit juice at least once a day and the children loved it. George Cree, a baker from Albany, New York, who was one of the passengers from Glasgow, offered to relieve the second cook who had been doing all of the baking. Cree baked excellent bread and also made cakes and treats that lifted everyone's spirits.[10]

The Reverend Dr. G.P. Woollcombe thought it was really quite amazing that this freighter without normal passenger facilities was actually able to house and feed almost three hundred people for ten days. Although young Ruby Mitchell was sure she slept for as much as twenty-four or forty-eight hours, she remembered the bunks as pretty crude. "We were sort of sleeping, you know, together," in the rows of bunks. "You had to, sort of, crawl out" of the bunks to get into a large aisle. The rows of bunks were quickly given names, such as "Times Square" or "Fifth Avenue" or "Montreal" or "Quebec," depending on who occupied them. The sleeping facilities and toilets (of which there were only three) needed to be monitored and cleaned and people volunteered to look after those matters. Bedding had to be aired and was strung up on lines on deck when the weather permitted. A "Captain's Inspection" was held every day and both Dr. Jenkins and Captain Gainard checked on how people were doing. Clothing was still in short supply for people who had lost everything. The college girls in particular gave up the new clothes they had bought in their travels across Europe, but the crew gave out clothing also. Captain Gainard, who was enormously proud of his crew, said that three of his sailors took turns wearing one pair of shoes. Chief Officer Jubb showed people how to make sandals out of rope and canvas. Three-year-old Rosemary Cass-Beggs was carried about the ship until some shoes were made for her. There was not enough water for showers, but an engineer gave John Coullie a bucket of hot seawater with which he washed the oil out his wife's hair and his own. Some of the men also borrowed razors and were able to shave. People could wash their clothes with hot seawater and dry them on the grating in the engine room, but many had to wear the same clothes until they got to Halifax.[11]

The first several days on board the *City of Flint* for the *Athenia* survivors who had transferred from the *Southern Cross* were hectic and unsettling. Many were traumatized by the whole experience and some sick with worry about missing family members. The deteriorating weather conditions raised peoples' anxieties even further. "The first night on board [the *City of Flint*] I thought I'd die," said Dorothy Dean, who remembered a terrible storm. Not only were the ship's movements violent but there were also loud noises from both the deck and cargo hold when the waves hit the ship. Caleb Davis told his parents when heavy seas pounded "that little tub," the ship did in fact "jump around." Reverend Woollcombe commented, "Above us we heard from time to time loud bangs, and so many of us suddenly roused from our sleep by the unusual noise," and remembered the "Bang" when the *Athenia* was torpedoed. Some loose cargo rolled around, water poured through ventilators and one of the hatches, and at one point the makeshift lighting system went out. "Women called out in temporary terror, and children began to scream." Dorothy Dean said, "It was awful. . . . No one slept." Over the next several days the weather gradually moderated. But sleep remained difficult for many people because of the heat. The beds were directly over the engine room. Captain Gainard realized that it would be better if those among the survivors who were reasonably fit were kept busy, so almost everyone was given tasks, and it worked. The children were encouraged to run around and play games on deck—"I Spy" and "Animal, Vegetable, Mineral" were favorites. Adults helped to clean, wash dishes, stand watch, and serve as lookouts. Even a ship's newspaper was created. Dorothy Dean and several of the young girls listened to the radio, took notes or shorthand, and typed up the news they had heard. Captain Gainard later said of Helen Crosby, a Swarthmore College student who had paid for her passage, "She worked until she had blisters on her hands. We had to tie her down to make her rest."[12]

One of the first important tasks to be carried out was to put together a list of all of the names of the *Athenia* survivors on board the *City of Flint*. The fact that survivors had been brought into Glasgow and Galway on 5 September, together with the problem of separating families on a "women and children first" basis while getting into lifeboats, meant that there was a serious difficulty for officials in England and Ireland in attempting to compile an accurate list of those who had survived and those who had not. This was compounded by the mystery of who was among the survivors taken on board the *City of Flint*. As soon as everyone was on board and looked after, Captain Gainard had the names of his survivors taken down and radioed to the U.S. Maritime Commission offices in New York and London. These names began to complete the list of who was saved and who was lost. One puzzle was that of a baby girl without her parents. Those looking after her could not quite make out what she called herself. It sounded like she said "Rose Marie Caspicks," possibly from Oxford. Her desperate parents in Glasgow could figure it out, however: she was Rosemary Cass-Beggs, and they were the only family on board the *Athenia* from Oxford. She had been carefully looked after in the lifeboat, on the *Southern Cross*, and now on the *City of Flint* by Mrs. Winifred Davidson of Winnipeg. The Cass-Beggs cabled friends in Canada to meet the *City of Flint* and baby Rosemary in Halifax.[13]

The injured and sick were looked after in the ship's small hospital and then lodged in the officers' cabins. Dr. Jenkins had plenty of broken limbs and bruises to look after and was very much appreciated. However, one of the *Athenia* survivors was Dr. Lulu Sweigard from the physical education department at New York University, with some medical experience. After she was cleaned up, given some clothes and a bit of rest, she became Dr. Jenkins' able and forceful assistant. Dr. Jenkins said of her that "on one occasion she worked for over thirty-six hours without rest" and that she was indispensable to the organization of assistance to people on the ship. She was joined by several other *Athenia* survivors, Mina McKellar and Mrs. E. A. Martineau, both graduate nurses, and by Hugh Swindley, who felt he could relieve the doctor of some of the menial tasks. One little girl, ten-year-old Margaret Hayworth from Hamilton, Ontario, had a serious cut on her head but nothing obviously wrong with her, but as she lay motionless beside her mother in the wheelhouse Captain Gainard became concerned. He called the doctor, and the child was found to have suffered a severe brain concussion as a result of the explosion on the *Athenia* and she developed a fever due to the swelling of her brain. The following day her complexion had changed and she looked worse. Dr. Jenkins found that her temperature had risen to 105 degrees. She and her mother were moved to the hospital and the doctor concluded that he would have to give her a spinal tap to reduce the temperature. Dr. Jenkins, Dr. Sweigard, Professor Childs, the chief officer, and the steward all worked to devise a suitable needle to perform the operation. Eventually they came up with the right tool, which was sterilized and worked in the operation. Margaret Hayworth's fever was reduced, but she was still in danger. Because of the concern for the child, when the Moore-McCormick Line passenger ship SS *Scanpenn*, sailing from New York to Sweden and the Baltic, radioed that she was nearby and would give any help needed, the *City of Flint* answered back that they could use some medical assistance and food supplies. The two ships altered course and, despite being enclosed in fog, sought each other out and made a successful rendezvous on the evening of Thursday, 7 September. The doctor from the *Scanpenn* came aboard bringing very helpful medical supplies and consulted with Dr. Jenkins. While he agreed that Dr. Jenkins had done all the correct things they realized that Margaret was very sick. Prayers were said for the little girl at the nightly services.

Indeed, although the child seemed to improve, and even talked, on the evening of 9 September she began to decline and early next morning Margaret Hayworth died. Her mother, Mrs. Georgina Hayworth, was understandably distraught and particularly upset at the thought of the child being buried at sea. Dr. Jenkins and the chief officer therefore embalmed the body as best they could by wrapping it in layers of sheets and spices of clove and cinnamon.[14] Margaret Hayworth was brought back to Hamilton where she was given a very public funeral.

The *Scanpenn* also sent some fresh vegetables, candy, cigarettes, and magazines, so the ship's stores were helpfully replenished. Captain Gainard was given a parcel labeled "for the little ones, in care of the Master of the *City of Flint*." This package was filled with toys and candy that a woman on the *Scanpenn* had been taking to her grandchildren in Sweden. She decided that the children on the *City of Flint* were in greater need. Captain Gainard radioed back to the *Scanpenn* his many thanks to "The Countess of Sweden" for her noble gesture. These treats provided the excuse to try to bring some cheering up to both the children and the adult survivors of this great sea disaster. One problem was that there was not enough candy for all of the children. The volunteer baker, George Cree, made delicious cakes and cookies that more than compensated for the shortfall. A "children's party" was held at three o'clock the next day. "The children flocked to it," Patricia Hale remembered, "joyous at the sight of the cake." As the ship proceeded west across the Atlantic other entertainments were arranged also: talent contests, limerick readings, and "fashion" shows, featuring the outlandish, makeshift apparel the survivors were wearing. Ruby Mitchell and her friend Margaret Calder got a huge laugh with their costumes—Ruby with her man's shirt from the *Southern Cross* together with a lady's sunsuit, and Margaret with a sailor's top and a towel wrapped around her as a skirt. Dr. Jenkins, several members of the crew, and one or two children became outstanding performers. Little Rosemary Cass-Beggs won a prize singing "Daisy, Daisy." The ultimate festivity was the "Captain's Dance" the last evening. The "Entertainment Committee" was kept very busy.[15]

Captain Gainard had decided when he picked up the *Athenia* survivors that he would not return them to Britain but would carry them across the Atlantic where they were headed. The *City of Flint* was bound for New York Harbor, but a North American port several days closer was Halifax, Nova Scotia. So Halifax became the immediate destination. The public shock of the sinking of the passenger liner and further anxiety about the safety of the survivors while on board the *City of Flint* prompted the U.S. government to take some protective action. Two U.S. Coast Guard cutters were sent out to meet the *City of Flint* and to escort her across the Atlantic and into Halifax. The USCGC *George M. Bibb* and *George*

W. Campbell joined the *City of Flint* during the night of 9 September. Captain Gainard turned his searchlight straight up into the clouds, which could be seen for miles, and the cutters responded with their lights and then took up stations on either side of the *City of Flint*. At 8:15 the following morning the three ships hove to, and the cutters sent boats over to the *City of Flint* with medical officers, men, supplies, and fresh food. Ten of the seriously injured survivors, including two with broken arms, one with a broken ankle, and one with a cracked rib, were put in metal stretchers and placed again into the cargo net and lowered over the side into the Coast Guard boats and taken to the cutters, along with the wife of one of the injured, where they would have more room and more complete medical service.[16] For the most part, however, the Coast Guard doctors approved of what had been done for the survivors and gave the *City of Flint* a good inspection. They also brought additional blankets and fresh vegetables and meat and, most welcomed by the survivors, toothbrushes and combs. The college girls received lots of good-natured teasing when they discovered lipstick and makeup just as the young Coast Guard officers arrived on the ship—they were subsequently known as the "Killer Dillers." The two cutters escorted the *City of Flint* for several days, and their gleaming white presence was greeted with emotion and was a source of reassurance to many of the *Athenia* survivors.

As the ships approached the Nova Scotia coast, a plane with newspaper photographers buzzed the vessel to get the first pictures of the ship. This so startled and upset many of the *Athenia* survivors, who feared that they were being bombed, that a request was made for no special ceremonies or celebrations when the *City of Flint* arrived in Halifax. However, the photographs showed many people on deck waving cheerfully to the airplane. Special permission was granted for the Coast Guard cutters to enter Halifax, and they left their position with the *City of Flint* early on the morning of 13 September to enter the harbor first. Captain Gainard had radioed the Halifax Harbor authorities forty-eight hours earlier that he had 265 passengers of Canadian, British, American, and other citizenship, and no sick, although of course many were without passports, visas, or entry permits. The ship's papers were not in order, but the emergency overruled protocol. Within minutes he was granted "free pratique," or permission to land his passengers, thanks in part to the careful preparations by the American consul general in Halifax, Clinton E. MacEachran. When the ship approached the harbor entrance the pilot came on board and took the *City of Flint* into Halifax.[17] The first of the *Athenia* survivors were home.

Tugboats brought the *City of Flint* into Pier 21 at the Ocean Terminal in Halifax at 10:30 a.m. on Wednesday, 13 September. The two Coast Guard cutters *Bibb* and *Campbell* anchored in the harbor. Although Captain Gainard had requested that there be no actual celebrations, a very large number of people had turned out to see the ship and welcome the survivors ashore. The crowd gave three cheers for the survivors and sang "Oh, Canada" as the ship was moored to the pier. The first to board the *City of Flint* was the premier of Nova Scotia, Angus L. Macdonald. Forty newspapermen and press photographers went on the ship also. Present at the dock were provincial minister of health, Dr. F. R. Davis, the mayor of Halifax, Walter Mitchell, and officials from Canadian immigration, the Canadian Red Cross, the Canadian navy, the Royal Canadian Mounted Police, and the Boy Scouts, as well as Consul General MacEachran, representatives from the U.S. Maritime Commission, the ship's agent, the American Red Cross, and the Cunard White Star Line. When praised by reporters as a hero, Captain Gainard shrugged off the compliment with the gruff statement: "There is no such thing as a hero. You're either a man or a bum." Cpt. Alan Reid represented the Maritime Commission and told Captain Gainard, "That was a swell job skipper." He passed on a letter from Adm. Emory S. Land, head of the commission, praising the efforts of Captain Gainard and his crew "for your outstanding service to humanity, according to the finest traditions of the sea." This was a sentiment echoed by many others from the ship. Dr. Lulu Sweigard noted that Captain Gainard and his crew had worked very hard and made great sacrifices for *Athenia* survivors. "He seemed never to snatch any rest," she concluded. Dr. Jenkins said that if he ever were to have a similar experience, "I should want it to be with Captain Gainard." The *Montreal Gazette* commented that "if King George could bestow the Victoria Cross on a ship, it would go to the *City of Flint* in the opinion of the survivors of the *Athenia*." Captain Gainard responded to all of this praise by saying, "I've got the finest crew a man ever wished to sail with. I ran the ship. They did the rest. God bless every one of them."[18]

Elaborate preparations had been made by Canadian Immigration and representatives of the Cunard White Star Lines, acting on behalf of the Donaldson Atlantic Lines. A number of doctors were in attendance, as well as registered nurses and volunteer nurses from the Red Cross. The U.S. consul was taken by a police boat out to the USCGC *Bibb* and *Campbell* to make arrangements for several of the seriously injured and sick to be brought into hospital in Halifax and the Americans to be taken to New London, Connecticut. Four large rooms had been reserved in the terminal building, two for men and two for women and a nursery for children, and adjacent were washrooms, bathing facilities, and dressing rooms. Ruby Mitchell delighted in her first real bath since the sinking and also exchanged her man's shirt for a dress and sweater from T. Eaton's & Company. The Canadian Red Cross had clothing available for those who were dressed in borrowed or makeshift gear. Close by there were also reception rooms where the survivors could be reunited with family and friends and where generous amounts of food were served. Boy Scouts stood at the bottom of the gangway to direct survivors where they wanted to go. Canadian and U.S. Immigration officials set up tables in the terminal where people could present themselves, after meeting with family or having a bath, to deal with the paperwork of arrival, whether they had the proper documents or not. In addition to assisting with the paperwork, these officials were also able to assist survivors in making telephone calls or sending telegrams to family members across Canada and the United States. By the end of the afternoon all of the people who had come off the *City of Flint* had been processed, including at least 109 American citizens. The Stewarts booked into the Lord Nelson Hotel in Halifax. Douglas had not had a change of clothes since 3 September, and the bath in the hotel was "the most welcome one we had ever had." Their two sons drove down from Montreal, bringing fresh clothes and a joyful reunion. The Cunard White Star Line had arranged, for those disembarking in Halifax, that a special Canadian National Railway train of sixteen sleeping and dining cars be available to leave for Montreal at 6:15 in the evening. The infant Nicola Lubitsch and nurse Carlina Strohmayer were met by the glamorous actress who had traveled from Hollywood, Sari Maritza, the wife of Sam Katz, the MGM executive that had alerted Ernst Lubitsch that his daughter was on the *Athenia*. Nicola's mother, Vivian Gayle Lubitsch, was still in England hoping to get passage back to the United States. Mrs. Davidson and Rosemary Cass-Beggs were met in Halifax and assisted onto the train, Rosemary being given a Panda bear that replaced the one lost on the *Athenia*. In Montreal friends of the Cass-Beggs, Dr. James and Caroline Gibson, met them at the train station. "She was smiling brightly and sweetly," Caroline Gibson said, "a precious little mite in all that mob." "Auntie" Davidson, who had looked after Rosemary for almost two weeks, found it hard to say goodbye: "I had to kiss her and walk away quickly."[19]

From Montreal people could make their way on to other parts of Canada or the United States. The husbands of Isobel Calder and Christina Horgan came to Montreal to meet them, but Ruby Mitchell's mother was at the train station in Toronto to greet her. When the train came in, young Ruby was the first person let off the carriage. There on the platform was her mother. "She just hugged me and hugged me and hugged me," Ruby remembered years later, "and I guess we both cried." Ruby's Toronto relatives were there too and they all went home for breakfast, although Ruby concluded that one of them must have made the breakfast because her mother would not let go of her. Many Americans came into New York by train at the Pennsylvania Station on Friday, 15 September. A chartered Canadian Colonial Airways flight into Newark, New Jersey, brought four-year-old Gale McKenzie and her mother; young Erika Hubscher; Mr. and Mrs. Alex Craig; Ernest Zirkl; and Charles Foster back to the United States to be met by the acting mayor of New York City. Eastern Airlines sent a charter flight to Halifax to carry newspaper reporters to meet the *City of Flint* and to bring back to Newark five of the Texas college girls, Mary Catherine Underwood, Constance Bridge, Anne Baker, Dorothy Fouts, and Betsy Brown. Consul General MacEachran was pleased to say that he had heard no word of dissatisfaction about these facilities and arrangements from any of the *Athenia* survivors. Indeed, the people coming off the *City of Flint* were relieved and grateful for everything that had been done for them. The ship carried on with her twenty-six remaining passengers and survivors and docked at Hoboken, New Jersey, on Saturday, 16 September. Among the *Athenia* survivors were Janet Olson of Honolulu, Dr. Lulu Sweigard of New York, Kay Schurr of Brooklyn, Gerda Sachs of Bavaria, Germany, and Mrs. Maria Kurilic and her five-year-old daughter from Czechoslovakia. Mrs. Kurilic was met by her husband, William, who had emigrated to the United States several years earlier. What should have been a joyous reunion was tempered by the anxiety that their son Jan, a boy of ten, was still listed among the missing.[20]

CHAPTER 9

MATTERS OF STATE

*I regret to inform the House that a signal was received in the Admiralty at about
11 p.m. last night giving the information that the steamship* Athenia *had been
torpedoed in a position about 200 miles north-west of Ireland at 8:59 p.m.*

—WINSTON S. CHURCHILL[1]

The outbreak of war in September of 1939 brought about the culmination of the worst fears of people in the West. There was a recognition that in many ways life would never be the same again. One of the very first things that the government of Prime Minister Neville Chamberlain did on Sunday, 3 September, was bring Winston Churchill into the cabinet as first lord of the Admiralty. In retrospect it is difficult to understand how anyone could have resisted the inclusion in the government of the figure who is now recognized as one of the giants of the twentieth century. Churchill, however, came with many political liabilities and had been in the political wilderness during the 1930s. To begin with, he had changed political parties twice—from Conservative to Liberal and then back to Conservative—so he was regarded by many as untrustworthy and an opportunist. Furthermore he had been first lord of the Admiralty in the Great War and had been the leading promoter of the attempted invasion of Turkey at Gallipoli, which had ended in disaster and had forced him from office in 1915. More recently in the 1930s, Churchill had led criticism of his own party, first under Stanley Baldwin and then Neville Chamberlain, for failing to rearm sufficiently to maintain Britain's strategic position in world affairs and for failing to resist Hitler and aggressive German expansion. As the international crisis unfolded during the first half of 1939, however, Churchill's earlier criticisms of the government appeared increasingly to have outlined the very course of action the government should have taken. When the war came, therefore, Chamberlain turned at last to Churchill to bring into his government a conspicuous and militant opponent of Hitler, untainted by any association with the policy of "appeasement" that had characterized the government's previous efforts. Churchill joined the cabinet when it met late on Sunday afternoon. Here was discussed, among other things, the deployment of the fleet in response to the presumption that several German battleships had put to sea. After the meeting, while the *Athenia* itself was under attack, Churchill walked from Downing Street to the Admiralty, where he was taken to his old office and to the board room where he met with the First Sea Lord, Admiral of the Fleet Sir Dudley Pound, and several others of the senior Admiralty staff. This meeting was largely occupied with introductions, and Churchill eventually dismissed these officers with the charge "Gentlemen, to your tasks and duties." However, rather prophetically the first lord also inquired of the director of naval intelligence about the disposition of German U-boats and of the deputy chief of the naval staff about the escort ships that would be available for convoy duty.[2]

At 2230, 10:30 p.m., the Malin Head radio station in Ireland picked up the distress signal from the *Athenia* and forwarded it to the Admiralty. "Important Admiral Rosyth. Intercept 2059 jamming near. SSSS SSSS SSSS ATHENIA GFDM torpedoed position 5644 1405." The commander in chief northern approaches was thus alerted that the *Athenia*, whose signal code was GFDM, was under attack by a submarine (SSSS), had been torpedoed, and her distress signal was being interfered with, or jammed. The ship's position was 56° 44′ N, 14° 5′ W, roughly sixty miles south of Rockall Bank. The Malin Head radio station continued to forward additional messages, relaying among other things that there were 1,400 people on board and that the ship was sinking rapidly. The Valentia radio station in southwest Ireland sent similar signals to England during the night by way of the Lands End radio station. The three destroyers *Electra*, *Escort*, and *Fame* were detached from their escort duties with HMS *Renown* and sent to assist. Churchill had left the Admiralty building before these radio reports came into the Admiralty, but he was informed of the sinking early the following day and was able to make a very brief report to the cabinet when it met at eleven on Monday morning. The ship was outward bound and had been sunk about two hundred miles northwest of Ireland at about two o'clock in the afternoon, he incorrectly reported, on 3 September. The passengers and crew had been able to get into the lifeboats, and destroyers had been sent to assist. There were perhaps 300 American citizens traveling on the ship, the first lord said, and he concluded that "the occurrence should have a helpful effect as regards public opinion in the United States."[3]

Later in the day, when the House of Commons sat, Churchill was able to give a somewhat expanded account of the attack on the *Athenia*. "I regret to inform the House that a signal was received in the Admiralty at about 11 pm last night giving the information that the steamship *Athenia* had been torpedoed," he said, and he gave the position of the ship as being some two hundred miles west of Ireland. Recent messages from the captain of the ship indicated that there had been 1,400 people on board, of whom about 300 were Americans. Apart from those killed in the torpedo explosion, the captain said, all of the remaining passengers and crew had been able to get away in the lifeboats. Destroyers had been dispatched to assist and should have reached the ship by ten o'clock that morning. Churchill also described the size of the vessel and noted that it was a Donaldson Line passenger ship that had sailed from Liverpool on Saturday 2 September for Montreal, and that she had been steaming at about fifteen knots well north of the usual steamer course, as ordered by the Admiralty. Churchill then explained to the House Germany's obligations to comply with the "Submarine Protocol" of the 1930 London Naval Treaty, which Germany had signed in 1936. He read out the relevant text, which said that "submarines must conform to the rules of international law to which surface vessels are subject." That is, except in situations where a merchant ship resisted, a submarine "may not sink or render incapable of navigation a merchant ship without having first placed passengers, crew, and ship's papers in a safe place," and "safe place" did not mean lifeboats unless they were in close proximity to land and the weather conditions were favorable. This spelled out Germany's duties under the provisions of the London Naval Treaty and was a strong signal that Britain intended to denounce any German inclination to adopt its First World War policy of "unrestricted submarine warfare." Several of these points were pursued in questions from members of the House. Mr. Albert V. Alexander, a former first lord of the Admiralty himself, expressed the "horror, disgust and indignation" that the country would feel at the sinking of a passenger liner and he asked whether steps were being taken for the United States, which was looking after British interests in Germany, to make representations to the German government. Commander Sir Archibald Southby asked if the *Athenia* was armed and whether any warning had been given before the attack. Churchill reported that no warning had been given and the *Athenia* was in no way an armed merchant cruiser. The sinking of the *Athenia* was discussed in the House of Lords on Monday afternoon also. Questions were asked about Germany's obligations under international law to provide for the safety of the passengers and crew of merchant vessels. Lord Stanhope, who had just preceded Churchill as first lord of the Admiralty and was currently government spokesman in the House of Lords, reported that Germany had recently abrogated the Anglo-German Naval Treaty although not the "Submarine Protocol" of the London Naval Treaty. He also emphasized, as had Churchill, that the *Athenia* was neither armed nor carrying munitions.[4]

On Wednesday, by which time survivors had been brought into Glasgow and Galway, the first lord answered more questions about the *Athenia* and was able to give more accurate information concerning the time of the attack, names of ships that had participated in the rescue of the survivors, and the important fact that at the time 125 passengers and crew were unaccounted for. Churchill repeated that the ship was not armed, and that the survivors had reported that the *Athenia* was not only torpedoed but that the submarine had also fired its deck gun at the ship and cruised around the *Athenia* on the surface. In the course of the questioning it was emphasized that in order to have been in position to sink the *Athenia* the submarine would have had to have left Germany some considerable time before the declaration of war.[5]

At the cabinet meeting the previous morning the *Athenia* was discussed in the context of the widening war. Churchill argued that "the attack on the *Athenia* was not an isolated incident." He pointed out that "there was definite evidence that four ships had been attacked," one of these by gunfire and two of them sunk. The sinking of the *Athenia* and several other ships in the opening hours of the war became part of the argument to place almost all of the merchant shipping in and out of Britain under convoy protection, which had been alluded to in Churchill's remarks to the House of Commons on Monday. After correspondence with Admiral Pound and others, Churchill met with his senior staff at the Admiralty at 9:30 in the evening on Wednesday, 6 September, and the decision was made that from the following day, 7 September, outward-bound ships leaving from Liverpool and the Thames would sail in convoys. Convoys of ships sailing along the east coast of Britain from the Firth of Forth to the Thames and ships coming across the Atlantic would be organized shortly. As Churchill later wrote in his memoirs, "the sinking of the *Athenia* upset those plans [organizing convoys only along the east coast], and we adopted convoy in the North Atlantic forthwith."[6]

Of course for both the British government and the British public there was no doubt that the *Athenia* was sunk by a German submarine. However, questions still remained. As a result several reports were written attempting to explain at least some of what had happened. Captain James Cook made a very brief statement for the Admiralty on 26 September in which he described the ship putting out to sea on 2 September, the explosion at 7:30 the following evening, and the process of lowering the lifeboats and getting the passengers away from the ship. Somewhat similarly, Chief Officer Copland gave a very simple statement largely for purposes of a press release in which he swore that there were no guns or munitions on board. The American naval attaché in London was given a report from the Admiralty that was sent to Washington on 14 November, which said that the *Athenia* had been struck by a torpedo from a submarine at 7:39, that the submarine had been seen, although the markings could not be read because of the smoke, and that a shell may also have been fired at the ship. Perhaps understandably the Admiralty was more interested in the role of its destroyers in the rescue than in the attack on the ship. The most complete and informative examination of the sinking of the *Athenia* was a thirty-two-page report put together by the Ministry of Transportation, although its focus was on how the disaster was dealt with by the ship's crew, how the lifeboat procedure worked, and how the rescue was accomplished by the freighters and naval vessels.[7] Very little of this material was ever released to the public, which acquired its information from the newspapers and the survivors' accounts they carried. In fact no public inquiry was ever held to determine what happened and who was responsible. The definitive answer to the question of who had sunk the *Athenia*—the legal evidence—would come only after the war was over.

The sinking of the *Athenia* within hours of the declaration of war came as a shock and British public opinion, as registered in the press, was uniformly critical. *The Times* ran headlines on Tuesday morning: "THE TORPEDOED ATHENIA. NO WARNING GIVEN AND ALL RULES BROKEN." By Tuesday it was able to provide quite a bit of information about the details of the ship and its passengers and the rescue by the Swedish yacht, several freighters, and two Royal Navy destroyers. Captain Cook was quoted about the sinking, and the statements from Ambassador Joseph P. Kennedy and from the White House were analyzed. *The Times* also mentioned the *Athenia* in two editorials, both of them emphasizing how Adolph Hitler had broken his commitments, in the one instance to observe the "Submarine Protocol" and in the other to disregard his statement the previous week in the Reichstag that he would not make war on women and children. "The speed with which Herr Hitler has broken his word and committed falsehood to paper during the last few days has surpassed even his own previous record," *The Times* pointed out. Captain Cook was interviewed and quoted at length, saying among other things, "There is no doubt about it, my ship was torpedoed."[8]

The sinking of the *Athenia* was a particular blow to Glasgow, the city where the ship had been built, the homeport for the Donaldson vessels; and it was from Glasgow that the ship had first sailed on Friday. Beyond these considerations, however, many of the crewmembers came from the Glasgow area, so many families had someone on the ship or knew someone on it. Moreover the local newspapers immediately understood the larger implications of the sinking. Indeed the *Glasgow Herald* printed a brief announcement as "late news" in its Monday, 4 September issue, "MANY AMERICANS ON TORPEDOED LINER," while the rescue operation was still under way. Captain James Reid, spokesman for the Donaldson Line, told the newspaper that the ship carrying 1,400 passengers and crew had been torpedoed. The *Herald* printed an editorial about the sinking titled "Crimes at Sea," which argued that the attack on the passenger liner was a "deliberate act of 'frightfulness,'" that was "so contrary to the rules of 'civilized' warfare that even the Nazi regime itself has made haste to disown it" (referring to the German foreign office denial that any of its submarines were in the area where the *Athenia* was sunk). *The Evening Citizen*, coming out on Monday afternoon carried a brief amount of news about the *Athenia* released by the Ministry of Information, and it published the text of the message from Captain Cook to the Donaldson offices, saying that the ship had been torpedoed west of Ireland and that those passengers not killed in the explosion had been picked up by rescue ships. "GERMAN SUBMARINE BROKE PLEDGE: GAVE NO WARNING," ran its headline. The *Daily Record & Mail* published an editorial on 5 September saying clearly Germany in 1939 "is as insanely committed to the policy of 'frightfulness' as was the Kaiser's regime of 1914–1918." The paper concluded that "the German leopard has not changed its spots." The paper also published lists of local people who were among the crew.[9] Public opinion in Britain, as reflected in the newspapers, concluded that Germany had begun the war at sea in 1939 right where it had left off in 1918 and that from the accounts of the survivors of the *Athenia* the war was going to be as horrible as could be imagined.

National journals echoed many of the sentiments of the daily newspapers. *The Spectator*, which was published on Friday, 8 September, ran an article titled "Frightfulness from the First," picking up the theme of Glasgow papers. "The decision of the German Government to begin the war with an exhibition of that form of frightfulness which concentrated the execration of the world on Germany twenty-five years ago would be incredible if the facts were not so incontestably established," *The Spectator* declared. *The Spectator*'s columnist "Centurio" raised the question of whether the *Athenia* would have in America the effect of the sinking of the *Lusitania* and work to push the United States into the war, joining the Allies. The *New Statesman and Nation*, published the following day, Saturday, made a similar argument in an article called "The First Frightfulness." "The Germans started their unrestricted U-boat attacks, with all the old brutality, within an hour or two of the outbreak of war." The *London Illustrated News* published vivid full-page pictures of distressed survivors coming into Galway from the *Knute Nelson*, and first issue of *The War Illustrated* carried both photographs and a feature article on "The Dastardly Sinking of the 'Athenia.'"[10]

It was Labor Day weekend in the United States on 2 to 4 September. In Washington, D.C., President Franklin D. Roosevelt gave a "fireside chat" to the nation over the radio on Sunday evening, in response to the declaration of war against Germany by Britain and France. Roosevelt warned the American people that "when peace has been broken anywhere, the peace everywhere is in danger," but he said that the United States would officially issue a proclamation of neutrality, which it did the following Tuesday. He deplored the rise of the resort to force in the world and regarded this state of affairs to be contrary to the values of the American people. "I hope the United States will keep out of this war," Roosevelt said. "I believe that it will," but he also realized that people could not remain "neutral in thought." "Even a neutral cannot be asked to close his mind or his conscience," the president concluded. With remarkable clairvoyance, he observed that "every ship that sails on the sea, every battle that is fought, does affect the American future." No more than an hour after the president's broadcast, Sunday evening radio programs were interrupted with the news bulletin that the *Athenia* had been sunk with over two hundred Americans on board, and by 8:50 Monday morning the first of Ambassador Kennedy's several *Athenia* cables was received by the State Department. Early on Monday also the Under Secretary of State, Sumner Welles, and senior State Department officials met to draft a neutrality proclamation and to send a message to Ambassador Kennedy, giving him advice about the repatriation of American citizens.[11]

The president's press secretary, Stephen Early, meeting with newspaper reporters did emphasize that the *Athenia* was carrying refugees home to Canada and the United States. "I point this out," he said, "to show that there was no possibility, according to the official information, that the ship was carrying any munitions, or anything of that kind." The reporters observed that the news of the sinking "was received with horror at the White House," and President Roosevelt much later publicly called German submarines "the rattlesnakes of the Atlantic." At a press conference later in the day, while talking about the complications of getting American citizens home from Europe, the president raised the matter of the *Athenia*. He noted, "in view of the ATHENIA sinking, that they [American citizens] are taking a greater risk than if they came in an American flag ship or a neutral ship," although he also mentioned that under American neutrality law citizens had a right to return on belligerent ships for ninety days after the outbreak of war. When asked about whether naval escorts would be provided for American ships, Roosevelt said that U.S. ships would have the flag painted boldly on the sides of their hulls and would sail with their lights on and without taking evasive action. In response to questions about how the *Athenia* was sunk, Roosevelt said that the naval attachés at the London embassy were investigating and that at the moment he had only newspaper reports of survivor statements. At another press conference at the end of the week, Roosevelt said the State Department was going to release the findings of the naval attachés about the cause of the sinking. Privately senior figures in Roosevelt's cabinet, such as Secretary of the Interior Harold L. Ickes, concluded that the sinking of the *Athenia*, filled with women and children, was "a typical act of German terrorism." Meanwhile the secretary of state and his senior staff were meeting on Monday and Tuesday to decide how the department should respond to the terrible news of the sinking of the ship, the problem of providing for the stranded American survivors, and the delicate issue of making a public statement that would not compromise the appearance of American neutrality during the very first week of the war.[12]

Many Americans learned of the sinking of the *Athenia* on Sunday evening while listening to dance orchestras on the radio. Special bulletins interrupted programs to announce that the British liner had been sunk, and some broadcasts included lists of U.S. citizens known to have been on the ship, spreading concern across the country. Newspapers across America gave extensive coverage to the story of the *Athenia*, focusing on both the beginning of the war and the involvement of American citizens. The *New York Times* ran the headline on Monday morning, 4 September, "BRITISH LINER ATHENIA TORPEDOED, SUNK; 1,400 PASSENGERS ABOARD, 292 AMERICANS; ALL EXCEPT A FEW ARE REPORTED SAVED." There were also articles in great detail about the ship, the White House reaction to the sinking, and a list of people either on the ship or believed to be on the ship, including the wife of the mayor of Saratoga Springs, the ten-month-old daughter of movie producer Ernst Lubitsch, a number of college girls from Texas, and the former lieutenant governor of Saskatchewan, Sir Richard Lake, and his wife. The *New York Herald Tribune* immediately picked up on what was worrying politicians: "If the torpedoing of the *Athenia* should have resulted in heavy loss of life, it presents the world with a parallel to the *Lusitania* sinking in 1915." "BRITISH STEAMER, 1400 ABOARD, TORPEDOED AND SUNK AT SEA," wrote the *Boston Herald* on Monday morning, and the *Boston Globe* added that a "Smith College Professor Is Aboard."[13] On Tuesday the *New York Herald Tribune* reported, "British Aghast at Sinking of the Athenia; Nazis Deny It," noting that the Germans had suggested that the ship had probably struck a British mine. During the next several days the *New York Times* provided survivor accounts, more elaborate lists of passengers on the ship, and eventually descriptions of the relief efforts. Later the paper gave extensive coverage to the American investigation of the sinking and to the German denials of responsibility. On Wednesday, 6 September, the paper published an editorial observing that "the sheer stupidity of such an act made it seem incredible at first." It argued that "no rational mind could believe that Germany would open the war with an attack on an unarmed passenger ship carrying Americans." If the attack were authorized it was madness and if it were unauthorized it was an indication of dangerous indiscipline within the German navy. The *Wall Street Journal* gave a brief account of the sinking of the *Athenia*, noting that the survivors had claimed to have seen a submarine. It also published the German government's denial that any of its submarines were involved. The *Washington Post* also reported on the sinking of the ship and attempted to provide information about the passengers headed for North America. The *Post* also tried to measure President Roosevelt's reaction to the sinking, news of which came immediately after his fireside chat to the nation. Although Roosevelt himself made no public comment, the paper speculated on the statements of Stephen Early, the president's secretary, that the ship was an innocent vessel and could not have been carrying any munitions. "President is Silent; White House Aides Appear Horrified," the *Post* observed. The columnist Dorothy Thompson, writing in the *Post*, called the sinking an act of "cold and criminal calculation."[14]

Time magazine gave extensive coverage to the sinking of the *Athenia*. In its 11 September issue, the magazine emphasized White House secretary Stephen

Early's assurance that the ship had not carried any munitions. It also ran a feature story about Axel Wenner-Gren and the role his yacht, the *Southern Cross*, had in the rescue of *Athenia* survivors. *Time* also reported the German claim that first the ship had been destroyed by a British mine and then that it had been sunk by the British themselves as in a cynical gesture to influence opinion in the United States. The following week *Time* reported on young John F. Kennedy's meetings in Glasgow with the American *Athenia* survivors, together with a photograph, and their demands for a naval protection on their return trip home. *Life Magazine* did not run any photographs relating to the *Athenia*, but did provide an artist's dramatic two-page rendering of the sinking of the ship. When the *City of Flint* arrived in Halifax, Nova Scotia, *Time* published a full report, along with the details of the funeral of young Margaret Hayworth in Hamilton, Ontario, together with a photograph of her parents and a poem written in her memory by Dr. Richard L. Jenkins.[15] The liberal weekly *The Nation* questioned the credibility of the German denial of responsibility for the sinking of the *Athenia*. "Destroy and then deny is the slogan of the Nazis at war (undeclared); it is the logical sequence to the slogan of the Nazis at peace—make promises in order to break them." The *New Republic* magazine also challenged the German denials in the 13 September issue. "There seems no doubt, however, that she [the *Athenia*] was sunk by a German submarine—and this in spite of the denials from Berlin," the publication observed. The following week the *New Republic* concluded that by sinking the *Athenia* and several other ships the Germans had quickly reverted to their First World War plan of unrestricted submarine warfare.[16] Press opinion in the United States held Germany responsible.

Both the American government and the public wanted answers about the sinking. How had it happened and who was responsible? Ambassador Kennedy had sent his naval attachés to Galway to interview Captain Cook almost as soon as he learned of the sinking. Before the end of the week Captain Alan G. Kirk and Commander Norman R. Hitchcock had submitted a report. They had interviewed Captain Cook, Chief Officer Copland, as well as the Officer-of-the-Watch Porteous, the quartermaster-of-the-watch, the quartermaster off watch, the chief engineer, several crewmembers, and many passengers. The most important statement was the conclusion that "a torpedo struck the port side of the *Athenia*," that a submarine, as witnessed by the chief officer and quartermaster, had surfaced and fired a gun or an explosive signal, possibly at the *Athenia*'s radio mast. They agreed that the ship had been hit on the port side by a torpedo that exploded in the fire room and engine room, that the concussion had shattered an oil tank and the stairs up from the third-class and tourist-class dining rooms, trapping some passengers and crew. Quick action by the officers on the bridge in closing the watertight doors had slowed the sinking of the ship and allowed the surviving passengers and crew to get into the lifeboats. On the basis of interviewing the witnesses to the attack it was possible to say that the ship had been sunk by a submarine, but because no one had seen the markings of the submarine, and Germany had denied that it had been one of theirs, it was not possible to actually say who was responsible. President Roosevelt mentioned the report in his press conference on 8 September and announced that the State Department would release a verbatim copy of what the naval attachés had sent. It would be released without comment, he said, "comment being, I think, unnecessary."[17] This could be taken to mean that everyone knew who had sunk the *Athenia*, but the president was not prepared to actually say it. In fact the question of the responsibility for the sinking of the *Athenia* entered the political debate in the United States over neutrality and nonintervention in the war in Europe. Despite public indignation, there were few demands for reprisals or other government action. Such a course of action was politically impossible in September and October of 1939 as the administration set about to revise the neutrality legislation.

A confidential internal report on the *Athenia* was written by the senior legal officer in the State Department, Green H. Hackworth. He had no difficulty concluding that the ship had been sunk by a submarine, but in the end, however, he too was unable to find legal proof of whose submarine had fired the torpedo. Over the next several months the State Department and the embassy in London continued to press the British for whatever evidence they had that would give proof of responsibility, but firm answers to that question would come only after the end of the war. Thus despite all of the public outrage and commentary, perhaps because the *Athenia* was not followed by a sustained campaign against passenger liners carrying Americans, the sinking of the *Athenia* was not allowed to play the role of the *Lusitania* in confronting Germany with an ultimatum.[18]

In Canada the events following the German invasion of Poland on 1 September had set in motion measures to prepare for the probable entry into the war by Great Britain. Prime Minister William Lyon Mackenzie King called a meeting of the cabinet and set a date for the reconvening of parliament on Thursday, 7 September. The War Measures Act was put in force through an "Order in Council," giving the government the authority to act decisively, and Canadian forces were put on alert. Canadians woke up on Sunday morning to learn that Germany had not complied with the ultimatum from Britain and France to halt their invasion of Poland and that war now existed between Britain and Germany. Following the broadcast from London by the king, the prime minister spoke to the nation late in the afternoon stating that Canada would be "at the side of Britain." (Canada would not itself go to war until Sunday, 10 September.) Mackenzie King was discouraged by President Roosevelt's radio speech in which the president said that the United States would declare its neutrality in the war and would expect to stay out of it. While dressing on Monday morning, Mackenzie King was informed of the sinking of the *Athenia* sailing to Montreal and the loss of both Canadian and American lives. Although he deplored the loss of life among the passengers and crew, "it might be the best thing that could have happened," he concluded. "I could not help but feel that this would bring home to the Americans the need for their intervention and that it was a terrible rebuke to Roosevelt, [and] the speech he had made."[19] Mackenzie King noted the loss of the *Athenia* with a logic similar to that of Churchill's comment in cabinet.

In London the Canadian High Commission was fully staffed on Sunday, 3 September. Lester B. "Mike" Pearson, first secretary and the number two person at the High Commission, had recently been flown back to London on a Pan American Clipper from his holiday with his family and friends at Lac du Bonnet, Manitoba. By Monday morning Pearson, High Commissioner Vincent Massey, and the staff at Canada House were plunged into attempting to sort out the fate of the 434 Canadians on board the ship. Although the people of both Glasgow and Galway tried to assist the survivors as much as they could, it became clear that the Canadian government would have to take some responsibility for these people; they needed clothing and temporary accommodation. High Commissioner Massey cabled Ottawa on 8 September that he had made arrangements for Canadian Pacific Railway steamships to transport the survivors back to Canada, but he said they would also need monetary assistance. He requested that the Canadian Red Cross assist in the way that the American Red Cross had made available $10,000 for both the Glasgow and the Galway survivors. Mackenzie King gave his authorization, and on 11 September External Affairs replied that funds would be available "to meet all needs regardless of the ability of recipients to make repayment."[20] Some $10,000 was made available.

The sinking of the *Athenia* was a shock to Canadian public opinion. In Canada newspapers ran banner headlines announcing the declaration of war by Britain and the sinking of the *Athenia*. The *Globe and Mail* ran a headline on Monday, "ATHENIA IS TORPEDOED, LINER CANADA-BOUND, 1,400 ABOARD, SUNK OFF HEBRIDES." The *Toronto Star* said specifically, "GERMANS SHELL WOMEN AND CHILDREN SCRAMBLING FOR ATHENIA LIFEBOATS, SURVIVORS TELL OF SUBMARINE ATTACK." The *Montreal Gazette* told what little was known of the rescue of survivors by the Swedish yacht, the two freighters, and the Royal Navy destroyers. The *Gazette*'s editorial noted that "Germany is running true to form, the form of 1914–18, the first example being the ruthless sinking, and without warning, of an unarmed passenger ship." The paper concluded that more of these sorts of acts were to be expected.[21] In western Canada, due to the time zone differences, the *Winnipeg Tribune* actually published several late editions on Sunday, 3 September, with news about the *Athenia*. The third extra edition ran the headline "BRITISH SHIP

SUNK BY ENEMY TORPEDO" and, obtaining copy from a French news agency dated 4 September, reported, "1,400 Aboard as Liner Sinks Near Hebrides." The Monday paper carried an editorial called "Frightfulness," in which the *Tribune* claimed, "It was just like the Nazis to 'do a *Lusitania*' on the first day of the war with Britain. The brutality of this action is matched only by its stupidity." Thinking in terms of the possible U.S. involvement in the war, the editorial noted that "the shock to neutral, especially American, opinion was immediate." On Tuesday the *Winnipeg Free Press* had a long editorial quoting passages from the "Submarine Protocol" of the London Naval Treaty, which Germany had signed in 1936, and declaring that "treaty breaking is no new thing for the Nazis, but the sinking of the *Athenia* calls attention to the first formal breach of their international obligations which they chose to commit on the outbreak of their war with Great Britain." The paper concluded that while the survivors would be joined by many others in the course of the war, "the *Athenia* and her passengers will stand in history as the first victims of the war which will be waged, on the Nazi side at least, without regard for either law or humanity."[22]

During this first week of September Canada remained officially still at peace. While frantic measures were being taken by the government to get the country on a war footing, the technicality of peace allowed the United States to continue to sell war material—airplanes, guns, strategic goods—without violating its own neutrality laws prohibiting sales to belligerents. Mackenzie King called for an emergency session of parliament on Thursday, 7 September, at which a speech from the throne outlined the government's determination to provide for the defense of Canada and to stand by Britain's side in the war, although quite what that meant was not clear. The debates in parliament, however, were overwhelming in support of Great Britain. In his strong appeal to Quebeckers that it was in their interest to support the war, Ernest Lapointe, minister of justice and the government's leading member in Quebec, made the argument that the sinking of the *Athenia*, sailing to Canada with some five hundred Canadians on board, had made the war a Canadian matter. Thomas L. Church, a member of parliament from Toronto-Broadview, Ontario, said that the House "owed a duty" to the passengers of the *Athenia* who had been attacked while on an innocent voyage, to support a declaration of war. On Saturday, 9 September, parliament adopted the measure to go to war without a roll-call vote. The following morning High Commissioner Vincent Massey was driven from London in his son's sports car to Windsor Great Park where King George VI signed the proclamation.[23]

The first Canadians arrived home when the American freighter *City of Flint* came into Halifax on 13 September. The joy for their safe arrival was overshadowed by the realization that young Margaret Hayworth, ten years old, had died of her head injuries on board the ship. A massive funeral was held at St. Andrews Presbyterian Church in Hamilton, Ontario, on 16 September with family and schoolmates and many dignitaries in attendance, including the lieutenant governor of Ontario, Albert E. Matthews, and the premier of Ontario, Mitchell Hepburn, and representatives of the prime minister. "A Canadian child is still in death, and for the murder of Margaret Hayworth the world's jury finds Hitler guilty." Rev. C. L. Cowan quoted the First World War heroine nurse Edith Cavell, who had been executed by the Germans in 1915. He said men of God must go to the mountain to pray, but he also urged that people resist "the things that make war."[24] Flags were flown at half-mast throughout the province and the whole country was stirred. Historian Michael L. Hadley noted that "the event was a propagandist's coup" and concluded that it "linked" the crimes against humanity of the First World War with the Second World War.[25] Margaret's younger sister, Jacqueline Hayworth, age six, had been holding on to her mother' skirt on the *Athenia*, but she had became separated when her mother and sister got into the lifeboat. In the crowd someone picked her up and took her to another lifeboat station. She reached Canada together with twenty-nine others on a British ship on 22 October.[26] More survivors began arriving back in late September and October on various Canadian Pacific Railway liners. By that time events had begun to overtake the shock of the sinking of the *Athenia*. The war, with its many shocks and horrors, became a reality for almost six more years.

CHAPTER 10

THE GERMANS

By order of the Führer: No hostile action is to be taken for the present against passenger ships, even in convoy.

—KRIEGSMARINE TO ATLANTIC FORCES, 4 SEPTEMBER 1939[1]

N ews of the sinking of the *Athenia* came over British radio as an unwelcome surprise to the German government. The confused negotiations that had gone on between 1 and 3 September, and the reluctance with which Britain and France declared war, convinced many in the German government that it would still be possible to keep the conflict limited to Poland. However, a negotiated settlement with Britain and France, not to mention the possible intervention of the United States, would be jeopardized by an inflammatory incident like the deliberate torpedoing of a passenger liner. Although Hitler's reactions are not known, he did take action immediately after the fact to prevent any further complications. The naval command sent a clear warning to both surface vessels and U-boats on 4 September. "By order of the Führer: No hostile action is to be taken for the present against passenger ships, even in convoy." This was specifically spelled out, "in order not to provoke neutral countries, the United States in particular."[2] Would it work?

The public action of the German government was to deny any responsibility. On Monday morning, 4 September, the Secretary of State for Foreign Affairs Baron Ernst von Weizsäcker, telephoned the naval operations staff to ask about responsibility for the sinking and was told that there were no German submarines in the area. He then phoned the American chargé d'affaires, Alexander C. Kirk, to call on him in order that he might officially "deny" that the *Athenia* had been sunk by any "German naval units." Von Weizsäcker emphasized that there were no German U-boats anywhere near where the *Athenia* had been sunk. He also specifically mentioned that the German navy was "under strict orders to refrain from any action contrary to international law and the agreements signed by the German Reich." Von Weizsäcker made arrangements for Kirk to cable a message to this effect to the State Department in Washington through The Hague, in the Netherlands, which arrived by 9:15 a.m. on Tuesday. William L. Shirer, the American journalist in Berlin, learned of the sinking of the ship from New York on Monday, but he recorded in his diary that the Germans both denied responsibility and forbade any mention of it in the press until Tuesday, 5 September. Then the German foreign office invited American journalists for a briefing on the sinking of the *Athenia*, at which they said that the ship could not have been sunk by a German U-boat and that it probably hit a mine or suffered an internal explosion or possibly was sunk by the British themselves in order to influence American public opinion.[3]

On Friday, 8 September, Kirk cabled the Secretary of State again, conveying the statement issued by the high command of the German navy that all units of the fleet were under orders to comply with international law, that there were no German ships in the vicinity of the *Athenia* and therefore could not have been sunk by a German vessel, and that British attempts to blame Germany, despite denials, were merely agitation. Kirk also reported that several German newspapers claimed that the *Athenia* had been sunk by Churchill's orders to generate animosity toward Germany in the United States. Both Churchill and Chamberlain were denounced in the German press. The following week Kirk forwarded the text of a message from Grand Admiral Erich Raeder to a journalist in Amsterdam in which he said the charge that the German submarine had sunk the *Athenia* was an "abominable lie," and that the nearest U-boat was 170 miles away. Admiral Raeder also called attention to the instructions to all U-boat commanders that they "conform absolutely to international law and treaties." The admiral also went so far as to call in the American naval attaché, Cdr. Albert E. Schrader, on 16 September and tell him that all of Germany's submarines were now back in port and none of them had sunk the *Athenia*. Commander Schrader reported Raeder as saying, "no German U-boat had torpedoed the ATHENIA, the investigation was considered closed as far as the [German] Navy was concerned and the Navy now has only an academic interest in how the ship was sunk." The admiral asked that Commander Schrader inform his embassy of this.[4]

Germany, in fact, began a serious publicity campaign to deny any involvement in the sinking of the *Athenia*. The *New York Times* reported the German newspaper articles that rejected the possibility of German involvement. Fritz Kuhn, a leader of the German-American Bund, soon to be convicted of embezzling funds from his organization, served as a key spokesperson in the United States for German noninvolvement and put the blame entirely on the British, whose interests would be served by the sinking. The German Library of Information in New York published a feature article in its newsletter, *Facts in Review*. It published extensive passages of von Weizsäcker's statements about the *Athenia* and denied German involvement in the sinking and charged Winston Churchill "once more [Churchill had also been blamed for the sinking of the *Lusitania* in the Great War] with the full responsibility for the sinking of the liner 'Athenia' and the resultant loss of some 220 lives." Another German publication, in English, made much the same argument: "The S.S. *Athenia* sunk by three British Destroyers." Even toward the end of October, almost a month after the *U-30* had returned to port, Dr. Joseph Goebbels, German propaganda minister, gave a radio speech denouncing Churchill for ordering the sinking of the ship and lying about it. "Your impudent lies, Herr Churchill! Your infernal lies!," William L. Shirer remembered Gobbels shouting repeatedly. The following day, 23 October, the leading Nazi newspaper, *Vöelkischer Beobachter*, ran the headline "CHURCHILL SANK THE 'ATHENIA.'" The British Broadcasting Corporation monitored German radio broadcasts, noting the German interpretations of events. Various explanations were put forward: the ship struck a British mine, there was an internal explosion, the ship was hit by a British torpedo, German citizens were deliberately kept off the ship in order to eliminate objective witnesses, the stricken ship was actually sent to the bottom by gunfire from British destroyers, all of this as part of the cynical plan of the First Lord of the Admiralty Winston Churchill to bring the United States into the war.[5] The British took the position that the multiplicity of German explanations illustrated how desperate the Germans were to avoid the truth.

The immediate reaction of the president or his secretary of state is not recorded, but Secretary of the Interior Harold L. Ickes considered German denials of responsibility and allegations of British sabotage to be "absurd on the face of it," in light of the claims of numerous passengers and crew who had seen a submarine. "More German stupidity such as took us into the last war," he concluded. Former President Herbert Hoover was suspicious about how the British released information about the *Athenia* in bits and pieces that seemed to change regularly. "The whole thing looks suspicious to me," he wrote to John C. O'Laughlin, of the *Army and Navy Journal*. To sink the passenger liner "is such poor tactics that I cannot believe even the clumsy Germans would do such a thing," and he noted that the Germans had denied any involvement. Hoover was not the only one to question whether the Germans had anything to gain by sinking the *Athenia*. Senator Robert Rice Reynolds of South Carolina, a Democrat and a leading "non-interventionist," concluded that while Britain had more to gain than Germany, observing that "it [the sinking of the *Athenia*] created considerable American opinion toward helping Britain and hurting Germany." He further stressed that "the sinking of the *Athenia* was of the greatest advantage to the Russians to achieve their ultimate purposes," that is to say, encouraging the western powers to war among themselves. The American public, however, was less distracted by these elaborate theories. In a poll taken in late September the American Institute of Public Opinion found that 60 percent of those questioned believed that the Germans had sunk the *Athenia* and only 9 percent the British. When *Fortune* magazine asked a similar question in December, even more people, 66.7 percent, thought the Germans had sunk the ship.[6]

In the meantime, two significant events had occurred, one public and one held secret. First, an American passenger on the *Athenia*, Gustav A. Anderson, when interviewed by the State Department and several congressmen in Washington after returning on the *City of Flint*, claimed that he had been told by Chief Officer Copland that the ship had been carrying guns with which to fortify coastal defenses in Canada and that the *Athenia* would be itself fitted with guns in order to serve as an armed merchant cruiser on the return trip. He said also that the ship was finally sunk by the British destroyers. Anderson, an Evanston, Illinois, lawyer and travel company operator, was known to be anti-British in his sentiments, but his remarks were a serious challenge to the British claims of the innocent nature of the ship and the final responsibility for the sinking. If the allegations of carrying weapons were true, the ship could not claim the protection of "Submarine Protocol" of the London Naval Treaty. Anderson's remarks were given wide newspaper coverage, in the United States and on the other side of the Atlantic. The *New York Times* gave Anderson's testimony a full page. Members of Congress unsympathetic to either President Roosevelt or Great Britain seized on Anderson's remarks as an argument to suspend judgment about how the *Athenia* might have been sunk. Anderson's statements, together with German denials of responsibility for the sinking, touched a chord among both the "isolationists" and the anti-British element in the country. Congressman Francis Case from South Dakota wrote to the State Department as a kind of character witness. Case had been a fraternity brother of Anderson's years ago at Northwestern University, and he had recently heard him talk about the *Athenia*. The experience had been "wearing," Case said, but he had never heard anyone question Anderson's "integrity or sincerity."[7]

However, Anderson's claims met with an immediate contradiction. Another *Athenia* survivor, Catherine Schurr, wrote to the *New York Times* denying any evidence of either guns or the preparations for conversion to an armed merchant cruiser. She said that because she and Anderson were picked up in the night by the *Southern Cross* and then transferred to the *City of Flint* Anderson could not have known how the *Athenia* eventually sank until he reached Halifax. Other passengers wrote directly to the Secretary of State attempting to refute Anderson's claim that there were guns on board. Dr. Edward T. Wilkes related a conversation with Captain Cook on board the *Knute Nelson* in which Cook said the attack might have been justified if his ship had been carrying munitions, but "we didn't have a single gun, so help me God." Caroline Stuart, now home in Plainfield, New Jersey, wrote to the chief special agent of the State Department to point out what a troublemaker Anderson had been on the *City of Flint*. He had refused to follow the rules on the rescue ship and he had told her companions that "we must get a good story ready for the newspapermen who would meet the ship in Halifax." The Texas University girls had seen Anderson in Europe during their travels and regarded him as "obnoxious." "To be in the limelight seemed to be the main factor in Mr. Anderson's life."[8] Anderson's allegations also flew in the face of numerous affidavits from *Athenia* survivors that the State Department had collected in the aftermath of the sinking. In Britain, Chief Officer Copland gave a sworn statement that while he was acquainted with Anderson he had never discussed weapons with him and that in fact the *Athenia* carried no weapons at all. Norman Donaldson was quoted as saying the charge was "tommyrot and absolute nonsense." The British government was understandably alarmed by Anderson's allegations and issued a press release that denied the claims made by both the German government and Anderson about how the ship had been sunk. The British and Canadian governments sent letters to the Department of State refuting the statements of Anderson and denying any weapons or military component to the *Athenia*. Ambassador Kennedy was given reports from British intelligence about Anderson's pro-Nazi statements while he stayed at the Savoy Hotel in London in July. None of this, however, provided any explanation for Anderson's extraordinary statements.[9] Anderson remained in the news for some weeks, giving lectures on his experiences on the *Athenia*.

The second event was a continuation of the *Athenia* story, but it took years to play out completely. As described earlier, while in the process of sinking the *Fanad Head* and taking off supplies from the freighter on 14 September, the *U-30* itself came under attack from dive bombers from the aircraft carrier HMS *Ark Royal*. Two of the three British planes crashed and the pilots were rescued by the German seaman Adolph Schmidt, who in turn was wounded when the third airplane strafed the submarine. *Oberleutnant* Lemp submerged the U-boat and after a six-hour attack by more airplanes and destroyers he was able to bring his submarine to the surface, where he radioed naval command reporting his action and asking permission to take the wounded Schmidt and the two injured British pilots to neutral Iceland for medical treatment.[10]

Seaman Schmidt was put ashore in Reykjavik on 19 September and sent to a hospital, but he carried with him damaging information and this worried Lemp. During the attack on the *Athenia*, Schmidt was called to the conning tower of the submarine and had seen the stricken ship and the passengers on deck; "I myself observed much commotion on board the torpedoed ship," as he put it. Before taking him off the submarine, *Oberleutnant* Lemp had him swear an oath never to disclose what he had seen on 3 September. After he got on shore he heard about the sinking of the *Athenia* and concluded correctly that this was the ship that he had seen, information about which he was sworn to keep secret. When British troops occupied Iceland in 1940, Schmidt became a prisoner of war and was taken to a prison camp in Lethbridge, Alberta. While a prisoner Schmidt was interrogated many times but never revealed the information that he held about the responsibility of the *U-30* for the sinking of the *Athenia*. However, at the end of the war both Admiral Dönitz and Admiral Raeder were arraigned before the International Military Tribunal in Nuremburg for war crimes. In the process of building their case against to the two admirals, the British legal team uncovered the fact that the original pages in the logbook of the *U-30* for 3 September 1939 had been removed and replaced by what were obvious forgeries, with different paper and in type from a different typewriter. They then searched the records for surviving crew members of the submarine and identified Adolph Schmidt in a prisoner-of-war camp in Lethbridge, Alberta. With the defeat of Germany, Schmidt felt that he was no longer bound to his oath. He provided an affidavit for the International Military Tribunal that he had witnessed the attack on the *Athenia* by the *U-30*.[11] Schmidt's testimony identified the responsibility for the sinking of the ship and revealed the complicity of senior officers in the German navy and the government in the falsehoods and cover-up surrounding the *Athenia*.

Lemp, meanwhile, still had to get the *U-30* back to Wilhelmshaven. This was no easy task. The attack on the submarine by the British destroyers had damaged the engines as well as other parts of the equipment. Only one of the two diesel engines still worked and it did not produce enough power to move the vessel very fast. Nevertheless on 27 September the *U-30* made its way into port. The crew looked bedraggled, which was typical for submarine crews, and they had picked up a turkey in Iceland that had become their mascot rather than a celebratory dinner. Admiral Dönitz met the ship at the dock and *Oberleutnant* Lemp, realizing that he had created a serious problem for the German government, asked to speak with him privately. "I noticed immediately that he was looking very unhappy," Dönitz remembered later, "and he told me at once that he thought he was responsible for the sinking of the *Athenia*." The admiral admitted that "in accordance with my previous instructions he had been keeping a sharp lookout for possible armed merchant cruisers." However, after the attack Lemp heard the distress signals and concluded that he had torpedoed the passenger liner *Athenia*. Dönitz had Lemp flown to Berlin to explain the situation to Grand Admiral Raeder. Orders came back from the High Command of the Navy (the *Oberkommando der Kriegsmarine*) that the whole matter was to be kept secret, that the high command would deal with the political explanations, and that a court-martial would not be appropriate. Dönitz had the crew of the *U-30* sworn to secrecy and the pages in the U-boat's logbook recording the attack on the *Athenia* removed and replaced with forged material—the only time during the war that this was done. The forgeries were uncovered as such by the British examining German records after the war. In his own war diary as well, Dönitz recorded that the *U-30* had sunk only the *Blairlogie* and the *Fanad Head*. The admiral also questioned Lemp closely on his return to Wilhelmshaven and said he was satisfied that while Lemp had not taken sufficient care he had not deliberately disobeyed orders. Lemp was placed under "cabin arrest," Dönitz said, but this was not serious punishment. In fact Lemp was really seen as a hero who had sunk three ships, been instrumental in bringing down two airplanes (albeit inadvertently), captured two enemy pilots, made provisions for an injured crew member and the captured pilots, taken his ship to record depths, survived a destroyer attack, and against all odds nursed his crippled U-boat back to Wilhelmshaven. These were the very qualities that were wanted in U-boat commanders and it would not set the right tone to punish such a captain in the opening days of the war. In October Lemp was given his first Iron Cross and promoted *Kapitäleutnant.*[12]

In view of these German efforts to keep the crew of the *U-30* from speaking and to cover up the truth about the responsibility for the sinking of the *Athenia*, it is significant that U.S. Naval Intelligence was able to pick up information that identified a German submarine as the cause. The American naval attaché in Berlin, Cdr. Albert E. Schrader, reported on 17 October that the U.S. consul general in Hamburg had passed on information five days earlier from a "responsible source" that "the S.S. ATHENIA is believed by at least several German U-boat commanders to have been sunk on the unfortunate order of some over-zealous German commander who had been ordered to sea prior to the outbreak of war and who, therefore, had not seen the new Prize Law of Hitler's special order." The basic information was quite correct, although *Oberleutnant* Lemp was fully aware of the prize law then in force, and in fact he was the reason for Hitler's "special order." Hitler also ordered that the truth about who torpedoed the *Athenia* not be released and continued throughout the war the false accusation that Winston Churchill had arranged the sinking. Only at the war crimes trials in Nuremburg in 1946 did the truth come out.[13]

Lemp went on to have a remarkable career as a submarine commander, but he also created even greater problems for Nazi Germany. When the *U-30* was repaired he put to sea again in December 1939 and was able to make an important attack on the battleship HMS *Barham.* One of his four torpedoes struck the ship and while the *Barham* was not sunk it was sent to the shipyard for three months. The *U-30* also placed mines off the entrance to Liverpool that sank one tanker and four freighters and closed down the port for a period of time. The *U-30* was the first U-boat to enter the newly acquired submarine base in Lorient on the French coast in July 1940. After eventually sinking sixteen more ships, Lemp was given the Knight's Cross and a new submarine, the *U-110.* However, on 9 May 1941, his luck ran out. In a "wolf pack" attack on a westbound convoy about four hundred miles southwest of Iceland, the *U-110* successfully sank three freighters, *Esmond, Bengore Head,* and *Gregalia,* and damaged *Empire Cloud.* Coincidentally the chief officer of the *Esmond* was B. M. Copland, formerly of the *Athenia.* Copland had the distinction of surviving a second sinking at the hands of *Oberleutnant* Lemp. In the ensuing destroyer attack the *U-110* was badly damaged and forced to the surface. Expecting to be rammed by the destroyers surrounding him, Lemp ordered his crew to abandon ship. However, HMS *Bulldog*, under Commander A. J. Baker-Cresswell, put a motor launch over the side and Sub-Lieutenant David Balme led a boarding party that clambered onto the now empty *U-110*. They retrieved an Enigma cipher machine and all the codebooks and charts, and the U-boat was taken under tow, although it sank before it could be brought into Iceland. Lemp had previously got into the water safely but drowned, possibly attempting to swim back to the *U-110* when he realized that British sailors were going to board the abandoned vessel.[14] The acquisition of a working Enigma cipher machine was an enormous breakthrough for British cryptanalysis and contributed substantially to the ability of the British to read German navy radio messages in the Battle of the Atlantic throughout the rest of the war. This was a major British triumph. It was Lemp's second major blow to the German war effort.

Although the war rapidly unfolded in the autumn of 1939, the echoes of the *Athenia* refused to stop. In the aftermath of the sinking of the *Athenia* and the possibility of other British or French passenger liners being attacked, the Department of State and American diplomats in Europe had a very difficult time making arrangements to bring American citizens home. A number of ships sailing under the American flag were chartered specifically to take citizens back. On 26 September Ambassador Kennedy cabled the secretary of state that he had learned that the United States Lines ships *Iroquois* and *Acadian* would be picking up passengers in Britain and Ireland. These were small coastal ships, not really intended for Atlantic crossings, but they were understood to carry between 675 and 900 people, respectively. The *Iroquois*, fully illuminated as a neutral and with large American flags painted on the hull, took on passengers first at Liverpool on 1 October and then at Cobh, or Queenstown, Ireland, the following day and proceeded west into the Atlantic. On 4 October, however, Grand Admiral Erich Raeder personally handed a note to the American naval attaché in Berlin, Commander Schrader, informing him that sources in Ireland had reported that the *Iroquois* would be sunk off the east coast of the United States, in Schrader's words, "under *Athenia* circumstances for apparent purpose of arousing anti-German feeling." The presumption being, in keeping with German accusations at the time, that Churchill had arranged for an explosive device that would without warning destroy the ship and many of its passengers. Raeder urged that the ship be inspected immediately while still at sea in order to avert a disaster.[15]

President Roosevelt was immediately informed of this by cable and reacted by sending Coast Guard and Navy vessels to meet the *Iroquois* at sea in order to assist in the event that an explosion took place. The captain of the *Iroquois* was ordered to undertake an exhaustive search of the vessel, although no explosive device was discovered. The incident also prompted the president to telephone Churchill on 5 October to consult about the matter. Several weeks earlier, on 11 September, Roosevelt had written a personal letter to Churchill inviting him to "keep me in touch personally with anything you want me to know about"; but before what became an extensive and personal wartime correspondence actually got started, this crisis intervened. Roosevelt again took the initiative and placed a transatlantic telephone call to speak directly with Churchill. The first lord was in fact having dinner with two of his senior Admiralty officials, Rear Admiral Bruce Fisher and Sir Stanley Goodall, when the butler, Frank Sawyers, announced that there was a telephone call. Churchill asked who it was and was told discretely by the butler that he did not know. Churchill said, "Well, say I can't attend to it now." The butler, however, insisted, "I think you ought to come, sir." It was President Roosevelt on the transatlantic telephone informing Churchill of the threat to the *Iroquois*. It was their first wartime conversation, and they discussed the *Athenia* and the *Iroquois* and what might be done in the circumstances. The solution became to give the warning the widest possible publicity. Churchill then broke off his discussion with his naval officers, consulted with Chamberlain, and replied to Roosevelt through the American embassy by telegram later that same night. He noted that the *Iroquois* was so far out into the Atlantic that it was beyond the reach of submarines, so that it could only be threatened by a bomb placed on board the ship in Ireland. "I am convinced full exposure of all facts known to United States Government, including sources of information, especially if official, [is the] only way of frustrating plot," he recommended. "Action seems urgent."[16] This was the beginning of that unique and celebrated relationship between Churchill and Roosevelt during the war, "the partnership that saved the west," as Joseph P. Lash called it. That "partnership" expanded after the Atlantic Conference in 1941 and after the United States entered the war, but it had its beginning in these events concerning the *Athenia* and the *Iroquois*.[17]

Churchill reported in cabinet the following morning that he had talked with the president by telephone and that he had been told that Admiral Raeder had warned the Americans that the *Iroquois* "would be sunk in circumstances similar to those attending the loss of the *Athenia*—the implication being that this would be the work of the British." The first lord concluded that the Germans had given this warning "so specifically" that it seemed possible that their agents had placed a bomb on the ship in Liverpool or Cobh. "The Germans no doubt hoped to claim credit for the friendly gesture of having warned the Americans and so enabled them to save the crew," he observed. Churchill thought that the *Iroquois* situation gave the Admiralty an opportunity to challenge German claims that the British had sunk the *Athenia*.[18]

In the United States, Roosevelt brought the matter of the *Iroquois* before his cabinet and confirmed Churchill's suggestion that the threat be given the widest possible publicity. The White House issued a press release on 5 October which said that the United States had been informed "officially" by Grand Admiral Raeder that "the *Iroquois* is to be sunk when it nears our American east coast." Following very closely the language of the naval attaché's cable, the announcement said, "The sinking of the *Iroquois*, Admiral Raeder said, would be accomplished through a repetition of the circumstances which marked the loss of the steamship *Athenia*." The details of the *Iroquois* affair were also circulated in the weekly *Department of State Bulletin* and in the press. In the end, no explosive device was found on the *Iroquois* and she proceeded to the United States without incident, arriving in New York on the evening of 11 October. Harold Ickes wrote in his diary that "of course no one in this country believes that the British would do a thing of this sort, but Hitler and his government have not ceased to insist that it was Churchill who personally gave the orders to sink the *Athenia* for the purpose of having it blamed on the German Government, in the hope of embroiling us with Germany." The *Iroquois* affair worked to effectively establish an enduring relationship between Roosevelt and Churchill and actually served to discredit German intelligence. For example, the *New York Times* observed that the German note "was regarded with amazement and disbelief" in the United States and "was too ridiculous to deny" in Britain.[19] Moreover, on a public level, the incident tended to reinforce the image of a German menace to the peaceful movement of innocent merchant ships at sea.

The American freighter *City of Flint* had played a dramatic role in the rescue and return of American and Canadian survivors of the sinking of the *Athenia*. However, the *City of Flint* and its gallant captain, Joseph A. Gainard, were not allowed to slip into obscurity in the performance of their normal duties. After putting its passengers ashore in Halifax and New York the *City of Flint* proceeded to Baltimore to unload its cargo and then sailed for Norfolk, Virginia, to discharge the old crew and sign on a new one. The ship then loaded general cargo at Norfolk, Baltimore, Philadelphia, and New York, consisting of tractors, machinery, lumber, asphalt, grease, lubricating oil, wax, cereal, flour, apples, lard, canned goods, and tobacco. The *City of Flint* put to sea on 3 October, bound for Liverpool within a day of the *Iroquois*'s sailing from Cobh. On the afternoon of 9 October the *City of Flint* encountered the German pocket battleship *Deutschland*, under the command of *Kapitän zur See* P. Wennecker, south of Cape Farewell, Greenland. The *City of Flint* was ordered to stop and not to send any radio signals. A boarding party commanded by *Leutnant* Hans Pushbach was sent from the German warship to inspect the ship's papers and cargo. The cargo of tractors, lubricating oil, and flour bound for Great Britain were deemed to be contraband. The ship was put under a prize crew of three officers and eighteen armed German sailors, and a northerly course was charted through the Denmark Strait, around Iceland to the Norwegian coast, and finally to Germany. The *Deutschland* had previously sunk two merchant ships, and taken thirty-eight prisoners from the British freighter *Stonegate* who were removed from the warship and brought on board. When asked if the *City of Flint* could accommodate passengers, Gainard said he had carried 236 passengers on his last trip. "They were survivors from the *Athenia*, which was sunk by an explosion—I didn't know the cause," he said with a touch of irony. Captain Gainard recounted that the German sailors were armed with guns and grenades. He thought it cru-cial to warn the crew not to attempt to retake the ship. It would be too dangerous and even if successful would place other American ships in jeopardy. In the end, neither the American sailors nor the British prisoners offered any resistance, so the relationship remained strained but civil. Gainard questioned the judgment of the decision to regard his cargo as contraband, but he realized that the situ-ation had the potential to escalate into an international incident, if not war.[20]

While still at sea the German prize crew had altered the ship's markings, changed the name to *Alf*, and painted the Danish flag on the side of the hull. Then on the excuse that they were running short of water, the ship put into Tromsø, Norway, on 21 October. The British prisoners were put ashore, but the ship was not released back to Captain Gainard. Instead the Norwegian authori-ties ordered that the ship's proper name and markings be restored and that it leave Tromsø at the end of twenty-four hours. (Under international law a ship commanded by a prize crew could put into a neutral port for emergency matters, but it must be released to its regular crew if the visit is prolonged or for other reasons.) However, it was unclear where they would go when they left Tromsø. Although they were supposed to be heading south toward Germany through the Norwegian inshore route, the weather to the south was deteriorating to storm conditions and it was also expected that both German and British warships would be looking for them. The next thought was to sail north along the Norwegian coast to Hammerfest, but the passage along the rocky fjord was fogbound. The German officer in command of the prize crew had alternative orders to bring the ship into Murmansk, the Barents Sea port of the Soviet Union where the German passenger ships *Bremen* and *St. Louis* and several freighters had earlier sought a haven. So the *City of Flint* sailed into Murmansk on 23 October. Russian port authorities removed the German prize crew from the ship, inspected the ship's cargo, and told Captain Gainard that he would be free to go as soon as the ship's papers had been processed. However, the papers were not returned, the ship sat in the harbor, and Gainard and the crew were not allowed to go ashore.[21]

When the German prize crew originally came on board, the ship's radio had been shut down. As a result of this the *City of Flint* had not reported in to the United States Lines on 14 October, and it was presumed that the ship had been captured or sunk. Its appearance in Norway alerted the world to the fact that the ship was under the control of the German navy, and its arrival in Murmansk now involved the Soviets as well. Newspapers reported on 24 October, "NAZIS SEIZE U.S. SHIP CITY OF FLINT, SAILING HER TO MURMANSK, RUSSIA," identifying the ship as the one that had carried out the rescue of the *Athenia* survivors. Indeed U.S. authorities learned that the ship was in Murmansk from the Soviet news agency Tass. Secretary of State Cordell Hull cabled the American ambassador to Russia, Laurence A. Steinhardt, urging him to find out from the Soviets what was happening, but President Roosevelt raised the matter at a press conference on Wednesday, 25 October, saying that they had been in touch with the ambassador and that "they don't know all the facts yet in Moscow, and the Russian Government is ascertaining, and so are we, what the facts are." Ambassador Steinhardt talked with Assistant Commissar of Foreign Affairs Vladimir P. Potemkin, over the next few days and attempted to explain the rights of neutrals under international maritime law, but he received evasive and contradictory answers. The ambassador's attempts to telephone Captain Gainard or to send one of his assistants to Murmansk by plane or train were also frustrated. Gainard was equally unsuccessful in sending messages to Steinhardt or even making a telephone call. In fact the Soviet authorities were ostentatiously uncooperative, and U.S. relations with the Soviet Union were seriously strained. Indeed the German chargé d'affaires in the United States, Hans Thompsen, took satisfaction in reporting that "the bitterness against Russia in the '*Flint* incident' is considerably stronger than against Germany."[22] Newspapers speculated on the fate of the ship and the meaning of the early removal of the German prize crew. The *New York Times* printed the headline "AMERICAN CREW SAFE ON CITY OF FLINT; RUSSIA FREES GERMANS, HOLDS THE SHIP." In fact the German prize crew returned to the *City of Flint* and the ship was ordered to sail from Murmansk on 27 October. The *New York Times* responded with "CITY OF FLINT, FREED, QUITS MURMANSK; GERMAN CREW REPORTED IN COMMAND." Soviet actions in this matter, soon to be further aggravated by the events of the Russo-Finnish War, did much to alienate American opinion, but the German chargé d'affaire also acknowledged in a report to his government that the seizure of the *City of Flint* was understood by the Roosevelt administration "as an unfriendly act on the part of Germany."[23]

Once again at sea, the *City of Flint* sailed close along the coast in northern Norwegian waters along the inshore route, avoiding possible capture by British warships. Eventually a Norwegian destroyer escorted the ship into Tromsø where the cargo and papers were checked once again. The ship then proceeded south, now escorted by three Norwegian warships, until on 3 November it put in to Haugesund and anchored, ostensibly for medical reasons but in fact to confer with the German consul. However, just after midnight on 4 November, sailors from the Norwegian minesweeper *Olaf Tryggvason* boarded the *City of Flint* and took the German prize crew into custody, as they were obliged to do. Under existing international law the ship had not been anchored in neutral waters for a valid reason. Command of the ship was once again restored to Captain Gainard, who was allowed to sail for Bergen on 11 December, where he consulted with the U.S. consul, Maurice P. Dunlap, and the American minister to Norway, Mrs. J. Borden Harriman. Captain Gainard and members of his crew had great praise for both the Norwegian government and Mrs. Harriman.[24]

Captain Gainard, the ship, and its crew had by this time achieved international prominence. They were welcomed and entertained in Norway. The news media wanted interviews and Captain Gainard made a radio broadcast to the United States recounting the ordeal. "The Capital Is Pleased," reported the *New York Times*, assessing Washington opinion, and it made the editorial comment that the ending of this story was so surprising and dramatic that it has "overshadowed in the American mind even the shocking tragedy of the *Athenia*, in which the *Flint* played her part as Good Samaritan." The practical question arose for Captain Gainard as to where to take his ship next. While being detained by the German prize crew, U.S. neutrality legislation had been changed to forbid American flag ships from entering war zones. The original destinations for the cargo in Glasgow, Manchester, Liverpool, and Dublin were no longer legally available. Gainard therefore sold his cargo in Norway and sailed for Narvik on 22 December where he picked up a cargo of iron ore for the United States. The *City of Flint* left Narvik on 7 January 1940, bound for Baltimore. "Few ships have had more adventures and been allowed to remain afloat," concluded the *Baltimore Evening Sun*.[25]

The capture and prolonged seizure of the *City of Flint* by the Germans, together with the *Iroquois* incident, kept before the American government and public the recollection of the tragedy of the sinking of the *Athenia*. The Soviet Union's assistance to Germany in holding the *City of Flint*, as well as their actions in Poland, the Baltic republics, and Finland, alienated American sentiments also. Although Americans wanted to stay out of the war in Europe, these events reinforced their suspicion and hostility toward both Germany and the Soviet Union and their sympathy and support for Britain and France. In the spring and summer of 1939 President Roosevelt had failed to get Congress to change the "arms embargo" provisions of the Neutrality Laws, which prohibited the sail of arms to any nation actually at war. However, the outbreak of war, the sinking of the *Athenia*, the threat to the *Iroquois*, and the seizure of the *City of Flint* were a graphic illustration to many that American people and interests were threatened by Germany even if the United States were neutral. The existing laws that placed an embargo on the sale of munitions to belligerents instead of protecting the country actually favored America's enemies while denying support to her friends. Former President Hoover, who opposed American intervention in the war, thought that Congress should amend the neutrality legislation to allow the sale of munitions to the Allies, and he felt the sinking of the *Athenia* created a propaganda issue that was likely to influence the legislators to do this. The president called Congress into a special session on 21 September and worked to get amendments to the Neutrality Laws that would enable the United States to sell weapons and war material to belligerents on a "cash and carry" basis; that is, belligerents could buy weapons for cash and carry them home on their own ships. This allowed the British and French, who had control of the sea, to purchase war materials, and effectively denied them to Germany, which had no way of transporting them. The *Athenia*, together with the *Iroquois* and the *City of Flint*, were thrust into this debate. Although opposition from the "isolationists," or "noninterventionists," in both parties remained, support throughout the country and in Congress was sufficient to pass the amendments to the neutrality legislation, which were signed into law on 4 November, the very day the Norwegian authorities returned the *City of Flint* to its American crew. This was a first step in providing full support for Britain, a step that would be followed by the Destroyer-for-Bases Agreement and the Lend-Lease Program. Daily newspaper reports from September to November about the fate of these ships—the *Athenia*, the *Iroquois*, and the *City of Flint*—and their survivors and crews were a constant reminder that the war had come to America whether it was neutral or not.[26]

As a hero of the rescue of the *Athenia* survivors, and himself the victim and survivor of the German seizure of his ship, Captain Gainard became a celebrity in the United States in the early days of the war. Gainard was praised in Congress by Massachusetts representative Edith Norse Rogers on 29 January 1940, saying she thanked God "for men of the caliber of Captain Gainard." Amherst College, which had been the institution of several of his passengers on the *City of Flint* in September of 1939, invited him to lecture about his experiences in February 1940. Gainard developed great respect for those Amherst students and faculty who had pitched in so willingly to create facilities on his freighter for the *Athenia* survivors. A friendship evolved that led to Amherst awarding him an honorary degree in November 1941. In late August 1940 Gainard was able to publish one of the first memoirs of the Second World War, *Yankee Skipper: The Life Story of Joseph A. Gainard, Captain of the* City of Flint, a generous recounting of his experiences in the *Athenia* rescue and the seizure by the Germans. Gainard was awarded the Navy Cross, the first in the war, and was recalled to active duty in the Navy in 1940. The USS *Big Horn* was his first command, a so-called Q-ship or Mystery Ship, one of several merchant vessels that were armed and sent out as decoys to draw an attack by submarines that would themselves be attacked by the hidden guns on the merchant vessel. He later commanded the attack transport USS *Bolivar*, in the Pacific. Captain Gainard died of natural causes in the U.S. Naval Hospital in San Diego in December 1943. The *Sumner*-class destroyer USS *Gainard* launched in September 1944, was named in his honor. The *City of Flint*, the old Hog Island freighter, was one of three ships sunk by a wolf pack on 27 January 1943, with a loss of seventeen of her crew of sixty-five men, while sailing in a convoy bound for North Africa.[27]

CHAPTER 11

THE RETURN TRIP

While we have every sympathy with the Athenia survivors, we definitely feel that this government is making every effort to make possible their early repatriation.

—CORDELL HULL, SECRETARY OF STATE[1]

How to get the *Athenia* survivors home to North America, not to mention all of the other Americans and Canadians hoping to get away from the war in Europe? These were incredibly complicated problems. As far as the *Athenia* survivors were concerned there was the awkward matter of who was financially responsible for them. When survivors were brought into Glasgow and Galway the local authorities stepped forward to provide food, clothing, shelter, and medical facilities, using local emergency funds and public subscriptions. The Donaldson firm and the shipbuilder contributed generous amounts to the relief funds. Both the American and Canadian Red Cross and the two governments also made significant contributions to the maintenance of their citizens among the survivors. This was all very good, but the survivors had purchased tickets to cross the Atlantic. Who, if anyone, was responsible to see that journey completed?

In 1939 if a person bought a ticket from a steamship company and the ship ran aground or had a collision this misfortune was an event for which the steamship company and its employees were held to be responsible, and the company was obliged to see that the survivors got to their destinations. However, if the ship were sunk by an act of war by the king's enemies, the steamship company could not be held legally responsible. The *Athenia* had been sunk by a German submarine, but Germany denied responsibility. Thus legal responsibility was difficult to establish. Moreover the *Athenia* had sailed before war was declared. Were the ship and its survivors eligible for war risk insurance? If legal responsibility could not be established, was there a moral responsibility, and on whom did it fall, the company or the government? These were vexing questions.

In this situation the Donaldson Atlantic Line took the position that its firm was under no legal obligation to provide for survivors of the *Athenia* because of the distress caused by an act of war. The British government recognized that some measures would have to be taken to transport the survivors to Canada and the United States. As early as 8 September the Treasury indicated that it was prepared to contribute up to £25,000 to see that this was done. The Board of Trade also realized that the Donaldson Atlantic Line was not in a strong financial position. The firm had not made a profit each year in the past decade, and indeed the loss of the *Athenia*, which was only partially covered by insurance, was a serious blow. Nevertheless the Board of Trade held that Donaldsons had a moral responsibility to contribute to the repatriation of the Canadians and Americans. Both the Board of Trade and Donaldson understood that it would cost roughly £30,000 to purchase tickets to take all of the *Athenia* survivors back to the United States and Canada. Norman P. Donaldson, the president of the firm, indicated that his directors authorized him to offer to pay half of these expenses if the Board of Trade agreed to pay the other half. The Board of Trade accepted this proposal. In the meantime the American State Department had arranged for a ship under charter to the United States Lines, the *Orizaba*, to take the American survivors home. However, the transatlantic fares on American ships were somewhat higher than on British ships, and costs were further aggravated by the fact that the war crisis had driven up the price of fares. The *Orizaba* made a minimum charge of $141 for each passenger. The final arrangement was that the Donaldson Line would pay $88 for each *Athenia* survivor, and on 21 September Norman Donaldson gave Ambassador Kennedy a check for £5,325 to pay for passage for American citizens. In fact the British government agreed to silently reimburse Donaldson through the Board of Trade for part of their share. The U.S. government agreed to pay the remaining $53 per passenger, lest it appear that destitute American citizens were forced to rely on charity from Britain to get home. Many of these survivors slept on cots put up in the public rooms.[2]

The State Department recognized even before war broke out that it would have to arrange for American ships to bring its citizens home. As early as 23 August a joint War, Navy, and Maritime Commission committee was created to make provisions. The *Athenia* survivors were just part of as many as 100,000 Americans in Europe. Ambassador Joseph P. Kennedy telephoned Under Secretary of State Sumner Welles on Tuesday morning, 5 September, and pointed out the extent to which American passenger liners still making the transatlantic run were booked solid until early October. Welles assured him that he was consulting with the chairman of the U.S. Maritime Commission at the time. At a cabinet meeting at the White House the same day it was decided to charter several American ships—the *Shawnee, St. John, Iroquois, Acadia,* and *Orizaba.* The small passenger liner *Orizaba* was to be directed to the United Kingdom and Ireland specifically to pick up the *Athenia* survivors. The ship was to have sailed on 6 September, but labor troubles complicated the signing of a crew. Arrangements were made for the ship to sail while the labor issues were being negotiated, and the *Orizaba* put to sea by early the next week.[3]

The *Orizaba* was a small passenger ship of 11,293 tons displacement and 443 feet (135.1 meters) in length, built in Philadelphia in 1917. The vessel served as a troopship in the First World War and was returned after the war to the New York and Cuba Mail Steamship Company, popularly known as the Ward Line. In the interwar years the *Orizaba* was operated between New York, Cuba, and Mexico, where the ship achieved some notoriety in 1932 when the American poet Hart Crane jumped from her deck into the sea to his death while return-ing from Mexico where he had held a Guggenheim Fellowship. In 1939 the ship was under charter to the United States Lines when the State Department made arrangements for it and the four other ships to be diverted to Europe to pick up stranded Americans. The ship was rated as having a capacity to carry 450 pas-sengers, but the United States Lines representative in London said that 370 was its maximum. An irritated Kennedy wrote to the Secretary of State that the ship was well past its prime and had only 192 berths. The ship would need an addi-tional 96 cots placed in public rooms and 82 in the existing cabins to accommo-date 370 people. Kennedy forwarded several angry letters from survivors, and he pointed out that after their harrowing experiences in a torpedoed ship, crowded lifeboats, and chaotic rescue ships, the *Athenia* survivors were "in an ugly frame of mind." Of course he also remembered their protests in Glasgow to his son Jack about the threat of German submarines and their demands that they be provided with a naval escort. Secretary Cordell Hull replied to Kennedy the same day, calmly assuring him that the *Orizaba* would not take any more passengers than was safe and that *Athenia* survivors who had made do with the facilities on the freighter *City of Flint* had no complaints. "While we have every sympathy with the *Athenia* survivors," Hull wrote, "we definitely feel that this Government is making every effort to make possible their early repatriation." The secretary concluded, without much sympathy, "They are certainly being shown preferen-tial treatment in getting away earlier than others who might otherwise be able to get accommodations in advance of them."[4]

Ambassador Kennedy also mentioned to Hull that he had been asked by Canadian high commissioner Vincent Massey whether Canadian citizens might arrange for passage on the *Orizaba*. The secretary said that carrying citizens of a belligerent country such as Canada might compromise the neutrality of the ship and that only spaces for American citizens could be provided. Kennedy pointed out instances in which families consisted of one spouse holding American citi-zenship and the other British or Canadian. "Are we to separate an American husband from his British wife?" Kennedy asked. Still more complicated were the circumstances in which children born in the United States held American citizenship. Should the families be broken up? "All are suffering from shock and exposure," he reminded the secretary. Strict enforcement of an American citizenship rule was too painful to contemplate. The secretary relented: "Under the circumstances you are advised that where one member of a family is an American citizen they have a right to travel on these specially diverted ships," Hull told Kennedy, "and that they may be accompanied by members of their family who are not American citizens if the latter have visas."[5] In fact a number of Canadians returned on the *Orizaba* also.

The *Orizaba* arrived in Glasgow on 18 September. Consul General Davis announced again that the ship would sail without a naval escort. "It is not necessary," he said, "as the *Orizaba* is from a neutral country." To make the point, however, the *Orizaba* had the American flag painted on the sides of the hull and even on the deck so that it could be seen from the air. The following day 150 *Athenia* survivors boarded the ship. Lord Provost Dollan wished them a safe trip home and told them, "When you pass the Statue of Liberty keep in your minds that we here are fighting for the same liberty which that statue represents." As the *Orizaba* eased out into the Clyde, Judith Evelyn was touched by the cries of "Good luck to ye!" and "Safe journey" from workers along the docks, all of this in contrast to the catcalls and jibes when the *Athenia* had sailed almost three weeks earlier.[6] The ship stood out through the Irish Sea and around Ireland into the Galway Bay anchorage on the evening of 20 September to pick up 97 survivors and a few others. Several families, separated in the chaos of the sinking of the *Athenia*, were reunited on the *Orizaba*, including Dr. Edward Wilkes and his son Daniel, although his wife, Matilda, and other son Jonathan had been lost. Bishop Browne came down to the waterfront to see off the survivors. The crowd at the pier sang "Come Back to Erin," "Tipperary," and "Auld Lang Syne," and gifts and handshakes were exchanged. Gárdá chief superintendent O'Coileain went out to the *Orizaba* on the tender and met with Captain Alfred M. Moore, who asked that greetings be extended to the Irish taoiseach, Eamon de Valera, whom he had know from earlier transatlantic crossings. A special message of thanks was also sent by the *Athenia* survivors to Mrs. Costello, the wife of the lord mayor, and to the people of Galway for their great efforts to organize the facilities and provide kindnesses for over 400 refugees arriving on the *Knute Nelson*. "You not only fed us, clothed us, and found us lodging but, most important of all, made us feel welcome."[7] The *Orizaba* weighed anchor and headed out of Galway Bay and into the Atlantic.

A week later, on 27 September 1939, the *Orizaba* steamed into New York Harbor on a cold, rainy afternoon. The small ship had been full and many of the 352 passengers had slept on cots in the liner's public rooms, as Ambassador Kennedy had warned, giving rise to a number of complaints. Judith Evelyn remembered that the *Athenia* survivors took the daily lifeboat drills much more seriously than the other passengers, and some of them did not undress for the whole trip. The voyage had not been uneventful either. Just before eight in the morning of Sunday the 24th, while still in mid-ocean, the ship's alarm bells had gone off, sending people out onto the decks in their nightclothes. Although the cause of the alarm bells was an electrical fault, the incident caused much distress and anxiety for the *Athenia* survivors who naturally thought they were under attack once again. On Wednesday afternoon, however, passengers ran on deck while the ship passed the Statue of Liberty as it appeared out of the mist. Tugboats nudged the *Orizaba* into the United States Lines slip at the West 18th Street Pier in Manhattan to a large cheering crowd. The *New York Herald Tribune* claimed that the "hardened seamen on the *Orizaba* looked on with tears in their eyes" as the *Athenia* survivors disembarked. Customs and Immigration authorities met with all those arriving, and a few were sent to Ellis Island. However, provisions had been made for the *Athenia* survivors who had lost their passports and identity papers. Their names had been cabled to the State Department and records of their papers and visas had been checked in advance. Traveler's Aid, the Red Cross, and several other relief agencies also stood by to assist people who were without cash, ongoing tickets, clothing, or luggage. The American Express Company sent agents to the dock who could replace lost travelers checks or write new ones on credit. All of this was a great relief to people without money who had worried about how they would get home once they arrived in New York.[8]

When the passengers streamed ashore newspaper reporters were able get the stories from the survivors themselves. Eighty-year-old Mary Little from Philadelphia, who had been to Europe eleven times, told of being led to a lifeboat by a steward with a candle, of wondering how she got into the lifeboat, and of being rescued by the *Knute Nelson*. Baby Stephen Levine, the son of Mrs. Mazie Levine, was the youngest survivor. He had his first birthday on board the *Orizaba* and was given one piece of cake to celebrate. Beatrice Jansen, returning home from teaching in an Episcopal school in Japan, remembered slipping on the deck of the *Athenia*, falling fifty feet into the sea, and swimming for fifteen or twenty minutes until she was pulled into a lifeboat. Young Russell Park, eleven years old, had got separated from his parents on the ship. He had suffered a blow on the head and was "still feeling funny," he said. On board the *Orizaba* he was reunited with Father O'Connor, the Catholic priest also from Philadelphia, whom he had known from the trip to Ireland earlier in the summer. Father O'Connor looked after him on the trip home, but Russell had received a telegram that his mother had survived and had returned on the *City of Flint*. He wanted to go home to Philadelphia as quickly as possible. "If someone will just let me off at the Thirtieth Street Station in Philadelphia, I will be all right," he said. Fortunately, his mother was at the pier to meet him, but with the sad greeting, "Daddy is gone."[9] Helen Hannay, one of the Texas college girls, was met by her father, Judge Allen B. Hannay of the U.S. District Court in Houston.

Ambassador Kennedy sent a cable commending "the heroic way she conducted herself." He thought her family would be proud to know "she united three or four mothers with their families even though it necessitated going down into [the] ship's hold where water was coming in." The mayor of Saratoga, New York, Addison Mallory, greeted his wife, son, and mother as they came off the ship. Andrew Allan remembered women on the street corners in New York with placards saying, "Keep our boys out of war!" NBC canceled a radio interview with him about the *Athenia* because, he suspected, they thought "it might be construed as pro-British propaganda." There were horror stories too. Mrs. Donald McLeod of Washington, D.C., told of seeing people with their clothes burning after the explosion. Mary McGoorty had put her seven-year-old child Margaret into a lifeboat. "That's the last I ever saw of my daughter."[10]

Americans came home on other ships also. Remarkably the first *Athenia* survivor to sail into New York was Damon Boynton, a thirty-year-old assistant professor at Cornell University. Boynton had been rescued by the HMS *Electra* and brought into Greenock at about 8:30 in the morning on Tuesday, 5 September. He was taken into Glasgow and learned that the Anchor Line passenger ship *Cameronia* was sailing that afternoon. He was able to purchase a ticket and got on the ship ten minutes before it sailed, thereby arriving in New York on 13 September while the *City of Flint* was entering Halifax. After a brief recuperation and shopping expedition for clothes, two of the Texas college girls, Rowena Simpson and Genevieve Morrow, sailed from Southampton on the *Washington* on Sunday, 9 September, and were met in New York a week later by Genevieve's parents and Rowena's brother for a joyous reunion. Rowena later told her father that if it had not been possible to book return tickets on a passenger ship she was certain that he would "get Captain Eddie [Edward V. Rickenbacker, a First World War flying ace and currently president of Eastern Air Lines] to secure passage for us on one of the Clippers, or provide an Eastern Air Lines plane."[11] Less than a week after the *Orizaba* came into New York the *American Banker* arrived in Boston on 2 October with 108 American citizens, of whom 5 were *Athenia* survivors. By 16 October the Anchor Line ship *Cameronia* returned to New York to put into Pier 47 in the North River carrying 58 Polish immigrants and 4 Czechoslovaks from the *Athenia*. Among them was nine-year-old Czech boy Jan Kurelic, whose mother and sister had been placed in a different lifeboat and rescued by the *City of Flint*. The boy had been sent to Ellis Island, but Traveler's Aid reunited him with his mother and they were about to join the father, an American citizen in Garfield, New Jersey. The Cunard White Star ship *Georgic* moored at its pier on Monday morning, 23 October with 341 passengers, including 3 *Athenia* survivors, 1 of whom was the Countess of Winchelsea and Nottingham, the former Margaretta Drexel of Philadelphia.[12] Some people were too unnerved by the experience on the *Athenia* to get back on another ship heading across the Atlantic and either waited until the spring or until after the war. The State Department noted that by the end of September the crowds of people attempting to get home to the United States had begun to ease up.

During the first week of the *Athenia* crisis, the Canadian high commissioner in London, Vincent Massey, negotiated with the Canadian Pacific Railway steamship line to arrange passage for Canadian survivors. Massey informed the government that the Canadian survivors were "restless as to the arrangements." He was not sure what the Donaldson Atlantic Line was planning to do, but he acknowledged that they were under no legal obligation to pay for the passage of these people. Massey seemed confident that Donaldson would make some gesture, although he recognized that "if no refund is available to 'Athenia' passengers we shall of course have to advance passage money." External Affairs was anxious that Donaldson Atlantic did not appear to accept any responsibility for these expenses. Moreover Canadian Pacific insisted on charging the full "wartime" fare for the *Athenia* survivors, even though the convention among British steamship companies was to honor all or part of another company's ticket. Although Canadian Pacific was willing to reduce the wartime fare by about one third, its assumption seemed to be that the Canadian government would pay for its citizens in distress. Norman Donaldson asked Canadian Pacific to charge 75 percent of its prewar fare, but Canadian Pacific held firm. Because Donaldson and the Board of Trade had paid the American government £5,325 for the expenses of the *Orizaba*, the Canadian Pacific felt that it could expect at least as much. Eventually Canadian Pacific was paid £5,199.[13] How that amount was divided between the Donaldson Atlantic Line, the Board of Trade, and the Canadian government is not clear.

The Canadian Pacific Railway liners operating on the Atlantic run were the *Duchess of Atholl, Duchess of York*, and *Duchess of Richmond*. The first two sailed from Glasgow on 13 and 14 September and were escorted part way by two British destroyers. About two hundred miles out from England the destroyers began a vigorous attack on a suspected submarine, dropping depth charges—all witnessed by the fearful *Athenia* passengers on the liners. Many of the *Athenia* survivors were so anxious about the possibility of being attacked by another U-boat that they refused to undress for bed or in some instances even go below deck to their cabins. Angus Beattie, of Joliette, Quebec, admitted that "I didn't go to my cabin for the first night." Seasickness added to their discomfort. The *Duchess of York*, carrying 163 survivors, came into Quebec on 21 September and the *Duchess of Atholl*, bringing 104, slipped into Montreal on the evening of 22 September. The Cass-Beggses, who had not received the reassuring cable from their friends the Gibsons that Rosemary had arrived safely on the *City of Flint* just over a week earlier, disembarked from the *Duchess of York* as quickly as possible and telephoned to learn that all was indeed well. "We then went and treated ourselves to a wonderful afternoon tea," she recalled, "the first meal we really remember eating since the *Athenia*." They took the next train to Ottawa, where they were met at the station by their friends and little Rosemary, wearing a blue dress, walking between them. "I'm glad to see you, Mummy. Did you have the bottom part of your 'jamas on in the lifeboat, cause I didn't!"[14] Relief.

Canadians had, of course, arrived home earlier on both the *City of Flint* and the *Orizaba*, but these ships brought fresh stories of the sinking of the *Athenia*. Eleven-year-old Billie Eadie was still wearing a sailor cap given to him on HMS *Escort*; he told of being thrown against a steel bulkhead by the concussion of the torpedo explosion. "I kept as calm as I could for mother's sake," he said proudly. Angus Beatie, a farmer from Joliette, Quebec, had been rescued in the *Knute Nelson* and brought into Galway. "I distinctly heard three shells fired after we were torpedoed," Beatie said, although he did not hear them hit. While he was still in England James Goodson had attempted to get into the war by trying to enlist in the Royal Air Force. However, he was told he would have a better chance of being accepted by going back to Canada and signing up through the Commonwealth Air Training Programme. He sailed from Liverpool on the *Duchess of Atholl* through stormy seas on the "Drunken Duchess," as he called the ship.[15]

On 16 October the *Duchess of Richmond* came into Quebec City and picked up a contingent of Canadian Red Cross workers to assist the survivors. The ship docked the following day in Montreal, bringing home sixty-nine people from the *Athenia* as well as its normal complement of passengers. By late Sunday afternoon twenty survivors from the Toronto area came into Union Station, to be greeted by a huge crowd. "This is a more welcome sight than the rescue ship," said Charles Hill, who was met by his wife and two daughters. The *Globe and Mail* concluded that it was fitting that this reunion coincided, within a few days, with the Canadian Thanksgiving holiday. The *Duchess of York* sailed again from England on 15 October with sixty *Athenia* survivors, and the *Duchess of Bedford* sailed on 29 November with just two. Lester Pearson informed the Department of External Affairs on 8 November that there were only twenty-seven Canadians known to the High Commission that would need repatriation, although he acknowledged that there may have been others who had not identified themselves and who had decided to stay in the United Kingdom for the foreseeable future.[16]

Once the *Athenia* survivors were home and safe the question arose about compensation for lost property. All those who got off the ship did so with only the clothes they were wearing—everything else went down with the ship. Was the

Donaldson Atlantic Line responsible? The German government? The British? A. D. Simpson, the father of one of the Texas college girls, Rowena Simpson, and the president of the Houston National Bank of Commerce, wrote to the State Department on behalf of several families asking questions about payment. These girls had been asked to list their losses when they made affidavits for the American consuls in Glasgow and London. Could claims be filed against the Donaldson Atlantic Line or against Germany through a Mixed Claims Commission? His daughter had paid $260 for a ticket home on the American passenger liner *Washington* and slept on a cot in a cabin with seven other people. Her friends picked up by the *City of Flint* or placed on the *Orizaba* came home free. Would there be some kind of equitable compensation paid? W. Arthur Strain, whose travel company had made arrangements for the Texas girls, inquired of the State Department raising many of the same issues. As people asked these questions, the Washington, D.C., law firm of George A. Nugent began to solicit survivors to file claims. In March of 1940 a $700,000 claim was made in a suit in the New York federal courts against Donaldson Atlantic, the Anchor lines, and Cunard White Star.[17] Nugent organized the "American War Claimants Protective Committee." This group circulated elaborate questionnaires to *Athenia* survivors and offered to represent the survivor's claims on the basis of a 25 percent contingency fee. The British embassy in Washington, which still worried about possible bad publicity resulting from the charges by Gustav Anderson that the *Athenia* had been carrying guns, consulted with the State Department about the suit. Green H. Hackworth, the senior legal adviser, had serious reservations about Nugent; however, while his assistant felt that the *Athenia* survivors might have a claim on the basis of negligence the embassy was assured that the State Department would take no part in any litigation. The reaction of the Canadian government was simply to bar Nugent and the American War Claimants Protective Committee's use of the Canadian postal service, deeming them to be of a "fraudulent character." However, the British high commissioner in Canada wrote to the colonial office, pointing out that there were over one thousand claims, amounting to millions of dollars, at the Cunard White Star headquarters in Montreal filed against the Donaldson Atlantic Line. The arguments were also made that the ship was carrying too many passengers, that there were not enough lifeboats or crew, and that there was negligence in looking after the passengers. The letter from the Donaldson Line to the passengers when they came on board, apologizing that the services on the ship would be inconvenienced by the larger than normal number of passengers, contributed to this argument. This was important in view of the legal ambiguity about what sunk the ship. To protect itself, Donaldson, in turn, entered a countersuit in the New York courts to limit the amount of any liability on its part, arguing that it could not have foreseen that the ship would become the victim of an act of war.[18]

By September of 1940 the British government decided to make ex gratia payment to people making claims concerning death, injury, or loss of personal possessions through the sinking of the *Athenia*. Payments would be made by the Ministry of Shipping after the claims had been examined by the assessors at the War Risk Insurance Office (although this office was created after the *Athenia* incident). The Canadian government was troubled by the fact that the British would make payments to British subjects, Canadians, and Americans who had filed claims or been parties to suits, but would not advertise the payments to *Athenia* sufferers in general. Elaborate forms had to be filled out and often several times, and not all losses could be claimed—money and jewelry were disallowed. In the end the British government accepted claim applications until 1949 and significant payments were made—$547,800 for injury and loss of lives and $297,200 for loss of personal property, or $845,000 altogether. Payments were made into the 1950s. It was also true that not everyone had made claims. Louis Molgat of Ste. Rose du Lac in Manitoba, a former French sailor, refused to join Manitobans seeking compensation. He and his three sons had survived; more could not be asked of the sea.[19]

It was thought by many that thanks should be given to the people involved in the rescue of the *Athenia* victims. Both the British and American governments had responded immediately after the sinking, sending official letters of thanks to Axel Wenner-Gren and to the governments of Sweden, Norway, and Ireland. Adm. Emory S. Land, the chairman of the U.S. Maritime Commission, wrote directly to Dr. Lulu Sweigard expressing the appreciation of the commission for the "great assistance rendered by you, a survivor yourself, to the Captain of the Maritime Commission Ship *City of Flint* in caring for, nursing, cheering, and directing the survivors," and he added a postscript, "You did a splendid job." Several parents of Texas college girls also raised money to purchase a rare book to be placed in the library of the University of Texas to celebrate the safe return of their daughters.[20] Forty-six of the *Athenia* survivors back in the United States and Canada, organized by James G. Davis, the head of the college department of the Boston book publisher Ginn and Company, put together a subscription $255.37 for the "mess fund" of the HMS *Escort* in time for Christmas 1939. The accompanying message read, "We can never forget your part in saving our lives and we shall treasure our brief moments in your company as one of life's bright memories." They were instructed by the State Department to make the draft out to "First Lord of the Admiralty" and send it to the American Consul General in Glasgow. John R. McDonald wrote to Lieutenant Commander S. A. Buss of HMS *Electra* on behalf of his fellow passengers to "thank you one and all for your capable and efficient rescue, your courtesy and most open hearted kindness to us all." When all of those in McDonald's lifeboat realized that they would be picked up by a ship from the Royal Navy, they knew the ship would be "home to us all . . . from the youngest child upwards."[21] The Donaldson Atlantic Line conveyed its appreciation by sending beautiful silver cigarette cases with the arms of the steamship company and an engraved remembrance of the rescue to all of the crewmembers of the destroyers.

The British government singled out several members of the crew of the *Athenia* in the New Years' Honours List. The citation commended the captain and the ship's crew for launching all twenty-six lifeboats under very difficult circumstances and made particular reference to the return to the *Athenia* of Chief Officer Barnet Mackenzie Copland and Boatswain William Harvey and their action to rescue the unconscious patient in the ship's hospital, Mrs. Rose Griffin, minutes before the ship sank. Chief Officer Copland was given the Order of the British Empire, Civil. "By his inspiration and example," the citation read, Copland "did much to ensure the very high standard of courage and morale among the rescued." Boatswain Harvey was awarded the British Empire Medal (Meritorious Service, Civil) for showing "outstanding coolness and efficiency on getting the boats away on the promenade deck, and setting a high example to the other men in this arduous and responsible work." He also was commended for volunteering to go back to the *Athenia* to help rescue the unconscious woman.[22] These were particularly generous endorsements of the ship's officers and crew in the crisis.

On the anniversary of the sinking, the Canadian government wanted to recognize those who had rescued *Athenia* survivors. Special silver plaques were commissioned by the Montreal silversmith, Henry Birks & Sons, which in its inscription expressed gratitude for the "gallant conduct in rescuing survivors from the passenger steamship *Athenia* torpedoed without warning by a German submarine off the North coast of Ireland on September 3rd 1939." A ceremony was arranged in Victoria, British Columbia, when the *Southern Cross* was in port on 4 September 1940, to present the plaque to Captain Karl A. Sjodahl and owner Axel Wenner-Gren. The lieutenant governor of the province, the mayor of Victoria, senior Canadian naval officers, and various people involved with the maritime trade were in attendance, although perhaps the most fitting person was Sir Richard Lake, the former lieutenant governor of Saskatchewan, who had himself been rescued the year before. A similar ceremony was organized at the Canadian Legation in Washington, D.C., on 26 September 1940 when plaques were presented to Adm. Emery S. Land, the chairman of the U.S. Maritime Commission, honoring the captain and crew of the *City of Flint*. A miniature of the plaque was also prepared for Captain Gainard, who was then serving in the Navy. At the same time a plaque was presented to the representatives of the owners of the *Knute Nelson*, Fred. Olsen & Company, in gratitude for their services.

The fact that Norway was by September of 1940 occupied by German troops meant that neither Captain Andersson nor any member of the crew were then able to receive the plaque.[23]

This recognition and gratitude for those who had contributed to the rescue of the victims of the sinking of the *Athenia* was all very well. However, as 1939 came to an end there was a sense of disappointment that the Allied stand against Hitler and Nazi Germany had not generated a more positive response from the United States. Winston Churchill was certainly one of the most "pro-American" figures in the British cabinet, but even he commented on this. In a memorandum written for the cabinet on 25 December Churchill pointed out, "The trend of American opinion since the war has been disappointing, and the movement to interpret neutrality in the strictest manner has gathered unexpected strength." Although he saw President Roosevelt as "our best friend," this had not resulted in bringing the United States into the war in 1939. The sinking of the *Athenia* had shocked, horrified, and fascinated the American public, but it had not led to a strong protest or an ultimatum by the U.S. government. The British embassy in Washington focused on this issue in its analytical report for the year. Commenting on the impact in America of the course of the war, the report said, "there was a tendency to discount the otherwise strong emotions aroused by events, such as the sinking of the *Athenia* and the German seizure of the American freighter *City of Flint*," and that the Soviet invasion of Finland generated much more indignation although no more action.[24] These events may actually have strengthened the so-called isolationist forces in the United States. Nevertheless it could be concluded that the sinking of the *Athenia*, the *Iroquois* fiasco, and the seizure of the *City of Flint* did accelerate the confidential correspondence and transatlantic telephone conversations between Churchill and Roosevelt that would eventually prove to be of the greatest importance. This was the beginning of the special relationship that distinguished Anglo-American leadership during the war. These events, by effectively identifying Nazi Germany in the public mind as aggressive, hostile, and dangerous to the United States, also helped to bring about a revision of the American Neutrality Laws that opened the door to American assistance to Britain through the sale of munitions and supplies under cash and carry provisions. The sinking of the *Athenia* was the first step in a long series of events that did eventually bring the United States into the war.

CHAPTER 12

HOME AGAIN, SAFE FROM THE SEA

Everyone has experiences that leave you with a scar.

—*Jacqueline Hayworth Bullock*[1]

And so the surviving *Athenia* passengers came home, some to pick up the pieces of shattered lives, others to start new lives. Separated on the ship, thirteen-year-old Peggy Hodge was reunited with her sister, sixteen-year-old Jocelyn, by the end of September. Jocelyn and her mother, Mrs. Mary Hodge, had been thrown into the sea when lifeboat No. 8 was overturned under the fantail of the *Southern Cross*. Only Jocelyn was pulled into another boat and eventually carried back to Canada on the *City of Flint*. Peggy had been in bed in the *Athenia* when it was struck, made her way to a different lifeboat, and was picked up by one of the destroyers and brought to Glasgow. She had flown back to New York on a Pan American Clipper on 28 September and reunited with her sister who was staying with their aunt in Toronto. Within six months of being rescued, twelve-year-old Ramona Allan of Oakland, California, won the women's junior singles figure-skating championship in Cleveland, Ohio.[2] Andrew Allan, who survived the destruction of his lifeboat and the loss of his father, the Reverend William Allan, sailed to New York on the *Orizaba*. He returned to Toronto where he immediately set to work putting together a book of his father's devotional radio talks as a memorial to him. His mother was unfortunately suffering from a stroke and following her death, Andrew Allan took the job with the CBC and moved to Vancouver where he began a distinguished career in first radio and then television as a writer and producer. He never married Judith Evelyn, with whom he had experienced the traumatic events of the sinking of the *Athenia*. She embarked on war work with the CBC in Montreal, Toronto, and Vancouver and then went to Hollywood to pursue her acting career. Her big break came when she opened brilliantly in *Angel Street* on Broadway in December 1941, playing opposite Vincent Price. She won the Drama League's medal in 1942 and went on to have a successful career on the stage and in movies and television in the 1950s and early 1960s. She is perhaps best remembered as "Miss Lonelyhearts" in the motion picture *Rear Window*.[3]

James Goodson came back to the United States and Canada from England and enrolled in Honors English at the University of Toronto, but concluded that he should be "doing my bit to stamp out Nazism." He received his pilot's wings at the No. 6 Service Flying Training School in the Commonwealth Air Training Programme in early December of 1941. He began a new life as an outstanding and colorful fighter pilot, first in the Eagle Squadron of the RAF and then with the U.S. Army Air Corps in the 336th Squadron of the 4th Fighter Group. Goodson became an ace, destroying thirty enemy planes, some in the air and some on the ground. However, in June of 1944 he was shot down himself over Germany and ended the war in a prisoner of war camp. Goodson left the Air Force in 1946 with the rank of lieutenant colonel, having been awarded the Distinguished Service Cross, the Distinguished Flying Cross, and the Silver Star, among other decorations. After the war he went to Harvard Business School and eventually became a senior executive in several major American companies in Europe. Norman E. Hanna of Bangor, Northern Ireland, made it to Canada on the *City of Flint*, got a job and settled in with his relatives in Montreal. However, haunted by the thought that he had shirked his duty by coming to Canada, he joined the Royal Canadian Air Force a year later and became a flying officer. In December of 1943, while flying Short Sunderlands out of Castle Archdale in County Fermanagh on antisubmarine patrol he was listed as missing in action.[4] Barbara Rodman returned safely to Garden City, New York, but when the United States entered the war in 1941 she volunteered with the Red Cross and returned to Europe, this time on the *Queen Mary* now fitted out as a troopship. William and Catherine Edmunds, missionaries in Africa who had been returning to the United States on leave in the late summer of 1939, survived the sinking of the *Athenia*, only to have a second narrow escape while sailing out to the Congo when the Egyptian liner *Zamzam* was sunk by a German surface raider in the South Atlantic in May of 1941.[5]

Dorothy Dean and her fifty-eight-year-old mother were rescued from a lifeboat by the *Southern Cross*, transferred to the *City of Flint*, and made their way to Halifax and then home to Vancouver. When the *Southern Cross* came into Vancouver the following July, Dorothy was able to go on board and personally give her thanks to Captain Karl A. Sjodahl and Chief Officer Hjalmer Rothman. While the *Southern Cross* was cruising along the Pacific coast, the Hollywood gossip columnist Louella Parsons reported that Ernst Lubitsch, whose film *Ninotchka* had just come out, and his wife, the British actress Vivian Gayle Lubitsch, dined on board with owner Axel Wenner-Gren when his yacht was in San Pedro harbor. They had come to say thank you for the rescue of their baby, Nicola, and her nurse, Carlina Strohmayer, who had been on the *Athenia*. Strohmayer, who had been in all the newspapers for her faithful protection of the infant, subsequently went into hiding in order to avoid a suit brought against her by her husband. Nicola Lubitsch grew up to become an actress herself.[6]

Three-year-old Rosemary Cass-Beggs was reunited with her parents who eventually arrived in Canada on the *Duchess of York*. However, "for years afterwards I had a nightmare," she remembered, "in which I was thrown from one sailor to another" in the lifeboat until "the last sailor threw me on over the end of the boat, into the dark waves." The family in fact sought psychological help from the distinguished Toronto child psychologist William E. Blatz, who referred to their experiences in his book *Hostages to Peace: Parents and Children of Democracy*. David Cass-Beggs was able to take up his appointment at the University of Toronto as a professor of electrical engineering, and he later became a key executive in the provincial hydroelectric corporations in Saskatchewan, Manitoba, and British Columbia. Barbara Cass-Beggs became a leading authority on music education for children, on Canadian folk music, and the author of several books. Rosemary returned to England as a young woman where she studied psychology at Oxford and made a life for herself as a freelance researcher, university teacher, and writer. She is the author of *The Penguin Book of Rounds*. Young Ruby Mitchell, back home in Toronto, was given a week to get her feet on the ground before going back to school. Lice had to be removed from her hair and the school took the precaution to warn the other children not to ask questions about her ordeal. Life resumed for a normal schoolchild, but for several years there was a reunion of *Athenia* survivors in Toronto every September. Mrs. Calder would take her, and Ruby remembered that the glamorous actress Judith Evelyn would always talk with her at these gatherings. Among the survivors was Andrew Allan, now a prominent figure in the CBC. One year she was able to introduce her mother to the woman in whose coat she had sheltered in the lifeboat. In some ways the harrowing experience was seemingly put behind her, but when she was about fifteen years old, just after the war ended, on the anniversary of the sinking of the *Athenia*, Ruby broke down and wept without stopping. The doctor was called and concluded that it was a nervous breakdown. Gradually she recovered, but the experience had touched her. Even years later, hearing the hymns that were sung that night in the lifeboat, "Oh God, Our Help in Ages Past," "Abide with Me," and "Jesus Loves Me," would bring tears to her eyes. Although his mother had lost her fur coat, new clothes, and jewelry and he his treasured football, Alexander Lamont remembered her saying comfortingly, "Just thank God we both survived."[7]

Dr. Rudolf Altschul and his wife, Anni, eventually arrived in Saskatoon on a Canadian National Railway train, where he began a long and distinguished career in the medical faculty of the University of Saskatchewan. Dr. John H. Lawrence returned to the University of California at Berkeley where he directed the Medical Physics Laboratory. He distinguished himself in nuclear medicine, winning the Enrico Fermi Award in 1983. (Lawrence's brother, Ernest, was one of the inventors of the cyclotron and won the Nobel Prize in Physics in 1939 and later worked on the Manhattan Project.)[8]

Father Joseph V. O'Connor went back to Philadelphia where the Oblate order placed him in his old high school, Northeast Catholic High. Father O'Connor offered to serve as an Army chaplain or a missionary in Africa, but the order wanted his talents as a teacher. Bernice Jansen recovered from her cuts and injuries, but did not return to St. Margaret's School in Japan. In 1941 she began teaching at an Episcopal school in the Diocese of Western Michigan, where she stayed until after the war. She then returned to overseas missionary work and served for twenty-five years at St. Stephen's Chinese Girls School and St. Andrews Theological Seminary at Manila in the Philippines. Rev. Gerald Hutchinson returned to Edmonton, Alberta, and to the university, became the national secretary of the Student Christian Movement for Canada, and began a career in the United Church of Canada. Rev. Elwood MacPherson, who together with his wife arrived in Quebec City on the *Duchess of York*, found himself to be something of a celebrity as an *Athenia* survivor. He was invited to speak about his experiences at thirty churches, schools, and service clubs in New Brunswick, Prince Edward Island, and the state of Maine. For years afterward he kept on his desk a three-inch-square block of the cork from his lifejacket, as a reminder of his own sea adventure.[9]

The Molgat family arrived in Halifax on the *City of Flint* and returned to Ste. Rose du Lac, a small town in central Manitoba where Louis had a general store. Of the brothers, Jean eventually took over the running of the store, while Gildas went into business and became the leader of the Liberal Party in Manitoba, a member of parliament, and later a senator. André grew up to be a surgeon in Winnipeg, and young Daniel, who had assured his mother that he would look after her if his father were lost, became a Canadian diplomat. After getting back to Glasgow, Barbara Bailey, who had been going to Canada to look after her brother's newborn baby, abandoned the whole idea of crossing the Atlantic. She moved to London, worked in the office of her father, a solicitor, drove ambulances, and served on fire watch. She met and married a Canadian soldier, and after the war sailed to Halifax on the recently restored Cunard White Star liner *Aquitania* in company with hundreds of other war brides. On 30 November 1941 in New York, nurse Margaret Brown of Toronto married seaman Robert Peck, a former sailor on the *City of Flint.* Their romance started when he assisted her out of an *Athenia* lifeboat onto his ship.[10]

Of the Texas college girls, a year later Rowena Simpson of Houston was married and living in San Antonio and Dorothy Fouts was soon to marry and settle in Grosse Pointe Park, Michigan. In 1942 Margaret Doggett married a young officer, Trammell Crow, who served as an auditor in the Navy. Their children used to tease him that their mother had seen more action during the war. "I suppose we will never forget it," remarked Anne Baker, one of the Texas college girls, a year later, "but it all seems like a long time ago."[11] But for some it was never long enough. Sixty years later Jacqueline Hayworth, the younger sister of Margaret, the girl who died on the *City of Flint*, remembered the instant she lost her grip on her mother's skirt as they got to the lifeboat. "It was the worst moment of my life, being separated from my mother." She concluded, "Everyone has experiences that leave you with a scar."[12]

The sinking of the *Athenia* off the northwest coast of Ireland on Sunday, 3 September 1939, was where the Second World War began. The declaration of war by Britain and France earlier that day transformed Hitler's attack on Poland into a major European conflict. For the next nine months people would talk about the "Phoney War," but the war at sea began almost immediately and was not a Phoney War. The sinking of the *Athenia* was only the beginning. It is well to remember that the first Americans to die in the Second World War were not those killed during the Japanese bombing of Pearl Harbor or even in the attack by U-boats on the USS *Kearney* and the USS *Reuben James* in the autumn of 1941. The first Americans killed in the Second World War were on the *Athenia*, the first day of the war. The *Athenia* brought the war to the United States even if it did not bring the United States into the war. Canadians have slowly come to acknowledge something of the same thing. The first Canadian service person killed in the war was not a fighter pilot over the English Channel or a foot soldier in France, but a member of the merchant fleet—Hanna Baird—a stewardess from Verdun, Quebec, serving in the crew of the *Athenia*. For the Canadians, for the Americans, as well as for the British, this is where the war began.

The sinking of the *Athenia* without warning was the first shot in the World War and the first shot in the Battle of the Atlantic, which was the longest battle of the war and coincided with the whole of the World War in the West. The Battle of the Atlantic began on 3 September 1939 and did not end until 7 May 1945, when a U-boat sank a Norwegian minesweeper off the south coast of England the day before V-E day, the official end of the war in Europe. U-boats sunk 2,452 Allied ships in the Atlantic, or 14,687,231 gross tons of shipping. The Royal Navy lost 52,000 sailors and the British merchant navy 31,000 seamen; the Royal Canadian Navy 1,965 sailors and the merchant navy 2,200 seamen (the highest rate of loss among Canadian forces). The U.S. Navy lost 39,000 sailors and the merchant navy 10,000 seamen. This was an unspeakable price to pay for victory, but the Allied navies and merchant fleets endured and prevailed. The cost to Germany was even higher. Of the 830 operational U-boats in the war, 696 were destroyed by the Allies—83.9 percent. There were 40,000 submariners in the

Kriegsmarine, of which 25,870 were killed, 63 percent—the highest casualty rate in the German forces. The casualty rate was even higher, 76 percent, if the 5,000 U-boat sailors captured by the Allies are added to the total. Just as in the First World War, Germany's U-boat policy was both catastrophic and unsuccessful.[13] The sinking of the *Athenia*, a conventional commercial passenger vessel on an innocent voyage, was cruelly symbolic of the illegality and mistakenness of the U-boat policy. Although it was not the most horrendous sinking during the war, the loss of the *Athenia* came as a great shock to world opinion, particularly in the United States and Canada. Whether unintended or a mistake or the actions of an impetuous submarine commander, the sinking of the *Athenia* anticipated the excesses of Nazi ruthlessness that went beyond imagination. The fact that 1,306 people were saved (although 112 were lost) can be attributed to the very gradual sinking of the ship, the relatively calm seas, and the coincidence that rescue ships were within five to ten hours' sailing time away, as well as to the efficiency and gallantry of the ship's crew. However, the sinking of the *Athenia* in the first hours of the war signaled that no ships in the Atlantic would be completely safe for the duration of the war. "Truly we had a marvellous escape," wrote Douglas Stewart shortly after returning to Montreal, "and are certainly thankful to be home again."[14] Not until 8 May 1945, for the first time since that fateful Sunday, 3 September 1939, could ships on the Atlantic sail home again, safe from the sea.

ATHENIA STATISTICS

Originating City of Passengers

Glasgow	420
Belfast	136
Liverpool	546
TOTAL PASSENGERS	1,102

Crew	316
TOTAL PASSENGERS AND CREW	1,418

Nationality of Passengers

Canadian	469
American	311
British (including Irish)	172
European	150
TOTAL PASSENGERS	1,102

Survivors on Rescue Ships

Knute Nelson	430	Passengers	1,009
HMS *Electra*	238[1]	Crew	297
HMS *Escort*	402	TOTAL SURVIVORS	1,306
City of Flint	236[2]		
TOTAL SURVIVORS	1,306		

The yacht *Southern Cross* rescued 376 people and distributed 236 survivors to the *City of Flint* and 140 to the destroyers.

Citizenship of Passengers Lost

Holders of British passports	50[3]
U.S. citizens	30
Polish citizens	7
German citizens	4
Stateless persons	2
TOTAL PASSENGERS LOST	93

Passengers and Crew Lost

Women lost	69
Men lost	27
Children lost	16
TOTAL PASSENGERS AND CREW LOST	112

Crew Lost	19[4]
TOTAL PASSENGERS AND CREW LOST	112

---

[1] Mrs. Rose Griffin, who had been taken off the *Athenia* unconscious on Monday morning, died in the hospital in Glasgow.

[2] Margaret Hayworth died on board the *City of Flint*.

[3] Most of the fifty people holding British passports were either natural born Canadians or were British subjects living in Canada and regarded as Canadian by the Canadian government, but Irish citizens were also lumped into this category.

[4] British subjects, including one Canadian, Hannah Baird, stewardess.

NOTES

ABBREVIATIONS USED IN NOTES

The richest single source of eye-witness accounts of the sinking of the *Athenia* is to be found in the U.S. State Department files. Almost all of the American survivors of the sinking were asked to provide signed affidavits to U.S. consuls or State Department officials explaining what they had seen and experienced. These affidavits were incorporated into the department's decimal document classification system. For example, the full citation for the affidavit of Florence Hargrave, an *Athenia* survivor, would be the following: Florence Hargrave, in Record Group 59, General Records of the Department of State, Decimal File, Records of the Department of State relating to the Internal Affairs of Great Britain, 851.857 ATHENIA/275, National Archives and Records Administration, College Park, Maryland. Inasmuch as the Record Group category and decimal number for these affidavits does not vary and only the individual document numbers change, these citations have been abbreviated for convenience to the following: Hargrave ATHENIA/275, NARA.

ADM	Admiralty, England
ADM	Admiralty, National Archives, London, England
CAB	Cabinet, National Archives, Londin,England
FO	Foreign Office, National Archives, London, England
FRUS	*Foreign Relations of the United States*
LAC	Library and Archives Canada
MT	Ministry of Transport, National Archives, London, England
NA	The National Archives, London
NARA	National Archives and Records Administration, College Park, Maryland
Parl. Deb.	*Parliamentary Debates*, England
RG	Record Group, General Records of the Department of State, National Archives and Records Administration
T	Treasury, National Archives, London, England

CHAPTER 1. THE HINGE OF FATE

1. [Rowena "Nino"] Simpson to A. D. Simpson, 15 August 1939 (cable), MSS 41, Box 8, folder 9, A. D. Simpson Family Papers, Houston Public Library.
2. James Goodson, *Tumult in the Clouds*, 1.
3. Judith Evelyn, "*Athenia* manuscript," 8–10, in possession of Ms. Cynthia Harrison, accessible at http://www.ahoy.tk-jk.net/macslog/ AtheniaManuscriptPreview.html (hereafter "*Athenia* manuscript"); and Andrew Allan, *Andrew Allan: A Self-Portrait*, 86–87.
4. For good analyses of the international crisis, see Donald Cameron Watt, *How the War Came: The Immediate Origins of the Second World War, 1938–1939*.
5. Neville Chamberlain, cited in A. J. P. Taylor, *English History, 1914–1945*, 429; and Watt, *How the War Came*, 29.
6. Chamberlain, cited in Taylor, *English History*, 442.
7. David Reynolds, *From Munich to Pearl Harbor: Roosevelt's America and the Origins of the Second World War*, 32–68; and Waldo Heinrichs, *Threshold of War: Franklin D. Roosevelt & American Entry into World War II*, 3–12.
8. For a useful discussion of the evolution of American attitudes toward the European situation in 1938 and 1939, see Philip E. Jacob, "Influences of World Events on U.S. 'Neutrality' Opinion," *Public Opinion Quarterly* 4, no. 1 (March 1940): 48–65.
9. Taylor, *English History*, 433; and Winston S. Churchill, *The Second World War: The Gathering Storm*, 411.
10. G. S. Messersmith to American Diplomatic Officers and Certain Consular Officers in Europe and the Near East, 21 March 1939, and John G. Erhardt to American Consular Officers in Great Britain and Northern Ireland, 22 August 1939, RG 84, Classified General Records, 1939–1962, Glasgow (Scotland) Consulate, 1939, Box 2, National Archives and Records Administration (hereafter NARA); Leslie A. Davis to John G. Erhardt, 31 August 1939, RG 84, Foreign Service Posts of the Department of State, Glasgow Consulate, 1939, Box 19, NARA; and Francis E. Hyde, *Cunard and the North Atlantic, 1840–1973: A History of Shipping and Financial Management*, 260–67.
11. Jeannette Jordan to Marion Potter, 26 August 1939, cable, Jeannette C. Jordan Papers, Wisconsin Historical Society; and Hargrave, affidavit, RG 59, General Records of the Department of State, Decimal file, Records of the Department of State relating to the Internal Affairs of Great Britain, 851.857 ATHENIA/275, National Archives and Records Administration, College Park (hereafter referred to by ATHENIA/document number, NARA); and Russell A. Park, "Aboard the *Athenia*," *World War II* (July 1989), 42.
12. Spiegelberg, ATHENIA/619, and Smith, ATHENIA/535, NARA.
13. *Toronto Star*, 4 September 1999; and Evelyn, "*Athenia* manuscript," 4.
14. Eva M. Blair, *Saved from the* Athenia: *A Personal Testimony to the Indisputable Presence of God during the Torpedoing of the R.M.S.* Athenia *Off the Coast of*

Ireland on September Third Nineteen Thirty-Nine, 7–10; Gerald Hutchinson Family Records, Edmonton; and Jansen to Green H. Hackworth, 4 December 1939, RG 59, ATHENIA/563, NARA.

15. Anni C. Altschul, "A Cousin in Ireland," Rudolf Altschul Fonds, University of Saskatchewan Archives.

16. Barbara Cass-Beggs, *Roots and Wings: A Memoir of My Life with David*, 93–96; and Ruby Mitchell Boersma Interview, 7 February 2006, Oral History Program, 31D 6, Canadian War Museum Archives.

17. Annette Brock to A. D. Simpson, 21 August 1939, Burke Baker to Major S. Greenwall, August 1939 (cable), Charles Cain Jr. to A. D. Simpson, 30 August 1939, A. D. Simpson to Jesse H. Jones, 30 August 1939 (cable), MSS 41, Box 8, folder 9, A. D. Simpson Family Papers; and *Dallas Morning News*, 3 September 2010. Also see Gladys B. Strain to Green H. Hackworth, 14 December 1939, ATHENIA/616, NARA.

18. [Rowena] Simpson to A. D. Simpson, 1 September 1939 (cable) and A. D. Simpson to R. T. Simpson, 1 September 1939 (cable), MSS 41, Box 8, folder 9, A. D. Simpson Family Papers.

19. Stephen Woodring, "Phenylthiocarbamide: A 75-Year Adventure in Genetics and Natural Selection," *Genetics* 172 (April 2006): 2015–23; and Joseph Gainard to the President, Amherst College, 29 September 1939, Captain J. A. Gainard folder, War Materials Collection, Amherst College Library.

CHAPTER 2. IN ALL RESPECTS READY FOR SEA

1. Chorus of a traditional Scottish song, played by a bagpiper at the sailing from Glasgow of Donaldson ships.

2. The loss of these paintings meant the book was never published. This was reminiscent of the loss of the Sangorski & Sutcliffe specially crafted, jewelled binding of the *Rubaiyat of Omar Khayyam*, which went down with the *Titanic* in 1912.

3. Max Caulfield, *Tomorrow Never Came: The Story of the S.S.* Athenia, 17–30.

4. The *Letitia* was converted first to an armed merchantman and then to a troopship; later she was transferred to the Canadian government and refitted as a very modern hospital ship to be used to return wounded Canadian soldiers to Canada. After the war the ship was renamed the *Captain Cook* and returned to passenger service. Alastair Dunnet, *The Donaldson Line: A Century of Shipping, 1854–1954*, 80; and Stephen Fox, *The Ocean Highway: Isambard Kingdom Brunel, Samuel Cunard and the Revolutionary World of the Great Atlantic Steamships*, 291–93. During the winter months she and her sister ship made runs from Liverpool to Halifax, Nova Scotia, Saint John, New Brunswick, and sometimes to Portland, Maine, and back; they were also used for holiday cruises into the southern latitudes; in January and December of 1938 the *Athenia* had served as a troop ship.

5. Caulfield, *Tomorrow Never Came*, 41; Dunnet, *The Donaldson Line*, 65; Derek M. Whale, *The Liners of Liverpool*, Part II, 6–7; and *Irish Times*, 5 September 1939.

6. Memorandum on behalf of Anchor Line Limited and Donaldson Atlantic Line Limited, submitted in support of a request by those Companies for Government assistance in respect of the Atlantic Passage liner business carried on by them, February 1939, TD49/107, Glasgow City Archives; and Whale, *The Liners of Liverpool*, 6–7. The Donaldson line had run at a loss from 1933 to 1935 but was recovering by the late 1930s. The war was devastating for the company, which lost eleven ships, mostly to torpedoes.

7. TSS *Athenia*, Lists of Crews and Voyages, TD49/72/4(2), Glasgow City Archives; and *Evening Citizen*, 4 September 1939; and *Connacht Tribune*, 9 September 1939.

8. TSS *Athenia*, Lists of Crews and Voyages, TD49/72/4(2), Glasgow City Archives; *Glasgow Herald*, 3 January 1940; and *Daily Record & Mail*, 5 September 1939.

9. Caulfield, *Tomorrow Never Came*, 22–23; Evelyn, "*Athenia* manuscript," 5; Rudolf Altschul Fonds, University Archives, University of Saskatchewan; and *Athenia* meeting of the Board of Trade 15 September 1939, Ministry of Transport (hereafter referred to as MT) 9/3127, The National Archives, London (hereafter referred to as NA).

10. Evelyn, "*Athenia* manuscript," 6; and Bella [Belle] Maranov from New York had similar recollections, in Terry Charman, *Outbreak 1939: The World Goes to War*, 91.

11. Caulfield, *Tomorrow Never Came*, 47–63.

12. Calder, ATHENIA/578, NARA; Blair, *Saved from the* Athenia, 12; *Irish Times*, 6 September 1939; *America*, 30 September 1939, 579; and Park, "Aboard the *Athenia*," 42.

13. Calder, ATHENIA/578, NARA; and Patricia Hale, "I Was on the *Athenia*," *Canadian Home Journal*, December 1939, 8.

14. Caulfield, *Tomorrow Never Came*, 26–27, 31–46; David A. Wilcox, "The *Athenia* Saga," 1–2, U/F U.530#18, Nova Scotia Archives and Records Management; Cass-Beggs, *Roots and Wings*, 96; and Circular letter from the Donaldson Atlantic Line, 1 September 1939, Gerald Hutchinson Family Records.

15. Daniel Francis, "The Sinking of the *Athenia*," *The Beaver* (April–May 2006), 30–36; and Blair, *Saved from the Athenia*, 13.

16. Charman, *Outbreak*, 120.

17. Caulfield, *Tomorrow Never Came*, 31–46.

18. Rev. Dr. G. P. Woollcombe, "My Experience in Connection with the Torpedoing of S.S. *Athenia* on September 3, 1939," Department of Transport Records, RG 12, file 7808-4, Library and Archives of Canada (hereafter

referred to as LAC); Mary Lou Kelley in Michael Poirier, "Survivors Recall *Athenia*'s Final Voyage," *Voyage* 49 (Autumn 2004): 28; and Allan, *Andrew Allan*, 86.

19. Evelyn, "*Athenia* manuscript," 8; Smith, ATHENIA/557, NARA; and Barbara Bailey, "*Athenia* Survivor," in *Fragments of War: Stories from Survivors of World War II*, ed. Joyce Hibbert, 13–14.

20. Charman, *Outbreak*, 192.

21. Report on the Sinking of the *Athenia*, MT 9/3278, NA; and Woollcombe, "My Experience," 1; Evelyn, "*Athenia* manuscript," 8; and Allan, *Andrew Allan*, 86.

22. Park, "Aboard the *Athenia*," 44; Connolly, ATHENIA/275, NARA; Blair, *Saved from the Athenia*, 14; Hale "I Was on the Athenia," 8; *Montreal Gazette*, 14 September 1939; and D .G. B. Stewart, "Homeward Bound on the *Athenia*," *The Canadian Banker*, October 1939, 80.

23. Bailey, "*Athenia* Survivor," 14; and Kate Ellen Hinds, ATHENIA/577, McPherson, ATHENIA/558, Singleton, ATHENIA/558, Calder, ATHENIA/578, Smith, ATHENIA/535, and Hutchinson, ATHENIA/318, NARA.

24. Anderson, ATHENIA/485, NARA; Charman, *Outbreak*, 238; Montgomery Evans, *A Ship Was Torpedoed*, 3–4; and Stork, ATHENIA/574, NARA.

25. Goodson, *Tumult in the Clouds*, 2–3.

26. Report on the Sinking of the *Athenia*, MT 9/3278, NA.

CHAPTER 3. SURFACE SHIP SIGHTED

1. Orders radioed to German submarines at sea following the declaration of war on 3 September 1939. Clay Blair, *Hitler's U-Boat War: The Hunters, 1939–1942*, 66.

2. Ibid., 55–57.

3. Ibid., 57–64.

4. Ibid., 66; and Caulfield, *Tomorrow Never Came*, 12–13. Signals went out to the Royal Navy at 11:17 a.m. to commence hostilities immediately. Admiral Karl Dönitz, 15 January 1946, *Trial of the Major War Criminals before the International Military Tribunal*, vol. 5, 267. Legro argues that U-boat commanders "were first and foremost taught to let no opportunity to attack pass," and furthermore that they "were not well trained to differentiate one target for another." See Jeffrey W. Legro, *Cooperation under Fire: Anglo-German Restraint during World War II*, 58.

5. Caulfield, *Tomorrow Never Came*, 62–63; and Adolph Schmidt, 15 January 1946, in *Trial of the Major War Criminals before the International Military Tribunal*, vol. 5, 265–67.

6. Smith, ATHENIA/535, Coullie, ATHENIA/537, and Bruce, ATHENIA/492, NARA; *Glasgow Herald*, 6 September 1939; and Stewart, "Homeward Bound on the *Athenia*," 81.

7. Blair, *Hitler's U-Boat War*, 66–67. Altogether four torpedoes were fired by the *U-30*, only one of which struck the *Athenia*. One or more of the other three torpedoes may have exploded at sea, leading the many witnesses on the *Athenia* to believe that the *U-30* fired its deck gun at the ship. That both the magnetic and contact detonators in German torpedoes had serious problems in the early stages of the war, may also be an explanation. Bernd Stegemann, "The Submarine War," in *Germany and the Second World War*, vol. 2, edited by Klaus A. Maier, Horst Rohde, Bernd Stegemann, and Hans Umbreit, 177–78; and Friedrich Ruge, *Der Seekrieg: The German Navy's Story, 1939–1945*, 61.

8. Högel cited in Andrew Williams, *The Battle of the Atlantic: Hitler's Gray Wolves of the Sea and the Allies' Desperate Struggle to Defeat Them*, 15–16; Cay Rademacher, *Drei Tage im September, Die letzte Fahrt der Athenia, 1939*, 175–80; and Hinsch cited in Caulfield, *Tomorrow Never Came*, 66–67.

9. Paul Kennedy, *The Rise and Fall of British Naval Mastery*, 239–50; Frank Uhlig Jr., *How Navies Fight: The U.S. Navy and Its Allies*, 75–100; and John Keegan, *The Price of Admiralty: The Evolution of Naval Warfare*, 251–55.

10. Arthur S. Link, *Wilson: The Struggle for Neutrality, 1914–1915*, 349–455. The sinking of the *Lusitania* has been extensively studied. See, for example, Thomas A. Bailey and Paul B. Ryan, *The Lusitania Disaster: An Episode in Modern Warfare and Diplomacy*; Colin Simpson, *Lusitania*; and Diana Preston, *Wilful Murder: The Sinking of the Lusitania*.

11. Ronald H. Spector, *At War at Sea: Sailors and Naval Combat in the Twentieth Century*, 103–21.

12. Captain S. W. Roskill, *The Strategy of Sea Power: Its Development and Application*, 149–50, 165. Two other pocket battleships were the *Admiral Sheer* and the *Lützow*, with six 11-inch guns. Germany also launched two battle cruisers in 1936, the *Scharnhorst* and the *Gneisenau*, with nine 11-inch guns, and the battleship *Tirpitz* in 1939, with eight 15-inch guns. As well, Germany built ten modern cruisers in the interwar years with from 5.9- to 8-inch guns. Bernd Stegemann, "Germany's Second Attempt to Become a Naval Power," in Maier et al. (eds.), *Germany and the Second World War*, vol. 1, 60–66; and Ruge, *Der Seekrieg*, 21–40. For a discussion of the primacy of the battleship in naval thinking during the first half of the twentieth century, see Kennedy, *The Rise and Fall of British Naval Mastery*, 1–9, 177–83; H. P. Willmott, *The Last Century of Sea Power*, Vol. 2: *From Washington to Tokyo, 1922–1945*, 119–44; and George W. Baer, *One Hundred Years of Sea Power: The U.S. Navy, 1890–1990*, 9–26. Also see Keegan, *The Price of Admiralty*, and Robert L. O'Connell, *Sacred Vessels: The Cult of the Battleship and the Rise of the U.S. Navy*. Seventy-nine U-boats were under construction when the war started, and between 300 and 658 more were projected. For German submarine statistics, see Stegemann, "Germany's Second Attempt to Become a

Naval Power," 76–78; and Marc Milner, *Battle of the Atlantic*, 15–16. Keegan mentions that in the 1920s Germany, prohibited from building submarines by the Versailles Treaty, had submarines constructed in the Netherlands and in Finland. Keegan, *The Price of Admiralty*, 260–61.

13. For an illustration of the problem the submarine presented at the 1930 London Naval Conference for nations with small navies in contrast with nations with large navies, see Christopher Hall, *Britain, America & Arms Control, 1921–37*, 102–3. W. T. Mallison Jr., *International Law Studies, 1966: Studies in the Law of Naval Warfare: Submarines in General and Limited Wars*, 1–53, quotation from 48; and Milner, *Battle of the Atlantic*, 12–13.

14. Edward P. Van Der Porten, *The German Navy in World War II*, 44; and H. L. Trefousse, *Germany and American Neutrality, 1939–1941*, 13–32.

15. Captain S. W. Roskill, *The War at Sea, 1939–1945: Defensive*, vol. 1, 103–4; Memorandum by an Official of the Foreign Minister's Personal Staff, 13 November 1939, *Documents on German Foreign Policy*, Series D, vol. 8, *The War Years, 1939–1940*, 8, 408; and Keegan, *The Price of Admiralty*, 271. The second British ship sunk was the merchant freighter, *Bosnia*, torpedoed by Günther Prien in *U-47* on 5 September. Blair, *Hitler's U-Boat War*, 78–80.

16. Winston S. Churchill, *The Second World War: Their Finest Hour*, 598. A very good discussion of the issues determining submarine policy can be found in Legro, *Cooperation under Fire*, 44–79.

17. Dan van der Vat, *The Atlantic Campaign: World War II's Great Struggle at Sea*, 5–6.

18. Milner, *Battle of the Atlantic*, 20; and Rademacher, *Drei Tage im September*, 279–90.

19. Schmidt, in *Trial of the Major War Criminals before the International Military Tribunal*, vol. 13, 266; and Williams, *Battle of the Atlantic*, 18; Blair, *Hitler's U-Boat War*, 85–87: and Richard Woodman, *The Real Cruel Sea: The Merchant Navy in the Battle of the Atlantic, 1939–1943*, 29–30.

CHAPTER 4. ABANDON SHIP!

1. Bloom, ATHENIA/275, NARA.

2. Mary Lou Kelly, in Poirier, "Survivors Recall *Athenia*'s Final Voyage," 29; and Calder, ATHENIA/578, NARA.

3. Report of the Sinking of the, ATHENIA, MT 9/3278, NA; and Bidwell, RG 59, ATHENIA/431, NARA.

4. Report of the Sinking of the, ATHENIA, MT 9/3278, NA; and Naval Attaché, London, to Director of Naval Intelligence, 7 September 1939, and Office of the Naval Attaché, London, Memorandum for the Ambassador, 6 September 1939, ATHENIA/491, NARA.

5. *Glasgow Herald*, 8 September 1939; Charman, *Outbreak*, 239; *Evening Citizen*, 7 September 1939; and *Glasgow Eastern Standard*, 9 September 1939.

6. Report of the Sinking of the, ATHENIA, MT 9/3278, NA; Charman, *Outbreak*, 238–39; Stewart, "Homeward Bound on the *Athenia*," 80; and Evelyn, "*Athenia* manuscript," 10–11.

7. Mickelsen, ATHENIA/481 3/9, and Grossman, ATHENIA/567, NARA; and Evans, *A Ship Was Torpedoed*, 4.

8. Dixon, RG 59, ATHENIA/276, NARA; and Evelyn, "*Athenia* manuscript," 12–13.

9. Report of the Sinking of the, ATHENIA, MT 9/3278, NA; and MacDonald, ATHENIA/275, /612, and Lewis, ATHENIA/275, NARA.

10. Bloom, ATHENIA/276, NARA; Hale, "I Was on the *Athenia*," 8; and Report of the Sinking of the, ATHENIA, MT 9/3278, NA.

11. McGoorty and Rodman, ATHENIA/275, /589, and Jansen to Green H. Hackworth, 4 December 1939, ATHENIA/563, NARA.

12. Levine, ATHENIA/318, Hannay and Bonnett, ATHENIA/275, NARA; and *Glasgow Herald*, 6 September 1939; and Smith, ATHENIA/557, and Singleton, ATHENIA/558, NARA.

13. Gifford, ATHENIA/275, and Ford, ATHENIA/318, NARA; Helen Edna Campbell, "Torpedoed at Sea: Aboard the S.S. *Athenia*, 1939," Thunder Bay Historical Museum Society, *Papers & Records* vol. 21 (1993), 3; and John Easton in Ahoy-Mac's Web Log, http://ahoy.tk-jk.net/Letters/JohnEastonandmotherLiluEa.html, 18/10/2007.

14. Cass-Beggs, *Roots and Wings*, 97.

15. Hinds, ATHENIA/318, NARA; and Ruby Mitchell Boersma Interview, 31D 6, Canadian War Museum Archives.

16. Lawrence, ATHENIA/581, NARA.

17. Douglas Bikow in Ahoy-Mac's Web Log, http://www.fogbugz.tkwebservice.com/default.asp?ahoy.2.641.5 , 15/12/2006; Calder, RG 59, ATHENIA/578, NARA; and Poirier, "Survivors Recall *Athenia*'s Final Voyage," 30.

18. Rev. Joseph V. O'Connor, "I Was Aboard the 'Athenia,'" *The Irish Digest* 6, no. 3 (May 1940): 36; Rev. Gerald Hutchinson Family Records; and *Montreal Gazette*, 23 September 1939.

19. Hannah, ATHENIA/318, NARA; and Goodson, *Tumult in the Clouds*, 3–5.

20. O'Connor, "I Was Aboard the 'Athenia,'" 36; and *Ottawa Citizen*, 3 September 1999.

21. David A. Wilcox, "The, ATHENIA Saga," 2 U/F U. 530 #18, Nova Scotia Archives and Record Management; and Boyle, ATHENIA/318, and Bridge, ATHENIA/275, NARA.

22. Bridge, ATHENIA/275, /507 ¼, NARA; *New York University Commercial Bulletin*, 16 October 1939; and Charman, *Outbreak*, 239.

23. Quine, ATHENIA/275, Bidwell, ATHENIA/431, /507 ¼, and Johnson, ATHENIA/559, NARA.

24. Coullie, ATHENIA/537, and McCubbin, ATHENIA/275, NARA; and *Glasgow Eastern Standard*, 16 September 1939; Insch, ATHENIA/600, NARA; and Park, "Aboard the *Athenia*," 44.

25. Morrison, ATHENIA/318, NARA.

26. Tinney, ibid.

27. Van Newkirk, ATHENIA/275, and Mowry, ATHENIA/627, NARA; *Toronto Star*, 4 September 1999; and interview with Hay "Scotty" Gillespie.

28. Norman Hanna to Mrs. S. Hanna, 15 September 1939, D 3265/1, Public Record Office of Northern Ireland; and Dick and Finley, ATHENIA/275, NARA.

29. Wilkes and MacLeod, ATHENIA/318, NARA.

CHAPTER 5. TO THE LIFEBOATS

1. Wilcox, "The *Athenia* Saga," 3, U/F U.530 #18, Nova Scotia Archives and Record Management.

2. Report on the Sinking of the *Athenia*, MT 9/3278, NA.

3. Ibid.

4. Ford, ATHENIA/318, Dick, ATHENIA/275, and Singleton, ATHENIA/558, NARA.

5. Rabenold, ATHENIA/275, and Rodman, ATHENIA/589, NARA; Evelyn, "*Athenia* manuscript," 14; Campbell, "Torpedoed at Sea," 3–4; and Report of the Sinking of the *Athenia*, MT 9/3278, NA.

6. McPherson, ATHENIA/275, and Park, ATHENIA/275, NARA.

7. *Toronto Star*, 4 September 1999; Richard Snow, *A Measureless Peril: America in the Fight for the Atlantic, the Longest Battle in World War II*, 53; Jeannette Jordan letter, 6 September 1939, Jeannette C. Jordan Papers; Hargrave and McCubbin, ATHENIA/275, and Smith, ATHENIA/557, NARA.

8. Woollcombe, "My Experience," 2–3, Department of Transport Records, RG 12, files 7808-4, LAC; Brian R. Meister, "Terror of War: The Tragedy of the *Athenia*," *Voyage* no. 9 (June 1991): 185; Hannah, ATHENIA/318, NARA; and Hale, "I Was on the *Athenia*," 9.

9. Steinberg and Connolly, ATHENIA/275, NARA; Report on the Sinking of the *Athenia*, MT 9/3278, NA; and Bailey, "*Athenia* Survivor," 15–16.

10. Dr. Lulu E. Sweigard, "The *Athenia* Disaster—My Story," *The Alumnus*, January 1940, 7; Janet Olson to Green H. Hackworth, 28 December 1939, ATHENIA/650, NARA; and John Coullie to Mother, 27 September 1939, P284, Imperial War Museum.

11. Anderson, ATHENIA/435, NARA; Wilcox, "The *Athenia* Saga," 3, U/F U.530 #18, Nova Scotia Archives and Records Management; and Rosemary Cass-Beggs Burstall, "A Three-Year-Old's Recollection of the Sinking of the Athenia," Maritime Museum of the Atlantic.

12. MacDonald, ATHENIA/275, /612, and MacLeod ATHENIA/318, NARA.

13. Jansen to Green H. Hackworth, 4 December 1939, ATHENIA/563, and Spiegelberg, ATHENIA/619, NARA; and Report of the Sinking of the *Athenia*, MT 9/3278, NA.

14. Gifford, RG 59, ATHENIA/275, NARA.

15. Insch, ATHENIA/600, NARA; Family Records; and Goodson, *Tumult in the Clouds*, 6; interview with Hay Gillespie; Hannay, and Bonnett, ATHENIA/275, and Smith, ATHENIA/507 ¼, NARA.

16. Smith, ATHENIA/535, NARA; and Ruby Mitchell Boersma Interview, 31D 6, Oral History Program, Canadian War Museum Archives.

17. Hugh S. Swindley to Mr. and Mrs. W. Trevor Jones, 20 September 1939, P284, Imperial War Museum; Bridge, ATHENIA/507 ¼, and ATHENIA/275, NARA; and Report on the Sinking of the *Athenia*, MT 9/3278, NA.

18. Kelly, ATHENIA/275, and Stuppel, ATHENIA/302, NARA; Report on the Sinking of the *Athenia*, MT 9/3278, NA; and Swindley to Mr. and Mrs. W. Trevor Jones, 20 September 1939, P284, Imperial War Museum.

19. Goodson, *Tumult in the Clouds*, 7–9.

20. Message from MALINHEADRADIO, 3 September 1939, ADM 199/140, NA; Van der Vat *The Atlantic Campaign*, 4; Lt. Commander J. Bostock to Captain S. N. O. Clyde, Western Approaches, 5 September 1939, ADM 1/10033, NA; and P. N. Walter, Commander, HMS *Fame* to Rear Admiral, Home Fleet, HMS *Aurora*, 13 September 1939, ADM 199/140, NA.

21. Report on the Sinking of the *Athenia*, MT 9/3278, NA; and Official Log of the *Athenia*, a copy in ATHENIA/636, NARA.

22. Report on the Sinking of the *Athenia*, MT 9/3278, NA; Official Log of the *Athenia*, copy in ATHENIA/636, NARA; and Charman, *Outbreak 1939*, 253.

CHAPTER 6. THOSE IN PERIL ON THE SEA

1. Dorothy Bulkley to Margaret and Birt, 28 September 1939, Manuscript Collection No. 3773, Dorothy Bulkley Papers, Western Reserve Historical Society.

2. Sweigard, "The *Athenia* Disaster—My Story," 7.

3. Charles Wharton Stork, "Sketches by an 'Athenian,'" *Saturday Evening Post*, 4 November 1939, 33; and Blair, *Saved from the* Athenia, 23.

4. Evelyn, "*Athenia* manuscript," 15; Dorothy Bulkley to Marge and Birt, 28 September 1939, Dorothy Bulkley Papers; and Grossman, ATHENIA/567, Spiegelberg, ATHENIA/619, Insch, ATHENIA/699, and Smith, ATHENIA/535, NARA.

5. Bloom, ATHENIA/275, Ingram, ATHENIA/507 ¼, Rodman, ATHENIA/275, and Quine, ATHENIA/275, NARA; Jeannette Jordan mss, n.d., Jeannette C. Jordan Papers; Hugh S. Swindley to W. Trevor Jones, 20 September 1939, Imperial War Museum; Dorothy Bulkley to Marge and Birt, 28 September 1939, Bulkley Papers; and Campbell, "Torpedoed at Sea," 4.

6. Van Newkirk, ATHENIA/275, and Spiegelberg, ATHENIA/619, NARA; and Hugh S. Swindley to Mr. and Mrs. W. Trevor Jones, 20 September 1939, P284, Imperial War Museum.

7. *New York Sun*, 5 September 1939; Hannay, ATHENIA/275, Stuppel, ATHENIA/302, Mowry, ATHENIA/627, and Anderson, ATHENIA/485, Insch, ATHENIA/600, and Stork, ATHENIA/275, NARA; Goodson, *Tumult in the Clouds*, 9–10; Stork, "Sketches by an 'Athenian,'" 33; Evans, *A Ship Was Torpedoed*, 7; Swindley to Mr. and Mrs. W. Trevor Jones, 20 September 1939, P284, Imperial War Museum; and Evelyn, "*Athenia* manuscript," 15.

8. Interview with Dr. André Molgat; Bridge, ATHENIA/507 ¼, Insch, ATHENIA/600, and MacDonald, ATHENIA/610, NARA; Wilcox, "The *Athenia* Saga," 5, U/F U.530 #18, Nova Scotia Archives and Records Management; Report on the Sinking of the *Athenia*, MT 9/3278, NA; interview with Sir Richard Lake, Saskatchewan Archives; and Charman, *Outbreak*, 249.

9. Boyle, ATHENIA/318, Boynton, ATHENIA/528, Grossman, ATHENIA/567, Ingram, ATHENIA/507 ¼, Singleton, ATHENIA/558, MacLeod, ATHENIA/318, Johnson, ATHENIA/559, Rodman, ATHENIA/589, Smith, ATHENIA/667, Lawrence, ATHENIA/581, MacDonald, ATHENIA/612, and Levine, ATHENIA/318, NARA.

10. Bridge, ATHENIA/507 ¼, Jansen to Green H, Hackworth, 4 December 1939, ATHENIA/563, and Calder, RG 59, ATHENIA/478, NARA; Sweigard, "The Athenia Disaster—My Story," 7; Goodson, *Tumult in the Clouds*, 8–9; James Goodson, http://www.acesofww2.com/Canada/aces/goodson .htm; Jeannette C. Jordan Papers, n.d., Jordan Papers; *Montreal Gazette*, 14 September 1939; Rosemary Cass-Beggs Burstall, "A Three-Year-Old's Recollections of the Sinking of the Athenia;" and Ruby Mitchell Boersma, 31D 6, Canadian War Museum Archive.

11. Evelyn, "*Athenia* manuscript," 16–17; Dorothy Bulkley to Marge and Birt, 28 September 1939, Bulkley Papers; Francis, "The Sinking of the *Athenia*," 33; Hutchinson, RG 59, ATHENIA/318, NARA; Berta Rapp narrative, http:// ahoy.tk-jk.net/Letters/BertaRappOsiasRappweresur.html, 18/10/2007; and Swindley to Mr. and Mrs. W. Trevor Jones, 20 September 1939, P284, Imperial War Museum.

12. Alton, ATHENIA/318, Bridge, ATHENIA/275, Gifford, ATHENIA/275, and Rodman, ATHENIA/589, NARA; Blair, *Saved from the* Athenia, 24; and Stewart, "Homeward Bound on the *Athenia*," 82.

13. *Ottawa Citizen*, 3 September 1999; Francis, "The Sinking of the *Athenia*," 33; and Davis, ATHENIA/275, Hislop, ATHENIA/275, and Insch, ATHENIA/600, NARA.

14. Rabenold, ATHENIA/275, NARA; Shoen in Report on the Sinking of the *Athenia*, MT 9/3278, NA; Norman Hanna to Mrs. S. Hanna, 15 September 1939, D 3265/1, Public Record Office of Northern Ireland; *New York Daily*

News, 14 September 1939. Patricia Hale, who was struggling with an oar in No. 4, did not turn to look at the submarine but many of those around her pointed to it. Hale, "I Was on the *Athenia*," 9; and Caroline Stuart to F. C. Bannerman, Chief Special Agent, ca. October 1939, ATHENIA/481 6/9, NARA.

15. Charman, *Outbreak*, 240; and Report of Inspector C. D. Long examining the log of the *Knute Nelson*, San Pedro Harbor, 24 October 1939, RG 59, ATHENIA/476, NARA. The *Knute Nelson* itself was sunk by torpedoes on 27 September 1944 off the southern coast of Norway, with a loss of nine of her crew of thirty-two. *Knute Nelson* file, Fred. Olsen & Company, Oslo, Norway.

16. Stork, "Sketches of an 'Athenian,'" 33; F. Elwood MacPherson, *Voyage, Venture and Victory*, 14. Gerald Hutchinson Family Records; and Wilcox, "The *Athenia* Saga," U/F U.530 #18, Nova Scotia Archives and Records Management, 6–7.

17. Blair, *Saved from the* Athenia, 25; Rev. Gerald Hutchinson Family Records; and Bailey, "*Athenia* Survivor," 17.

18. MacPherson, *Voyage, Venture and Victory*, 14–15; Wilcox, "The *Athenia* Saga, U/F U.530 #18, Nova Scotia Archives and Record Management, 7; Wilkes affidavit, and Jansen to Green H. Hackworth, 4 December 1939, ATHENIA/318, /563, NARA; Bernice Jansen to A. B. Parson, 13 September 1939, Bernice Jansen file, Archives of the Episcopal Church; Report on the Sinking of the *Athenia*, MT 9/3278, NA; Ford, ATHENIA/318, Report of Inspector C. D. Long examining the log of the *Knute Nelson*, San Pedro Harbor, 24 October 1939, ATHENIA/476, NARA; and Anni C. Altschul, "A Cousin in Ireland," Rudolf Altschul Fonds; and Goodson, *Tumult in the Clouds*, 12.

19. Stewart, "Homeward Bound on the *Athenia*," 83; Hale, "I Was on the *Athenia*," 9; and *Toronto Star*, 4 September 1999.

20. Report on the Sinking of the *Athenia*, MT 9/3278, NA; Allan, *Andrew Allan*, 88; and Andrew Allan, "Reminiscences of the *Athenia*," Andrew Allan Fonds, MG 31, D56, LAC.

21. Fielder to Department of State, n.d., ATHENIA/638, NARA; Evelyn, "*Athenia* manuscript," 18–20; Goodson, *Tumult in the Clouds*, 11–12; Report on the Sinking of the *Athenia*, MT 9/3278, NA; and *Glasgow Herald*, 6 and 8 September 1939. Patricia Hale, who was rowing in lifeboat No. 4, recorded a similar near disaster. They had come up to the *Knute Nelson* but there were so many boats clustered alongside that they were not able to get a line or a mooring. They began drifting slowly toward the stern of the freighter and into the dangerous region of the propeller. The boatswain urged them to row with all their might to get clear. "By a miracle we escaped," she wrote. Hale, "I Was on the *Athenia*," 18.

22. John C. Coullie to Mother, 27 September 1939, P284, Imperial War Museum; Report on the Sinking of the *Athenia*, MT 9/3278, NA; and Anderson, RG 59, ATHENIA/435, NARA.

23. Francis, "The Sinking of the *Athenia*," 36; Hale, "I Was on the *Athenia*," 29; and Smith, ATHENIA/535, NARA.

24. Report on the Sinking of the *Athenia*, MT 9/3278, NA. Matters were further complicated when, as Macintosh's boat reached the stern of *Southern Cross*, five or six people in another boat climbed into No 8. Interview with Scotty Gillespie; *Winnipeg Free Press*, 18 September 1939; Report on the Sinking of the *Athenia*, MT 9/3278, NA; Fielder to Department of State, n.d., ATHENIA/638, NARA; Charman, *Outbreak*, 257–58; and Evans, *A Ship Was Torpedoed*, 8.

25. Ruby Mitchell Boersma Interview, 31E 6, Canadian War Museum Archive.

26. Hannay and Insch, ATHENIA/275, and Calder, ATHENIA/578, NARA.

27. Coullie to Mother, 27 September 1939, P284, Imperial War Museum; Woollcombe, "My Experience," Department of Transport, RG 12, file 7808-4, LAC;; Francis, "The Sinking of the *Athenia*," 35; Interview with Scotty Gillespie; and Evans, *A Ship Was Torpedoed*, 8–9.

28. Calder, ATHENIA/578, and Smith affidavit, ATHENIA/535, NARA.

29. T. J. Cain, *H.M.S. Electra*, 17–19; Jack Taylor, "A Report about HMS Electra," in Ahoy-Mac's Web Log, http://ahoy.tkjk.net/macslog/AreportaboutHMSElectraand.html, 07/12/2007; and Commander P. N. Walter, HMS *Fame*, to Rear Admiral, Home Fleet, 13 September 1939, ADM 199/140, NA.

30. Rodman, ATHENIA/589, Dick, MacPherson, and Stork, ATHENIA/275, NARA; and Campbell, "Torpedoed at Sea," 5.

31. Evelyn, "*Athenia* manuscript," 20–23; Report on the Sinking of the *Athenia*, MT 9/3278, NA; and Catherine Mackey affidavit, ATHENIA/275, NARA. Allan's recollections differed from the Donaldson report. He said there were six saved on the boat: two men—a steward and himself—and four women: Evelyn, a sick Scottish woman, a college girl, and an unidentified woman. Allan, *Andrew Allan*, 91; and Lieutenant Commander J. Bostwick to Captain S. N. O. Clyde, Western Approaches, 5 September 1939, ADM 1/10033, NA.

32. Evelyn, "*Athenia* manuscript," 24–27; Allan, *Andrew Allan*, 90–91; Report on the Sinking of the *Athenia*, MT 9/3278, NA; Campbell, "Torpedoed at Sea," 4–5; and Finlay, ATHENIA/507 ¼, and Bloom, ATHENIA/275, NARA.

33. Spiegelberg, RG 59, ATHENIA/619, NARA; and Report on the Sinking of the *Athenia*, MT 9/3278, NA.

34. Spiegelberg, ATHENIA/619, Hutchinson, ATHENIA/318, Hinds, ATHENIA/577, MacDonald, ATHENIA/275, and Van Newkirk, ATHENIA/275, NARA.

35. Report on the Sinking of the *Athenia*, MT 9/3278, and Report from CO HMS *Escort*, embodying the report from CO HMS *Electra*, ADM 1/18915, NA; and Goodson, *Tumult in the Clouds*, 10–11. The ship settled in about 197 feet (60 meters) of water and is now occasionally visited by divers.

CHAPTER 7. ON DRY LAND

1. H.M.S. ESCORT to A. C. North West Approaches, C. in C. Rosyth, N.O. in Charge Scapa Flow, N.O. in Charge, Clyde, Admiralty, 4 September 1939 (cable), ADM 199/140, NA.

2. Campbell, "Torpedoed at Sea," 6; D. MacLean to Rt. Hon. John Colville, M.P., 12 September 1939, T 161/996, The National Archives London (hereafter NA); and *New York Sun*, 5 September 1939.

3. D. MacLean to Rt. Hon. John Colville, M.P., 12 September 1939, T161/996, NA; *Daily Telegraph*, 6 September 1939; and *Globe and Mail*, 2 October 1939.

4. Park, "Aboard the *Athenia*," 48; Campbell, "Torpedoed at Sea," 6; and *Daily Record & Mail*, 5 September 1939.

5. Norman Donaldson to Lord Provost, 5 and 11 September 1939, G1/3/44, Athenia Disaster Fund, Glasgow City Archives; Minutes of the Corporation of Glasgow, April, 1939 to November, 1939, p. 2848, C1/3/100, Glasgow City Archives; and *Evening Citizen*, 6 and 11 September 1939.

6. Lord Provost Dollan to President Roosevelt, 5 September 1939, and Franklin D. Roosevelt to J. P. Dollan, 11 September 1939, Personal file #6211, Dollan, J. P., Franklin D. Roosevelt Presidential Library. The ambassador sent his immediate thanks. See Joseph P. Kennedy to Secretary of State, 5 September 1939, ATHENIA/83, and Memorandum for the Secretary's Office, 9 Sept. 1939, ATHENIA/224, NARA; F. H. La Guardia to Lord Provost, 7 September 1939 (cable), G1/3/44, Athenia Disaster Fund, Glasgow City Archives. Also see, Carol C. Adams to Lord Provost, 19 September 1939, Ernest A. Smith to Lord Provost, 14 September 1939, and Mrs. H. Altfield to Lord Provost, 29 October 1939, G1/3/44, Athenia Disaster Fund, Glasgow City Archives.

7. Jeanette Jordan to Family, 11 September 1939, Jeannette C. Jordan Papers; and Goodson, *Tumult in the Clouds*, 17–18.

8. Michael R. Beschloss, *Kennedy and Roosevelt: The Uneasy Alliance*, 190; Joseph P. Kennedy, "Diplomatic Memoir," chap. 34, 4–5, Joseph P. Kennedy Papers, John F. Kennedy Presidential Library. "Have talked with the head of Admiralty personally. They will have no further information until 12:00 o'clock our time when the first destroyer will have reached the scene of the catastrophe. Will of course keep you advised of all details and the Admiralty will give them to me as quickly as they arrive." Joseph P. Kennedy to Secretary of State, 3 September 1939, cable, received, 8:50 p.m., 4 September 1939, 5:20 a.m., 4 September 1939, 2:25 p.m., 4 September 1939, *Foreign Relations of the United States, 1939, Volume 2, General, The British Commonwealth and Europe* (hereafter referred to as *FRUS*), 282–84. Also see, Richard J. Whalen, *The Founding Father: The Story of Joseph P. Kennedy*, 272–73.

9. Memorandum of Telephone Conversation between Joseph P. Kennedy and Sumner Welles, 5 September 1939, ATHENIA/50½, Cordell Hull to American Embassy London, 7 September 1939, cable, ATHENIA/159D, NARA; and

Breckinridge Long, *The War Diary of Breckinridge Long: Selections from the Years 1939–1944*, ed. Fred Israel, 8; *New York Times*, 9 September 1939; and Leslie A. Davis to R. P. Ramsay, 18 October 1939, G1/3/44, Athenia Disaster Fund, Glasgow City Archives.

10. Dominion to External Affairs, 4 September 1939, cable, External to Dominion, 4 September 1939, cable, 7:00 p.m. and 9:00 p.m., Massey to External Affairs, 8 September 1939, 767.B.39, Sinking of the S.S. Athenia, Department of External Affairs Records, RG 25, file 767-39, Library and Archives Canada (hereafter LAC); *Evening Citizen*, 9 and 11 September 1939; and Vincent Massey to Lord Provost, 23 October 1939, G1/3/44, Athenia Disaster Fund, Glasgow City Archives.

11. *New York Daily News*, 6 September 1939.

12. Joseph P. Kennedy to Lord Provost Dollan, 6 September 1939 (cable), G1/3/44, Athenia Disaster Fund, Glasgow City Archives; Edward J. Renehan Jr., *The Kennedys at War, 1937–1945*, 111–13; and Joseph P. Kennedy to Jesse Jones, 8 September 1939 (cable), MSS 41, Box 8, folder 10, A. D. Simpson Family Papers, Texas and Local History Department, Houston Public Library. Also see, Whalen, *The Founding Father*, 273–74; *Daily Record & Mail*, 8 September 1939; Memorandum of telephone call from William Hillman by J. E. B. Jr., 7 September 1939, Box 21, Dave Powers Papers, John F. Kennedy Presidential Library; Michael O'Brien, *John F. Kennedy: A Biography*, 93–98; and *Glasgow Herald*, 8 September 1939.

13. Memorandum, John F. Kennedy, 8 September 1939, Box 21, Dave Powers Papers, John F. Kennedy President Library; and Joseph P. Kennedy to Cordell Hull, 8 September 1939, cited in Barbara Leaming, *Jack Kennedy: The Education of a Statesman*, 92–93.

14. *Daily Record & Mail*, 8 September 1939; *London Evening News*, 7 September 1939; and *Glasgow Herald*, 8 September 1939. John Kennedy was described in the *London Evening News* as having "displayed a wisdom and sympathy of a man twice his years." Also see Oral History Interview with Torbert H. MacDonald, 10, John F. Kennedy Presidential Library and Foundation.

15. *Evening Citizen*, 7 September 1939; Jack Kennedy to Lord Provost, 8 September 1939, and Lord Provost Dollan to Jack Kennedy, G1/3/44, Athenia Disaster Fund, Glasgow City Archives; and Leslie A. Davis to Joseph P. Kennedy, 24 September 1939, and Joseph P. Kennedy to Leslie A. Davis, 27 September 1939, RG 84, Foreign Service Posts of the Department of State, Glasgow Consulate, 1939, Box 19, NARA.

16. Survivors of SS Athenia, Cabinet Minutes, 4 September 1939, S11415, Taoiseach file, National Archives of Ireland; *Galway Observer*, 9 and 30 September 1939; and *Connacht Tribune*, 9 September 1939. Also see Francis M. Carroll, "'The First Casualty of the Sea': The *Athenia* Survivors and the Galway Relief Effort, September 1939," *History Ireland* 19, no. 1 (January–February 2011), 42–45.

17. *Connacht Tribune*, 9 September 1939. Ironically as the *Cathair Na Gaillimhe* was coming into Galway the light commission ship *Isolde* was steaming out toward the Atlantic to answer the distress signal of the SS *Bosnia*, which had been torpedoed and was sinking.

18. *Connacht Tribune*, 9 September 1939; *Irish Press*, 6 September 1939; *Galway Advertiser*, 26 March and 23 July 2009; and *Irish Press*, 6 September 1939.

19. O'Connor, "I Was Aboard the 'Athenia,'" 37; Linda Grave Johnson in Benjamin Grob-Fitzgibbon, *The Irish Experience during the Second World War: An Oral History*, 22, 141; *Irish Times*, 9 September 1939; *Connacht Tribune*, 9 September 1939; MacPherson, *Voyage, Venture and Victory*, 17–18; Blair, *Saved from the* Athenia, 28–30; *Irish Press*, 5 September 1939; and Goodson, *Tumult in the Clouds*, 14–15.

20. Anni C. Altschul, "A Cousin in Ireland," and J. S. Thomson to Rudolf Altschul, 13 September 1939 (cable), Rudolf Altschul Fonds, University of Saskatchewan Library.

21. Wilkes and Boyle, ATHENIA/318, NARA; *Irish Times*, 7, 9 September 1939; Goodson, *Tumult in the Clouds*, 15–16; Wilcox, "The *Athenia* Saga," 8, U/F U.530 #18, Nova Scotia Archives and Record Management; and Cass-Beggs, *Roots and Wings*, 98–102. Although the Cass-Beggses got to Dublin, they missed the train to Belfast and had to wait overnight before traveling north the next morning. Fortunately they were befriended by a fellow passenger whose home was in Belfast, but they did not get to Glasgow until late Thursday night. The fragmentary information they got from various shipping offices provided no information about a three-year-old girl. Jansen to A. B. Parson, 13 September 1939, Bernice Jansen file, Archives of the Episcopal Church, Austin, Texas.

22. Henry H. Balch to Secretary of State, 4 September 1939, cable, ATHENIA/37, NARA; John Cudahy to Secretary of State, 7 September 1939, ATHENIA/247, NARA; and Minister in Ireland to Secretary of State, 5 September 1939, cable, *FRUS, 1939*, vol. 2, *General*, 284. Cudahy left Ireland at the end of the year to serve briefly as ambassador to Belgium and Luxembourg from January 1940 until the German invasion in May.

23. John Cudahy to Secretary of State, 5 September 1939, cable, *FRUS, 1939*, vol. 2, *General*, 284. Cudahy sent a second telegram pointing out that his first assessment of the sinking agreed with that of the naval attachés. John Cudahy to Secretary of State, 7 September 1939, *FRUS, 1939*, vol. 2, *General*, 286–87; and John Cudahy to Secretary of State, 7 September 1939, ATHENIA/247, NARA.

24. Commandant Padraig O'Duinnin to C.S.O., G2 Branch, G.H.Q. Dublin, 6 September 1939, S.S. *Athenia* file G2/X/0431, Military Archives, Cathal Brugha Barracks, Dublin. Irish scepticism about a German submarine sinking the *Athenia* is captured in the report of the chargé d'affaire in Berlin, noting that Britain blamed Germany "without one vestige of proof."

Confidential report from William P. Warnock to Joseph P. Walsh, 21 November 1939, Catriona Crowe et al., eds., *Documents on Irish Foreign Policy, Volume VI, 1939–1941*, 96–97; and T. O'Coileain, Chief Superintendents Office, Galway, to Coimisineár, C Branch, 8 September 1939, SS *Athenia* file, G2/X/0431, Military Archives, Cathal Brugha Barracks, Dublin. The impossibility of making a positive identification of a submarine in the sinking of the *Athenia* may have led to the Irish government's note to the belligerent powers the following week prohibiting submarines from access to Irish territorial waters. See Aide mémoire to British, French, and German governments regarding restrictions on the use of Ireland's territorial waters, 12 September 1939, Crowe et al., eds., *Documents on Irish Foreign Policy, Volume VI, 1939–1941*, 23–24; *Irish Times*, 9 September 1939; and John Cudahy to Franklin D. Roosevelt, 15 September 1939, cited in T. Ryle Dwyer, *Behind the Green Curtain: Ireland's Phoney Neutrality during World War II*, 49.

25. Hull to American Consul Dublin, 5 September 1939, cable, ATHENIA/37, Balch to Secretary of State, 16 September 1939, ATHENIA/342, and Balch to Secretary of State, 3 October 1939, ATHENIA/376, NARA. Balch was commended by the secretary of state for his efficient handling of the relief effort for American citizens.

26. James Cormack to Vincent Massey, 12 September 1939, and "Assistance Rendered to Survivors of S.S. Athenia," Report to the Hon. Vincent Massey by James Cormack, and J. P. Ruttledge to Vincent Massey, 12 November 1939, 767.B.39, Sinking of the S.S. Athenia, Department of External Affairs Records, RG 25, file 767-39, LAC.

27. *New York Herald Tribune*, 6 September 1939; Radford Mobley to Marion E. Potter, 5 September 1939 (cable), Jeannette C. Jordan Papers; and Scott Eyman, *Ernst Lubitsch: Laughter in Paradise*, 275–76.

28. Sir Percy Lake to Right Hon. Mackenzie King, 5 September 1939, Sinking of the S.S. Athenia, Department of External Affairs Records, RG 25, file 767-39, LAC; [Mrs.] Molgat to Lord Provost, and Lord Provost to [Mrs.] Molgat, 7 September 1939, Athenia Disaster Fund, Glasgow City Archives; and For the Press, Americans Missing from S.S. Athenia, 17 September 1939, ATHENIA/379, NARA.

29. Tate to Mr. and Mrs. A. D. Simpson, 4 September 1939 (cable), A. D. Simpson to Gordon S. Reutochler, 4 September 1939 (cable), A. D. Simpson to W. B. Burton-Baldry, 4 September 1939 (cable), Burton-Baldry to Simpson, 4 September 1939 (cable), Gordon S. Reutochler to A. D. Simpson, 4 September 1939, A. D. Simpson to A. O. Tate, 6 September 1939, Burton-Baldry to Simpson, 5 September 1939, and Farris Campbell to A. D. Simpson, 6 September 1939, MMS 41, Box 8, folder 9, A. D. Simpson Family Papers, Texas and Local History Department, Houston Public Library. Burke Baker, the father of Anne Baker, wrote to Texas Congress member Albert Thomas complaining about the failure of the State Department to get accurate infor-

mation to the parents and families of survivors. He had been kept informed by Simpson, so could make unfavorable comparisons with the data supplied by the department. The secretary of state replied to the representative that the department had released names of those on the *City of Flint* on 5 September and actually telephoned Baker. Albert Thomas to Cordell Hull, 4 September 1939, Lindley Beckworth to Cordell Hull, 11 September 1939, Burke Baker to Albert Thomas, 13 September 1939, and Cordell Hull to Albert Thomas, 30 September 1939, ATHENIA/40, /210, and /295, NARA.

30. Secretary of State to American Legation, Dublin, 7 September 1939, cable, ATHENIA/146, NARA; *Galway Observer*, 16 September 1939; and Eamon deValera to Most Reverend Michael Browne, 11 September 1939, and Eamon deValera to Joseph Costello, 11 September 1939, S.11415, Taoiseach file, National Archives of Ireland.

31. O. D. Skelton to High Commissioner for Ireland, 17 January 1940, Department of External Affairs file 239/54, National Archives of Ireland; Clair Wills, *That Neutral Island: A Cultural History of Ireland during the Second World War*, 146; Secretary of State to American Legation, Oslo, 8 September 1939, cable, ATHENIA/163A, NARA; and *Irish Press*, 27 September 1939. See also Sir C. Dormer to Foreign Office, 6 September 1939, Foreign Office (hereafter FO) 371/23675, NA.

32. Sir Edmund Monson, Bt., to Herr Direktor Axel Wenner-Gren, 18 October 1939, FO 371/23097, NA; Axel Wenner-Gren to The President, 6 September 1939 (radio telegram), and Franklin D. Roosevelt to Axel Wenner-Gren, 7 September 1939, radio telegram, ATHENIA/141, NARA; and Trefousse, *Germany and American Neutrality*, 26–27.

CHAPTER 8. THE *CITY OF FLINT*

1. Caleb Davis to Mr. and Mrs. Leslie A. Davis, 4 October 1939, ATHENIA/518, NARA.

2. Joseph Gainard, *Yankee Skipper: The Life Story of Joseph A. Gainard, Captain of the* City of Flint, 106–15, quotation from 115.

3. Ibid., 117–26; and R. E. Harding to A. D. Simpson, 1 September 1939 (cable), MSS 41, Box 8, folder 9, A. D. Simpson Family Papers, Texas and Local History Department, Houston Public Library.

4. Gainard, *Yankee Skipper*, 123–26.

5. Ibid., 127–29; and Frank H. Gordy, ATHENIA/486, NARA. Captain Gainard noted that his ship sailed "thirty-six hours" after the *Athenia* left Glasgow; that would be 11:00 p.m. on 2 September. The *Athenia* subsequently sailed from Liverpool at 4:00 p.m. and steaming at least five knots faster would have been well west of the *City of Flint* when it was torpedoed. Gainard's engineer, Frank Gordy, says they sailed from Glasgow at 11:00 p.m. on 1 September. That would have placed the *City of Flint* west of the *Athenia*, requiring her to turn around to come back to pick up the survivors.

6. Caleb Davis to Mr. and Mrs. Leslie A. Davis, 4 October 1939, ATHENIA/518, NARA; and Gainard, *Yankee Skipper*, 132–34.

7. Gainard, *Yankee Skipper*, 136–43; and Hugh S. Swindley to W. Trevor Jones, 20 September 1939, P184, Imperial War Museum, London, England.

8. Gainard, *Yankee Skipper*, 111, 136–43; Evans, *A Ship Was Torpedoed*, 10; and Ruby Mitchell Boersma Interview, 31D 6, Canadian War Museum Archives.

9. Caleb Davis to Mr. and Mrs. Leslie A. Davis, 4 October 1939, RG 59, ATHENIA/518, NARA; Hale, "I Was on the *Athenia*," 30; Gainard, *Yankee Skipper*, 144–48; and Evans, *A Ship Was Torpedoed*, 10.

10. Hale, "I Was on the *Athenia*," 33; Gainard, *Yankee Skipper*, 155–57; and interview with Scotty Gillespie.

11. Ruby Mitchell Boersma Interview, 31D 6, Canadian War Museum Archive; Gainard, *Yankee Skipper*, 157–62; Snow, *A Measureless Peril*, 64; Woollcomb, "My Experience," Department of Transport Records, RG 12, file 7808-4, Library and Archives Canada (hereafter LAC); Cass-Beggs, *Roots and Wings*, 106–7; and John Coullie to Mother, 27 September 1939, P284, Imperial War Museum, London, England.

12. Dorothy Dean, in Francis, "The Sinking of the *Athenia*," 35; Caleb Davis to Mr. and Mrs. Leslie A. Davis, 4 October 1939, ATHENIA/518, NARA; G. P. Woollcombe, "My Experience," RG 25, LAC; and *New York Times*, 20 September 1939.

13. Gainard, *Yankee Skipper*, 152; Rosemary Cass-Beggs Burstall, "A Three-Year-Old's Recollections of the Sinking of the Athenia," Research file, Maritime Museum of the Atlantic, Halifax, Nova Scotia; and Cass-Beggs, *Roots and Wings*, 102–5.

14. *New York Times*, 14 September 1939; Gainard, *Yankee Skipper*, 158, 161, 164–65, 173–74; and Hugh S. Swindley to Mr. and Mrs. W. Trevor Jones, 20 September 1939, P284, Imperial War Museum, London, England.

15. Gainard, *Yankee Skipper*, 164–72; Hale, "I Was on the *Athenia*," 33; Ruby Mitchell Boersma Interview, 31D 6, Canadian War Museum Archive; and Cass-Beggs, *Roots and Wings*, 107.

16. Coast Guard Headquarters to *Bibb* and *Campbell*, from *City of Flint*, n.d., ATHENIA/415 7/11, NARA.

17. Gainard, *Yankee Skipper*, 175–82; and Rear Admiral E. L. Covell to Chief, Division of Protocol, 11 September 1939, and Cordell Hull to U.S. Consul, Halifax, 11 September 1939, ATHENIA/201, NARA. The figure 265 includes the 29 paying passengers and makes allowance for the 11 people removed to the Coast Guard cutters and the one deceased child.

18. *Globe and Mail*, 14 September 1939; Sweigard, "The *Athenia* Disaster—My Story," 15; *New York Times*, 14 September 1939; and *Montreal Gazette*, 14 September 1939.

19. Gainard, *Yankee Skipper*, 181–86; Stewart, "Homeward Bound on the *Athenia*," 84; *Halifax Chronicle*, 14 September 1939; Ruby Mitchell Boersma

Interview, 31D 6, Canadian War Museum Archive; Eyman, *Ernst Lubitsch*, 275–76; and Cass-Beggs, *Roots and Wings*, 107–9.

20. Ruby Mitchell Boersma Interview, 31D 6, Canadian War Museum Archive; *Houston Press*, 12 September 1939; *New York Journal-American*, 15 and 18 September 1939; *New York Times*, 16 and 18 September 1939; Clinton E. MacEachran to Secretary of State, 16 September 1939, ATHENIA/259, NARA; and Gainard, *Yankee Skipper*, 185–91.

CHAPTER 9. MATTERS OF STATE

1. 4 September 1939, United Kingdom, *Parliamentary Debates* (hereafter *Parl. Deb.*) (Commons), 5th ser., vol. 351 (1938–39), cols. 370–71.

2. Martin Gilbert, *Winston S. Churchill: Finest Hour, 1939–1941*, vol. 6, 3–5; Martin Gilbert, ed., *The Churchill War Papers: At the Admiralty, September 1939–May 1940*, vol. 1, 8–10.

3. Malin Head Radio to Admiralty, 2230 and 2356, 3 September 1939, Lands End Radio to Admiralty, 0050, 4 September 1930, ADM 199/140, The National Archives, London, England (hereafter cited as NA). Dan van der Vat mentions that Churchill was informed of the attack on the *Athenia* at 10:30, but gives no sources for this information. Van der Vat, *The Atlantic Campaign*, 5. The Admiralty records indicate only that the message from Malin Head was dated 10:30 and make no mention of when the first lord was informed. War cabinet minutes, 11:30 a.m., 4 September 1939, CAB 65/1, NA. Churchill also reported that one other merchant vessel had been sunk (the *Blairberg*) and that although convoys had not been generally established the Admiralty was supervising the routing of merchant ships. Harold Nicolson, coming up to London on Monday to attend parliament, learned of the sinking from the newspaper headlines. "How insane the Germans are to do this," he commented in his diary along the lines of Churchill and others, "at the very moment when Roosevelt has put out his neutrality proclamation." Harold Nicolson, *Diaries and Letters of Harold Nicolson: The War Years, 1939–1947*, vol. 2, 30.

4. 4 September 1939, *Parl. Deb.* (Commons), 5th ser., 351 (1938–39), cols. 370–74; and 4 September 1939, *Parl. Deb.* (Lords), 5th ser., vol. 114 (1938–39), cols. 983–86. Alexander was asked to be first lord of the Admiralty again when Churchill became prime minister in 1940. *The Times*, 5 September 1939.

5. 6 September 1939, *Parl. Deb.* (Commons), 5th ser., vol. 351 (1938–39), cols. 538–41.

6. War Cabinet: Confidential Annex, 5 September 1939, in Gilbert, ed., *The Churchill War Papers*, vol. 1, 26–27; Notes of a Conference, 6 September 1939, Admiralty, ibid., 40–41. There were some who felt that the sinking of the *Athenia* was not "part of a deliberate policy laid down by the German

government," in the words of Chief of the Air Staff Sir Cyril Newall. The shock of the sinking overrode those concerns. War Cabinet: Minutes, 13 September 1939, in Gilbert, *The Churchill War Papers*, vol. 1, 89. In his memoirs Harold Macmillan notes that although the British government was slow in employing economic measures against Germany, a full blockade of German imports was put in force immediately as a reprisal for the sinking of the *Athenia*. Harold Macmillan, *The Blast of War, 1939–1945*, 5; Winston S. Churchill, *The Second World War: The Gathering Storm*, vol. 1, 424; Roskill, *The War at Sea, 1939–1945*, vol. 1, 21–22; and Francis M. Carroll, "The First Shot Was the Last Straw: The Sinking of the T.S.S. *Athenia* in 3 September 1939 and British Naval Policy in the Second World War," *Diplomacy & Statecraft* 20, no. 3 (September 2009). Exceptions were also made for ships that could steam at speeds in excess of fifteen knots or less than nine knots.

7. Report of an Interview with Captain Cook, Master of the S.S. *Athenia*, 26 September 1939, ADM 199/140, NA. The Board of Trade held a meeting with the management of the Donaldson Line, but these discussions were concerned largely with financial responsibility. "ATHENIA" Meeting at the Board of Trade, 15 September 1939, MT 9/3127, NA. Draft Statement to be made available through the Press Bureau, ca. October 1939, FO 371/22841, NA. Memorandum for the Consul General from Commander Alan G. Kirk, 14 November 1939, ATHENIA/603, NARA; and The Sinking of the *Athenia*, MT 9/3278, NA.

8. *The Times*, 5, 6, and 7 September 1939. By Wednesday, 6 September, *The Times* correspondents had interviewed survivors brought into Glasgow and Galway and were reporting details of what was experienced during the attack, the ordeal in the lifeboats, and the reception of the survivors in both cities. These accounts were filled with the drama and horror of the ordeal. *The Times* began printing a list of the known survivors of the sinking and it also followed closely the reactions and statements of Ambassador Kennedy, the state department, and the White House. Roughly a week later *The Times* editorial concluded, "The great part of the world was startled and horrified to learn from the circumstances of the sinking of the *Athenia* that Germany had once more adopted without hesitation those methods of war at sea which provoked universal reprobation in the last War, and which she had freely and voluntarily renounced less than three years ago." *The Times*, 11 September 1939

9. *Glasgow Herald*, 4, 5, and 6 September 1939. The Wednesday, 6 September, issue of the paper carried interviews of survivors who had been brought into Greenock and Glasgow and many more photographs. These accounts gave vivid details about witnessing the submarine, the ordeal of the lifeboats at sea, and the generous treatment of survivors by the sailors on the destroyers. *Glasgow Evening Standard* also published extensive interviews with sur-

vivors, especially local crewmembers, in the course of the week. *Glasgow Evening Standard,* 4 September 1939. The weekly *Glasgow Eastern Standard* came out on Saturday, 9 September, too late to carry breaking news, but it too ran interviews with survivors spelling out the harrowing experiences that they endured. *Glasgow Eastern Standard,* 9 September 1939. Also see *Daily Record & Mail,* 5 September 1939.

10. *The Spectator,* No. 5802 (2 September 1939), 341; Centurio, "Land, Sea and Air," ibid., 347; and *New Statesman and Nation,* vol. 18, no. 446 (New Series) (9 September 1939), 363. The denial of responsibility by the German government was preposterous, the weekly said. "Needless to say, we do not lay mines on the tracks prescribed to our own shipping." The *New Statesman* speculated whether Germany would continue to "ignore the moral opinion of the world." Also see *London Illustrated News,* 16 September 1939, and *The War Illustrated,* 16 September 1939.

11. Rosenman, ed., *The Public Papers and Addresses of Franklin D. Roosevelt,* vol. 8, 460–64; Long, *The War Diary of Breckinridge Long,* 6; Joseph P. Kennedy to Secretary of State, 3 September 1939, cable, received 8:50 p.m., 4 September 1939, received 5:20 a.m., 4 September 1939, received 2:25 p.m., U.S. Department of State, *Foreign Relations of the United States* (hereafter *FRUS*), *1939: Volume 2, General, The British Commonwealth and Europe,* 282–84; and Harold Lavine and James Wechsler, *War Propaganda and the United States,* 40–41.

12. *New York Daily News,* 4 September 1939; Fireside Chat to the Nation, 11 September 1941, in Samuel I. Rosenman, ed., *The Public Papers and Addresses of Franklin D. Roosevelt,* vol. 10, 390; Press conferences, 5 and 8 September 1939, *The Complete Presidential Press Conferences of Franklin D. Roosevelt, 1939,* vol. 14, 138–43, 148; Harold L. Ickes, *The Secret Diaries of Harold L. Ickes: The Inside Struggle, 1936–1939,* vol. 2, 714; and Long, *The War Diary of Breckinridge Long,* 6–7. The precedent of the sinking of the *Lusitania* in 1915—and its impact on both the Wilson administration's policies and public opinion in the United States—which had taken place just twenty-four years earlier, was never far from the minds of senior people in the government, and perhaps particularly President Roosevelt who in 1915 had been assistant secretary of the Navy.

13. *New York Times,* 4 September 1939; and *New York Herald Tribune,* 4 September 1939. The *New York Daily News* ran similar headlines: "BRITISH LINER TOPEDOED AMERICANS AMONG 1,400 ON BOARD," and then published an "extra" edition, which read, "SUB SINKS BRITISH LINER." *New York Daily News,* 4 September 1939. Also see *Boston Herald,* 4 September 1939; and *Boston Globe,* 4 September 1939.

14. *New York Herald Tribune,* 5 September 1939; *New York Times,* 5, 6, and 9 September 1939; and *Wall Street Journal,* 5 and 6 September 1939. The *New*

York Herald Tribune, 6 September 1939, carried a by line that read, "U.S. Survivors Say Submarine Shattered the Athenia." *Washington Post*, 4, 5, and 13 September 1939. On Tuesday the *Post* began to provide lists of Americans sailing on the *Athenia* as well as survivors' accounts. The paper also published an editorial "Frightfulness Again" saying the German explanation that the ship struck a British mine was "possible" but "highly improbable." "There is certainly a very strong presumption that the *Athenia* was a victim of the kind of frightfulness with which the world became only too familiar during the [First] World War," and the paper cited the bombing of the villa outside of Warsaw of American ambassador Anthony J. Drexel Biddle Jr. as consistent evidence of German "schrecklichkeit"—frightfulness.

15. *Time*, 11, 18, and 25 September 1939. *Time* also featured a cartoon from the *New York World-Telegram* that showed a gorilla-like figure in a German submarine shaking its fist at the sinking *Athenia* and saying "Why don't you fight <u>fair</u>—like me!" Also see *Life Magazine*, 18 September 1939.

16. *The Nation*, 149, no. 11 (9 September 1939), 258. However, *The Nation* also observed that "the sinking of the *Athenia* indicates a warfare by Hitler designed like his diplomacy to terrorize by its brutality." This would eventually be self-defeating, *The Nation* concluded. Also see *New Republic*, 80, no. 1293 (13 September 1939), 141, and no. 1294 (20 September 1939), 173.

17. Joseph P. Kennedy to Secretary of State, 6 September 1939, cable, *FRUS, 1939, General*, vol. 2, 285–86; Naval Attaché, London, to Director of Naval Intelligence, 7 September 1939, ATHENIA /491, NARA; and Press conference, 8 September 1939, *Complete Presidential Press Conferences of Franklin D. Roosevelt*, vol. 14, 148.

18. Memorandum by Green H. Hackworth, 8 September 1939, ATHENIA/159 ½, Pierrepont Moffat to Green H. Hackworth, 24 October 1939, ATHENIA/457, Lord Lothian to Cordell Hull, 30 October 1939, ATHENIA/442, John G. Erhardt to Secretary of State, 14 December 1939, ATHENIA/636, NARA; and C. H. to J. Balfour, 8 February 1940, and J. Balfour to C. H. Boyd, 16 February 1940, FO 371/24247, NA. Ralph F. de Bedts argues that in 1939 the submarine was an accepted weapon and that the *Athenia* was not large enough and famous enough to have the same shock value as the sinking of the *Lusitania*. Perhaps more important still was the realization by Roosevelt and many others that President Wilson's *Lusitania* ultimatum to the Germans in 1915 had so narrowed his subsequent options that Germany's eventual return to "unrestricted submarine warfare" made war virtually inescapable. See Ralph F. de Bedts, *Ambassador Joseph Kennedy, 1938–1940: An Anatomy of Appeasement*, 155–56.

19. J. W. Pickersgill, *The Mackenzie King Record, 1939–1944*, vol. 1, 15–17; Mackenzie King Diary, 4 September 1939, MG 26 J, Library and Archives Canada (hereafter cited as LAC); and Churchill in War Cabinet Minutes, 11:30 a.m., 4 September 1939, CAB 65/1, NA.

20. Lester B. Pearson, *Mike: The Memoirs of the Right Honourable Lester B. Pearson*, vol. 1, *1897–1948*, 133–36; Vincent Massey to External Affairs, 8 September 1939 (cable), and Secretary of State for External Affairs to High Commissioner for Canada, 11 September 1939 (cable), Department of External Affairs Records, RG 25, file 767-39, LAC; and Mackenzie King Diary, 9 September 1939, MG 26 J, LAC; and Vincent Massey, *What's Past Is Prologue: The Memoirs of the Right Honourable Vincent Massey*, 282. In the High Commission the young diplomat Charles Richie was appalled at "the absurd wicked folly of these utterly unwarlike people being drowned." After observing the events of the past week he concluded, "This war has a quality which no other had." Charles Richie, *The Siren Years: A Canadian Diplomat Abroad, 1937–1945*, 44.

21. *Globe and Mail*, 5, 6, and 7 September 1939. The paper wrote that "Nazi Frightfulness Begins," picking out the word "frightfulness" that the Germans had used in the Great War to describe their policy. The paper viewed with contempt the attempt by the German government to deny responsibility for the sinking. "Not a nation on earth, human or inhuman, can be so gullible as to believe an act so typically German would be committed by any other power." The paper kept a focus on the *Athenia* over the next few days, never losing its sharp edge—"Sinking of the Athenia Called Murder, Not War." *Toronto Star*, 4 September 1939. "LINER ATHENIA IS TORPEDOED AND SUNK," reported the *Halifax Herald*, and "1400 ABOARD SHIP BOUND FOR CANADA," 4 and 5 September 1939, respectively. The *Halifax Herald* ran even larger headlines the next day, "EMPIRE AT WAR." See also *Montreal Gazette*, 5 September 1939.

22. *Winnipeg Tribune*, 3 and 4 September 1939. In the fifth extra edition the paper published the headline "FEAR WINNIPEGGERS VICTIMS OF U-BOAT" and began to list Winnipeggers who might have been on the ship. The *Winnipeg Free Press*, which did not publish on Sundays, brought out full headlines on Monday: "1,400 RESCUED FROM TORPEDOED ATHENIA; NO WARNING GIVEN, CHURCHILL SAYS." In its editorial column, the *Free Press* said, "War had scarcely been declared by Great Britain when proof of the intention of the Germans to again disregard all the rules of war, all considerations of humanity, was given by the sinking of the steamship *Athenia* by a torpedo from a German submarine." The editorial went on to say, "There was no possible excuse for sinking a passenger ship which was not taking munitions or any other supplies to a belligerent country, but was only bringing passengers away." The *Free Press* also published photographs of Winnipeggers feared on the ship, 4 and 5 September 1939, respectively. "ATHENIA TORPEDOED BY GERMAN SUB," the *Edmonton Bulletin*, another western Canadian paper, declared, and "BRITISH LINER SUNK WITHOUT ANY WARNING," *Edmonton Bulletin*, 4 September 1939.

23. Canada, House of Commons, *Debates*, 7–13 September 1939, quotations from 9 September 1939, 67 and 74; J. L. Granatstein, *Canada's War: The Politics of the Mackenzie King Government, 1939–1945*, 7–18; and Donald Creighton, *Canada, 1939–1945: The Forked Road*, 1–7.

24. *Globe and Mail*, 15 and 18 September 1939; and *New York Times*, 17 September 1939.

25. Michael L. Hadley, *U-Boats Against Canada: German Submarines in Canadian Waters*, 13–14.

26. *Winnipeg Free Press*, 23 October 1939; and *Toronto Star*, 4 September 1999.

CHAPTER 10. THE GERMANS

1. Cited in Blair, *Hitler's U-Boat War*, 68.

2. Cited in ibid.; and Trefousse, *Germany and American Neutrality*, 36–37. William Phillips, the American ambassador to Italy, recorded a conversation with minister of press and propaganda shortly after the sinking of the *Athenia*. The minister avoided any comment on the disastrous effect of the sinking of the ship on opinion in the United States and talked confidently about the likely end of the war once Poland was defeated. William Phillips, *Ventures in Diplomacy*, 238–39.

3. Memorandum by the Secretary of State, 4 September 1939, *Documents on German Foreign Policy, 1918–1945*, vol. 8, 3–4; Chargé in Germany to Secretary of State, 4 September 1939, *Foreign Relations of the United States* (hereafter *FRUS*), *1939, General*, vol. 2, 283–84; and Trefousse, *Germany and American Neutrality*, 35–36. The German minister to Ireland called on John Cudahy to convey the same message. John Cudahy to Secretary of State, 6 September 1939, ATHENIA/248, NARA; William L. Shirer, *Berlin Diary: The Journal of a Foreign Correspondent, 1934–1941*, 163; and Alexander C. Kirk to Secretary of State, 5 September 1939 (cable), ATHENIA/63, NARA.

4. Chargé in Germany to Secretary of State, 8 and 12 September 1939, *FRUS, 1939, General*, vol. 2, 287–89; Alexander Kirk to Secretary of State, 8 November 1939 (cable), ATHENIA/468, and Extract from "War Diary" of Commander A. E. Schrader, USN, 16 September 1939, ATHENIA/491, NARA.

5. *New York Times*, 6, 7, and 9 September 1939; "Blame for Athenia Catastrophe Placed on Churchill," *Facts in Review* 1, no. 12 (31 October 1939): 1–2; "The S.S. Athenia sunk by three British Destroyers," n.p., ATHENIA/524, NARA; Trefousse, *Germany and American Neutrality*, 36; *New York Times*, 23 October 1939; Alan Kirk to Secretary of State, 28 October 1939 (cable), ATHENIA/409, NARA; Shirer, *Berlin Diary*, 191; William L. Shirer, *The Rise and Fall of the Third Reich: A History of Nazi Germany*, 638; and Extracts from B.B.C. Digest, October and November, 1939, ADM 179/140, The National Archives, London (hereafter NA).

6. Ickes, *Secret Diaries of Harold L. Ickes*, vol. 2, 714; Herbert Hoover to John C. O'Laughlin, 4 September 1939, Herbert Hoover Subject Collection, Box 320, Hoover Institution Archives; *Congressional Record*, 76th Congress, 2nd Session, 21 October 1939, 689–91; and "Gallup and Fortune Polls," *Public Opinion Quarterly*, 4, no. 1 (March 1949): 100.

7. Anderson affidavit, ATHENIA/485, NARA; and *New York Times*, 18 and 23 October 1939. It was also proposed by the head of the Georgetown University Foreign Service School that the *Athenia* may have been torpedoed by a Soviet submarine, arguing that it would have been to the advantage of the Soviet Union to have the United States enter the war against Germany. *New York Times*, 14 November 1939; *Congressional Record*, 76th Congress, 2nd Session, 21 October 1939, 687–91; and Francis Case to Anna O'Neill, Legal Section, Department of State, 9 October 1939, ATHENIA/368, NARA.

8. *New York Times*, 21 October 1939; and Dr. Edward T. Wilkes to Cordell Hull, 18 October 1939, ATHENIA/434, NARA. Captain Joseph A. Gainard told the American minister to Norway that he knew Anderson while on the *City of Flint*. Anderson had said that he had seen the torpedo as it came through the water toward the *Athenia* and that he could make a lot of money selling the story. Gainard refused to let him use the radio of the *City of Flint* to reach the wire services, but Gainard said that Anderson had got a message sent through the SS *Scanpenn*'s radio operator. Anderson also told Gainard that "he had done a great deal of espionage work for Senator Borah." Senator William E. Borah of Idaho was chairman of the Senate Foreign Relations Committee, a powerful "isolationist" and the bane of the Department of State. See Florence T. Harriman to Secretary of State, 8 November 1939, ATHENIA/509, and Caroline Stuart to F. C. Bannerman, ca. October 1939, ATHENIA/481 6/9, NARA.

9. *New York Times*, 19 October 1939; Marquis of Lothian to Foreign Office, 18 October 1939, Action by Mr. Gustav Anderson in regard to the sinking of the SS "Athenia," 19 October 1939, FO 371/22841, NA; Loring C. Christie to Cordell Hull, 24 October 1939, Department of External Affairs Records, RG 25, file 767-39, LAC; British Ambassador to Secretary of State, 30 October 1939, *FRUS, 1939, General*, vol. 2, 290–91; and Joseph P. Kennedy to Secretary of State, 24 October 1939 (cable), ATHENIA/415, NARA.

10. Blair, *Hitler's U-Boat War*, 85–87; and Woodman, *The Real Cruel Sea: The Merchant Navy in the Battle of the Atlantic, 1939–1943*, 29–30.

11. Schmidt in *Trial of the Major War Criminals*, vol. 5, 265–67; Ann Tusa and John Tusa, *The Nuremburg Trial*, 183–85; and Andrew Williams, *The Battle of the Atlantic: Hitler's Grey Wolves of the Sea and the Allies' Desperate Struggle to Defeat Them*, 18. Sharp-eyed Women's Royal Naval Service first noticed the differences in the log pages while examining the German records. Richard Snow notes that the original log showed the dates in Roman numerals while the added pages recorded the dates in Arabic numerals. Snow, *Measureless*

Peril, 72. The tribunal sentenced Dönitz to ten years and Raeder to life in prison. Their equivocating and false statements about the responsibility for the sinking of the *Athenia* undermined their credibility and contributed to their conviction. Hans Fritzsche, deputy to Goebbels, was questioned at the trials about his role in the deception about the responsibility for the sinking of the *Athenia,* but he claimed to have had no knowledge of the cover-up and was acquitted. Also see Joe Heydecker and Johannes Leeb, *The Nuremburg Trials,* 223–24.

12. *Trial of the Major War Criminals,* vol. 5, 267–69; Blair, *Hitler's U-Boat War,* 95; and Peter Padfield, *War beneath the Sea: Submarine Conflict during World War II,* 59. Dönitz sheds no light on dealing with Lemp and the *Athenia* matter in his memoirs. Karl Dönitz, *Memoirs: Ten Years and Twenty Days.* Blair is particularly good in pointing out that Lemp's accomplishments were too valuable to be repudiated by a court-martial and punishment despite the embarrassment that the sinking of the *Athenia* caused the government.

13. Extract from "War Diary" of Cdr. A. E. Schrader, USN, 17 October 1939, RG 59, ATHENIA/491, NARA; and *New York Times,* 16 January 1939. The German navy's history of the U-Boat war, as published in English by Her Majesty's Printing Office, played down the sinking as the "unfortunate Athenia incident." It takes the view that Lemp mistook the ship for an auxiliary cruiser and only learned that it was a passenger vessel when he heard a BBC broadcast. After he returned to Germany he was sent to Berlin where he was told to keep silent about the matter. "He had acted in good faith, and as there was no question of negligence, no disciplinary action was taken." Great Britain Ministry of Defence, *U-Boat War in the Atlantic, 1939–1945: German Naval History,* 40–42.

14. Martin Middlebrook, *Convoy,* 63; David Kahn, *Seizing the Enigma: The Race to Break the German U-Boat Codes, 1939–1943,* 1–14, 161–69; Blair, *Hitler's U-Boat War,* 125, 178, 278–83; and Van der Vat, *The Atlantic Campaign,* 184–85. Lemp's old submarine, *U-30,* had a formidable record, sinking eighteen ships and then serving as a training vessel. It was eventually sunk in a bombing raid on 5 April 1945. Walter J. Boyne, *Clash of Titans: World War II at Sea,* 72.

15. Ambassador in the United Kingdom to Secretary of State, 26 September 1939 (cable), *FRUS, 1939,* vol. 1, *General,* 613–14. Admiral Raeder also demanded a receipt for his note. Naval attaché in Germany to Navy Department, 4 October 1939 (cable), *FRUS, 1939,* vol. 1, *General,* 625. Warren F. Kimball, having examined the Schrader papers in the Naval History Center, notes that issue first came up at a cocktail party in Berlin at which Admiral Raeder was in attendance. Warren F. Kimball, *Forged in War: Roosevelt, Churchill, and the Second World War,* 40, 349.

16. Franklin D. Roosevelt to Winston S. Churchill, 11 September 1939, in Gilbert, ed., *Churchill War Papers,* vol. 1, 76. Roosevelt had written a similar letter

to Chamberlain on 11 September, although the prime minister had little confidence in Roosevelt and sought no special communications or relationship with him. See William R. Rock, *Chamberlain and Roosevelt: British Foreign Policy and the United States, 1937–1940*, 210–11; Ambassador to the United Kingdom to Secretary of State, 6 October 1939 (1 a.m., cable), *FRUS, 1939*, vol. 1, *General*, 626; and Winston S. Churchill to President Roosevelt, 5 October 1939 (cable), in Gilbert, ed., *Churchill War Papers*, vol. 1, 212–13. This was the first message sent under the pseudonym "former Naval Person."

17. Joseph P. Lash, *Roosevelt and Churchill, 1939–1941: The Partnership That Saved the West.*

18. War Cabinets minutes, 6 October 1939, CAB 65/1, NA.

19. White House Statement on the Threatened Sinking of the SS "Iroquois," October 5, 1939, Rosenman, ed., *The Public Papers and Addresses of Franklin D. Roosevelt*, vol. 8, 533–34. The presumption that a bomb had been placed on the *Iroquois* while the ship was in Irish waters stirred an interest by the Irish government also. See Minister in Ireland to Secretary of State, 7 October 1939, and Memorandum of Conversation by the Assistant Secretary of State [A. Berle] with the Irish Minister, 9 October 1939, *FRUS, 1939*, vol. 1, *General*, 727. It may have been that the rumor of a bomb on the *Iroquois* came through the Irish Department of External Affairs to the German minister in Dublin. See, John P. Duggan, *Neutral Ireland and the Third Reich*, 76–77; "German Warning to the United States Regarding the S.S. 'Iroquois,'" *Department of State Bulletin* 1, no. 17 (21 October 1939): 407; Ickes, *The Secret Diaries of Harold L. Ickes: The Lowering Clouds, 1939–1941*, vol. 3, 32; and *New York Times*, 6 and 17 October 1939.

20. Gainard, *Yankee Skipper*, 192–221; and *New York Times*, 27 January 1940. The issues of international law and protocol involved in the whole *City of Flint* episode are discussed in Charles Cheney Hyde, "Editorial Comment: The City of Flint," *American Journal of International Law* 34, no. 1 (January 1940): 89–95. Richard Snow has provided a good account of this whole incident. See Snow, *A Measureless Peril*, 70–78.

21. Gainard, *Yankee Skipper*, 227–35.

22. *New York Times*, 24 October 1939; and chargé d'affaires to Foreign Ministry, 30 October 1939, *Documents on German Foreign Policy*, vol. 8, 359–60. President Roosevelt was particularly annoyed by Soviet disregard for the rights of the United States under international law and discourtesy to American diplomats in this affair. He ordered restrictions to be placed on Soviet diplomats in retaliation. See Memorandum for the Secretary of State, 22 December 1939, and Franklin D. Roosevelt to Sumner Welles, 12 January 1949, *F.D.R. His Personal Letters, 1928–1945*, ed. Elliott Roosevelt, vol. 2, 974–75, 987–88. For interesting commentary on this situation, see Basil Rauch, *Roosevelt from Munich to Pearl Harbor: A Study in the Creation of a Foreign Policy*, 162–63.

23. Press Conference, 25 October 1939, *Press Conferences of Franklin D. Roosevelt,* vol. 14, 245–46; Cordell Hull, *The Memoirs of Cordell Hull,* vol. 1, 704–5; and Secretary of State to Ambassador in the Soviet Union, 23, 24, and 25 October 1939, and Ambassador in the Soviet Union to Secretary of State, 24, 25, and 26 October 1939, *FRUS, The Soviet Union, 1933–1939,* 984–92. The fate of the *City of Flint* in Murmansk was raised in a number of subsequent press conferences, but the president and the State Department were not able to get any cooperation from the Soviets or even much information until the ship reached Norway and was released. For a good summary of the State Department's efforts, see "German Capture of the American Steamer 'City of Flint,'" *The Department of State Bulletin* 1, no. 18 (28 October 1939): 429–32; *New York Times,* 26 and 27 October 1939; William L. Langer and S. Everett Gleason, *The Challenge to Isolation: The World Crisis of 1937–1940 and American Foreign Policy,* vol. 1, 328–39; and Chargé d'Affaire to Foreign Ministry, 26 October 1939, *Documents on German Foreign Policy,* vol. 8, 343. Harold Ickes noted how anxious the president was over this incident and was angry enough to wish he had the freedom to seize and hold a German ship in American waters until the *City of Flint* was released. Ickes, *Secret Diary of Harold L. Ickes,* vol. 3, 48–50.

24. Minister Harriman sent a cable to the State Department containing a concise statement by Captain Gainard explaining what had happened in Murmansk. See Minister in Norway to Secretary of State, 9 November 1939, *FRUS, The Soviet Union, 1933–1939,* 1012–13; and *New York Times,* 27 January 1940.

25. *New York Times,* 4 and 6 November 1939. Critics of the Roosevelt administration argued that his "un-neutral" policies would lead to more incidents like the seizure of the *City of Flint* and would draw the United States into the war. See *Congressional Record,* 76th Congress, 2nd Session, 25 October 1939, 863, and Appendix to the *Congressional Record,* 687–89; Gainard, *Yankee Skipper,* 236–60; and *Baltimore Evening Sun,* 27 January 1940. The new so-called Cash and Carry provisions, which allowed the sale of munitions to belligerents but excluded U.S. ships from war zones, were signed into law on 4 November 1939. The German chargé d'affaires reported to Berlin that the *City of Flint* incident contributed to the revision of the neutrality laws that would not allow the sale of munitions to belligerents under the cash and carry provisions. Chargé d'Affaires to Foreign Ministry, 26 October 1939, *Documents on German Foreign Policy,* vol. 8, 343.

26. Reynolds, *From Munich to Pearl Harbor,* 63–68; Robert A. Divine, *The Illusion of Neutrality: Franklin D. Roosevelt and the Struggle of the Arms Embargo,* 286–335; Justus D. Doenecke, *Storm on the Horizon: The Challenge to American Intervention, 1939–1941,* 13–15; and Charman, *Outbreak,* 296–97. In this context Hoover wrote, "The sinking of the *Athenia* is going to be used for terrific propaganda purposes," and he then went on to urge that Republicans support what became called the "cash and carry" provisions of the Neutrality

Act. See Herbert Hoover to John C. O'Laughlin, 4 September 1939, Herbert Hoover Subject Collection, Box 320, Hoover Institution Archives.

27. *Congressional Record*, 76th Congress, 3rd Session, 29 January 1939, 763–64, and Appendix to the *Congressional Record*, 423–24. See the War Materials Collection, Cpt. J. A. Gainard folder, Archives and Special Collections, Amherst College; Gainard, *Yankee Skipper*, passim; and Samuel Eliot Morison, *The Battle of the Atlantic, 1939–1943*, 284–85, 356–57.

CHAPTER 11. THE RETURN TRIP

1. Hull to American Embassy, London, 16 September 1939 (cable), ATHENIA/245, NARA.

2. Memorandum on the "ATHENIA," 8 September 1939, "ATHENIA" Meeting at the Board of Trade, 15 September 1939, T. G. Jenkins to Norman P. Donaldson, 16 September 1939, Norman P. Donaldson to Board of Trade, 18 September 1939, and Joseph P. Kennedy to Norman P. Donaldson, 6 October 1939, MT 9/3127, NA; and T. G. Jenkins to N. G. Loughnane, 18 September 1939, T 161/996, NA; memorandum of telephone conversation Mr. Long had with Mr. Messersmith and with Mr. Truitt Re: Expenditure a/c Athenia survivors—Voyage of Orizaba, 13 September 1939, ATHENIA/224 ½, NARA; and *New York Times*, 17 October 1939. Donaldson appears to have also paid the U.S. Maritime Commission £3,020 for the 236 passengers carried on the *City of Flint*. Ambassador Kennedy in turn paid Donaldson £459 for the expenses of American survivors in Galway. For an additional fee people could also arrange for a cabin.

3. Whitney H. Shepardson, *The United States in World Affairs: An Account of American Foreign Relations, 1939*, 156; Memorandum of telephone conversation between Joseph P. Kennedy and Sumner Welles, 5 September 1939, 10:14 a.m., ATHENIA/50 ½, and American Citizen Committee to the President, 4 September 1939, ATHENIA/100, NARA; Long, *War Diary of Breckinridge Long*, 8–9; and David E. Koskoff, *Joseph P. Kennedy: A Life and Times*, 221–23. These five relief ships were sent to Europe in the war crisis in addition to the regular American transatlantic passenger liners such as the *Washington* or the *Manhattan*. The National Maritime Union wanted a $200 bonus, a 40 percent increase in wages for sailing into a war zone, and paid-up life insurance for $25,000.

4. Kennedy to Secretary of State, 16 September 1939 (cable), and Hull to American Embassy London, 16 September 1939 (cable), ATHENIA/245, NARA. In an early draft of the cable Hull said that before complaining the survivors should consider the conditions under which wounded American soldiers were returned to the United States in the First World War. With the *Athenia* in mind, Kennedy also created a stir in Britain when a week later he warned Americans not to attempt to sail home on belligerent ships, such as the Cunard White Star liner *Aquitania*. See Koskoff, *Joseph P. Kennedy*, 223.

5. Ambassador in the United Kingdom to Secretary of State, 15 September 1939 (cable), and Secretary of State to the Ambassador in the United Kingdom, 16 September 1939 (cable), *FRUS, 1939,* vol. 1, *General,* 603–7.

6. *New York Times,* 19 and 21 September 1939; *Glasgow Herald,* 19 September 1939; and Evelyn, "*Athenia* manuscript."

7. *Connacht Tribune,* 23 September 1939; and *New York Times,* 21 September 1939.

8. Evelyn, "*Athenia* manuscript"; *New York Herald Tribune,* 28 September 1939; *New York Times,* 28 September 1939; and *Washington Post,* 28 September 1939. There was one stowaway, seventeen-year-old William Clark from Scotland, who was actually born in the United States.

9. *New York Times,* 28 September 1939; *New York Herald Tribune,* 28 September 1939; and Park, "Aboard the *Athenia,*" 49.

10. Kennedy to Jesse Jones, 8 September 1939 (cable), MSS 41, Box 8, folder 10, Simpson Family Papers; Allan, *Andrew Allan,* 92; and *Washington Post,* 28 September 1939.

11. *New York Times,* 14 September 1939; *New York Herald Tribune,* 14 September 1939; A. D. Simpson to R. T. Simpson, 8 September 1939 (cable), Genevieve Morrow to Mrs. Dee Simpson, 15 September 1939 (cable), and Burton-Baldry to Simpson, 9 September 1939 (cable), MSS 41, Box 8, folder 9, and A. D. Simpson to Paul H. Brattain, 23 September 1939, MSS 41, Box 8, folder 10, Simpson Family Papers.

12. *New York Times,* 3, 17, 20, and 24 October 1939.

13. High Commissioner for Canada in Great Britain to Secretary of State for External Affairs, Canada, 8 September 1939 (cable), O. D. Skelton to High Commissioner for Canada in the United Kingdom, 23 October 1939, Department of External Affairs Records, RG 25, file 767-39, LAC; and Minutes on the liability of the Donaldson Line for the expenses of survivors, 12 September 1939 to 31 May 1940, J. C. Pattison to Lester B. Pearson, 15 May 1940, and Norman P. Donaldson to T. G. Jenkins, 20 June 1940, MT 9/3126, NA.

14. *Globe and Mail,* 25 September 1939. It was presumed that the U-boat was sunk. *Montreal Gazette,* 23 September 1939; MacPherson, *Voyage, Venture and Victory,* 20; High Commission, London, to Secretary of State for External Affairs (cable), 15 September 1939, and H. L. Keenleyside to A. L. Sauve, 19 September 1939, Department of External Affairs Records, RG 25, file 767-39, LAC; and Cass-Beggs, *Roots and Wings,* 104–5.

15. *Globe and Mail,* 23 September 1939; and Goodson, *Tumult in the Clouds,* 18–22.

16. *Globe and Mail,* 16 October 1939; and High Commission to Secretary of State for External Affairs, 12 October 1939 (cable), and Lester B. Pearson to Secretary of State for External Affairs, 8 November 1939, Department of External Affairs Records, RG 25, file 767-39, LAC.

17. A .D. Simpson to Dr. Henry F. Grady, 20 October 1939, ATHENIA/439, and W. Arthur Strain to Department of State, 11 November 1939, ATHENIA/482, NARA; *Washington Post,* 4 March 1940; and Marquis of Lothian to Foreign Office, 7 March 1940 (cable), FO 371/24247, NA.

18. Chancery to American Department, Foreign Office, 12 June 1940, and Minute, FO 371/24247, NA. Private citizens in the United States were similarly anxious about Nugent and his organization. United Kingdom High Commissioner in Canada to Secretary of State for Dominion Affairs, 6 March 1940 (cable), FO 371/24247, NA; and Kirlin Campbell Hickox Keating & McGrann to Cunard White Star, Limited, 10 September 1940, Department of External Affairs Records, RG 25, file 552, LAC.

19. Memorandum for Dr. Skelton, Compensation for Loss of Personal Effects by "Athenia" Survivors, 29 November 1940, and J. L. Ilsley, Minister of Finance, to Dr. O. D. Skelton, 20 December 1940, Department of External Affairs Records, RG 25, file 552, LAC; Summary of Claims, SS "Athenia," 27 April 1949, Athenia Claims, Department of External Affairs Records, RG 25, file 552, LAC. For the struggle to obtain compensation for items lost on the *Athenia* and also property confiscated by the Nazis in Europe, see Rudolf Altschul Fonds. Also see interview with Dr. André Molgat.

20. Admiral E. S. Land and Dr. R. L. Jenkins cited in Sweigard, "The *Athenia* Disaster—My Story," 6–7. Dr. Richard L. Jenkins, with whom she had worked on the ship, wrote to New York University praising Dr. Sweigard also, and commenting that the university was fortunate to have such a capable person on their staff. Jessie A. Ziegler to A. D. Simpson, 5 October 1939, folder 10, box 8, MSS 41, Simpson Family Papers.

21. Lorraine S. McCutcheon to Secretary of State, 13 November 1939, and G. S. Messersmith to Lorraine S. McCutcheon, 18 November 1939, ATHENIA/483, and James G. Davis to George S. Messersmith, 21 December 1939, ATHENIA/629, NARA; and John R. McDonald to Commander S. A. Buss, 5 September 1939, http://ahoy.tk-jk.net/macslog/Letterofthanksfroman Athen.html.

22. Naval Secretary to First Lord of the Admiralty, 7 December 1939, ADM 1/11519, NA; and *The Times,* 3 January 1940.

23. A. W. R. Wilby to Director of Marine Services, 5 September 1940, and Press release, 26 September 1940, and Memorandum, Department of Transport Records, RG 12. file 7808-4, LAC; and *Washington Post,* 27 September 1940.

24. War Cabinet Papers, 25 December 1939, in Gilbert, ed., *The Churchill War Papers,* vol. 1, 565–66; and Lord Lothian to Lord Halifax, 3 September 1940, in Thomas E. Hachey, ed., *Confidential Dispatches: Analysis of America by the British Ambassador, 1939–1945,* 4–5. This view was mirrored in contemporary analysis of American public opinion. See Jacob, "Influences of World Events on U.S. 'Neutrality' Opinion," 61.

CHAPTER 12. HOME AGAIN, SAFE FROM THE SEA

1. *Toronto Star*, 4 September 1999.
2. *Globe and Mail*, 30 September 1939; and *New York Times*, 11 February 1940.
3. Allan, *Andrew Allan*, 90–133; and Rev. William Allan, *Memories of Blinkbonnie: A Second Book of Musings*. Andrew Allan wrote a memoir about his father for the book. Also see *Globe and Mail*, 8 December 1941; and scrapbooks in Nancy Pyper Collection, University of Manitoba Archives.
4. *Globe and Mail*, 6 December 1941; James Alexander "Goody" Goodson, http://www.acesofww2/Canada/aces/goodson/htm; Goodson, *Tumult in the Clouds, passim*; and Norman E. Hanna to mother, 8 October 1941, D 3265/2, Public Records Office Northern Ireland; and Ian Montgomery to author, 4 June 2008.
5. *Garden City News*, 28 August 2009; and *Globe and Mail*, 20 May 1941.
6. Francis, "*The Sinking of the Athenia*," 32; Louella O. Parsons, "Close-Ups and Long-Shots," *Washington Post*, 17 September 1940. Lubitsch had directed films in both Germany and Hollywood, several of the most notable being *The Merry Widow*, *Design for Living*, and *Heaven Can Wait*. See Leonard Lyons, "The New Yorker," *Washington Post*, 6 July 1940.
7. Cass-Beggs, *Roots and Wings*, 110–13; and Rosemary Cass-Beggs Burstall to the author, 16 March 2009. The psychologist mentioned the Cass-Beggs' circumstances in his book on problems of violence and war. W. E. Blatz, *Hostages to Peace: Parents and the Children of Democracy*, 201. Also see Ruby Mitchell Boersma Interview, Oral History Program, 31D 6, Canadian War Museum Archive; and *Ottawa Citizen*, 4 September 1999.
8. Rudolf Altschul Fonds, University of Saskatchewan Archives.
9. William Conley to the author, 19 March 2010; Maribeth Kobza Betton to the author, 31 March 2010; Rev. Gerald Hutchinson Papers; MacPherson, *Voyage, Venture and Victory*, 20–21; and Graham MacPherson to the author, 16 July 2008.
10. Interview with Dr. André Molgat; Hibbert, ed., *Fragments of War*, 19–20; and *Globe and Mail*, 2 December 1941.
11. *Dallas Morning News*, 3 September 2010; and newspaper clippings, MSS 41, box 8, folder 10, Simpson Family Papers. In 1995 the Crow family founded the Tramwell and Margaret Crow Collection of Asian Art.
12. *Toronto Star*, 4 September 1999.
13. Admiral Dönitz had sent out a radio message on 5 May effectively ordering an end to operations, but this was not received by U-boats that were submerged. Van der Vat, *The Atlantic Campaign*, 380–82; and Milner, *Battle of the Atlantic*, 230. The submarine campaign was called "a costly failure" by two critics. See G. H. Bennett and R. Bennett, *Hitler's Admirals*, 1.
14. Stewart, "Homeward Bound on the *Athenia*," 84.

BIBLIOGRAPHY

MANUSCRIPTS

CANADA

Edmonton, Alberta

Rev. Gerald Hutchinson Family Records

Halifax, Nova Scotia

Maritime Museum of the Atlantic

—Rosemary Cass-Beggs Burstall, "A Three-Year-Old's Recollection of the Sinking of the *Athenia*," Research file

Nova Scotia Archives and Records Management

—Donald A. Wilcox, The *Athenia* Saga, U/F U.530 #18

Ottawa, Ontario

Canadian War Museum Archive

—Ruby Mitchell Boersma Interview, Transcript of Interview Number 31D 6 BOERSMA

—Seasoned Sailors, Set 2, No. 3, video interview with Rear Admiral Robert P. Welland, DSC and Bar

Library and Archives of Canada

—Andrew Allan Fonds, MG 31, D6, Vols. 18 and 41

—William Lyon Mackenzie King Diaries, MG 26, J

—The Reverend G. P. Woollcombe, "My Experience in Connection with the Torpedoing of the S. S. 'Athenia' on September 3rd 1939," Department of Transport Records, RG 12, file 8780-4

—Department of External Affairs Records, RG 25, files 552 and 767-39

—Department of Transport Records, RG 12, file 7808-4

Regina, Saskatchewan

Saskatchewan Archives

—Saskatchewan Historical Society Collection

—Sir Richard Lake file

Saskatoon, Saskatchewan
　University of Saskatchewan Library, University Archives
　　—Rudolf Altschul Fonds

Thunder Bay, Ontario
　Thunder Bay Museum
　　—Helen Edna Campbell Papers

Winnipeg, Manitoba
　University of Manitoba Archives
　　—Nancy Pyper Collection

IRELAND

Dublin
　Military Archives, Cathal Brugha Barracks, Department of Defence
　　—SS *Athenia* file, G2/X/0431
　National Archives of Ireland
　　—Department of Foreign Affairs file, 239/54
　　—Taoiseach file, S11415

NORWAY

Oslo
　Fred. Olsen & Company
　　—M/V *Knute Nelson* file

UNITED KINGDOM

Belfast, Northern Ireland
　Public Record Office of Northern Ireland
　　—Norman Hanna Papers, D.3265/1, 2 and 3A-B

Glasgow, Scotland
　The Mitchell Library
　　—Athenia Disaster Fund, G1/3/44
　　—General Accounts Ledger, No. 4, TD49/36
　　—Glasgow City Archives
　　—Memorandum on behalf of Anchor Line Limited and Donaldson
　　　Atlantic Line Limited, submitted in support of a request by those
　　　Companies for Government assistance in respect of the Atlantic
　　　Passenger Liner business carried on by them, TD49/107
　　—Minutes of the Corporation of Glasgow, C1/3/100
　　—TSS Athenia, Lists of Crews and Voyages, TD49/72/4(2)

Liverpool, England

    Merseyside Maritime Museum

        —Jean Lambert Letter, DX/2389

        —Harry Morgan, "A Sea Cruise to Remember"

        —Treharne Letters, DX/2393

London, England

    The Imperial War Museum

        —J. Coullie Letters, P284

        —Hugh S. Swindley Letters, P284

    The National Archives

        —Admiralty

         –ADM 1/-

         –ADM 199/-

        —Board of Trade

         –BT 385/-

        —Cabinet Papers

         –CAB 65/-

        —Foreign Office

         –FO 115/-

         –FO 371/-

        —Ministry of Transport

         –MT 9/-

         –MT 59/-

        —Treasury

         –T 161/-

UNITED STATES

Amherst, Massachusetts

    Amherst College Library, Archives and Special Collections

        —Biography file, J. A. Gainard

        —War Materials Collection, Cpt. J. A. Gainard folder

Austin, Texas

    Archives of the Episcopal Church

        —Bernice Jansen file

Bloomington, Indiana

    Lilly Library, University of Indiana

        —Montgomery Evans Papers

Boston, Massachusetts

John F. Kennedy Presidential Library and Foundation
—John F. Kennedy Personal Papers
–Childhood letters and correspondence, Series 4, Box 4
—Joseph P. Kennedy Papers
–Unpublished manuscript, "Diplomatic Memoir," Box 1, JPKP
—Dave Powers Papers
—Oral History Interview with Torbert H. MacDonald
Massachusetts Historical Society
—Nigel Hamilton Papers, Box 2

Childs, Maryland

Oblate Archives
—Father Joseph V. O'Connor file

Cleveland, Ohio

Western Reserve Historical Society
—Dorothy Bulkley Papers, MS 3773

College Park, Maryland

National Archives and Records Administration
—Classified General Records, 1934–1962, RG 84
–Glasgow Consulate, 1938–1942
—Foreign Service Posts of the Department of State, RG 84
–Belfast Consulate General, General Records, 1939
–Glasgow Consulate, General Records, 1939
—General Records of the Department of State, RG 59
–Decimal file, M-1455, Reels 73–77

Fayetteville, Arkansas

University of Arkansas Libraries
—Core Family Papers, MC 1380

Houston, Texas

Texas and Local History Department, Houston Public Library
—A. D. Simpson Family Papers
–Box 8, folders 9 and 10
–Box 9, folder 1

Hyde Park, New York

> Franklin D. Roosevelt Presidential Library
>> —Official file #48, "Scotland"
>> —Personal file #6211, "Dollan, P. J."
>> —Public Papers and Addresses, Press Conferences, 5 and 8 September and 5 October 1939, Press Conferences, 5 and 8 September 1939

Madison, Wisconsin

> Wisconsin Historical Society
>> —John Cudahy Papers
>> —Jeannette C. Jordan Papers

Philadelphia, Pennsylvania

> American Philosophical Society
>> —Bronson Price Papers

Stanford, California

> Hoover Institution Archives, Stanford University
>> —Herbert Hoover Subject Collection

Washington, D.C.

> Library of Congress
>> —Cordell Hull Papers

PERSONAL INTERVIEWS, EMAIL INTERVIEWS, TELEPHONE CONTACT, OR CORRESPONDENCE

Batton, Maribeth Kobra
Cass-Beggs Burstall, Rosemary
Conley, William
Gillespie, Hay "Scotty"
Harrison, Cynthia
Hutchinson, Robert
MacPherson, Graham
Molgat, Dr. André
Montgomery, Ian

PUBLISHED DOCUMENTS

Canada. House of Commons. *Debates.* 1939.

The Complete Presidential Press Conferences of Franklin D. Roosevelt, Volumes 13–14, 1939. New York: Da Capo Press, 1972.

Congressional Record. 76th Congress, 2nd Session, vol. 85, part 1. Washington, D.C.: Government Printing Office, 1939.

Crowe, Catriona, Ronan Fanning, Michael Kennedy, Dermot Keogh, and Eunan O'Halpin, eds. *Documents on Irish Foreign Policy, Volume VI, 1939–1941.* Dublin: Royal Irish Academy, 2008.

Documents on German Foreign Policy, 1918–1945. Series D, Vol. 8, *The War Years, 1939–1940.* Washington, D.C.: Government Printing Office, 1954.

Gilbert, Martin, ed. *The Churchill War Papers: At the Admiralty, September 1939–May, 1940.* New York: W. W. Norton, 1993.

Hachey, Thomas E., ed. *Confidential Dispatches: Analysis of America by the British Ambassador, 1939–1945.* Evanston: New University Press, 1974.

Roosevelt, Elliott, ed. *F.D.R. His Personal Letters, 1928–1945*, vol. 2. New York: Duell, Sloan and Pearse, 1950.

Rosenman, Samuel L., ed. *The Public Papers and Addresses of Franklin D. Roosevelt*, vol. 8. New York: Macmillan, 1941.

———. *The Public Papers and Addresses of Franklin D. Roosevelt*, vol. 10. New York: Harper and Row, 1950.

Trial of the Major War Criminals before the International Military Tribunal. vols. 5 and 13. Nuremburg: Allied Control Authority for Germany, 1947.

United Kingdom. *Parliamentary Debates* (Commons), 5th Series, vol. 351 (1938–39).

———. *Parliamentary Debates* (Lords), 5th Series, vol. 114 (1938–39).

U.S. Department of State. *Foreign Relations of the United States, 1939: Volume 1, General.* Washington, D.C.: Government Printing Office, 1956.

———. *Foreign Relations of the United States, 1939: Volume 2, General, The British Commonwealth and Europe.* Washington, D.C.: Government Printing Office, 1956.

———. *Foreign Relations of the United States, The Soviet Union, 1933–1939.* Washington, D.C.: Government Printing Office, 1955.

ONLINE MATERIALS

ACES OF WORLD WAR II WEBSITE

James Goodson. James Alexander "Goody" Goodson. http://www.acesofww2
.com/Canada/aces/goodson.htm (accessed 8 January 2010)

AHOY – MAC'S WEB LOG, WEBSITE OF THE NAVAL HISTORICAL SOCIETY OF AUSTRALIA, INC., AND MACKENZIE J. GREGORY

Bikow, Douglas. Douglas Bikow letters. http://www.fogbugz.tkwebservice.com/
default.asp?ahoy.2.641.5 (accessed 4 October 2009)

Easton, John. John Easton narrative. http://ahoy.tk-jk.net/Letters/
JohnEastonandmotherLilyEa.html (accessed 4 October 2009)

Evelyn, Judith. Judith Evelyn narrative. "*Athenia* manuscript," in the possession of Ms. Cynthia Harrison. http://www.ahoy.tk-jk.net/macslog/
AtheniaManuscriptPreview.html (accessed 4 October 2009)

McDonald, John R. John R. McDonald to Commander S. A. Buss, 5 September
1939. http://ahoy.tk-jk/macslog/Letterofthanks
fromAthen.html (accessed 4 October 2009)

Rapp, Berta. Berta Rapp narrative. http://ahoy.tk-jk.net/Letters/
BertaRappOsiasRappweresur.html (accessed 4 October 2009)

Taylor, Jack. "A Report about HMS Electra." http://ahoy.tk-jk.net/macslog/
AreportaboutHMSElectra.html (accessed 4 October 2009)

NEWSPAPERS AND JOURNALS

CANADA

Edmonton Bulletin
Halifax Chronicle
Halifax Herald
Montreal Gazette
Ottawa Citizen
Russell Banner
Toronto Globe and Mail
Toronto Star
Winnipeg Free Press
Winnipeg Tribune

IRELAND

Connacht Tribune
Galway Advertiser
Galway Observer
Irish Independent

Irish Press
Irish Times

UNITED KINGDOM

Daily Mail
Daily Record & Mail
Daily Telegraph
Evening Citizen
Glasgow Eastern Standard
Glasgow Herald
London Illustrated News
New Statesman and Nation
The Spectator
The Times
The War Illustrated

UNITED STATES

America
Baltimore Evening Sun
Baltimore Sun
Boston Globe
Boston Herald
Dallas Morning News
Department of State Bulletin
Facts in Review
Garden City News
Houston Press
Life Magazine
The Nation
New Republic
New York Daily News
New York Herald Tribune
New York Journal-American
New York Sun
New York Times
New York University Commercial Journal
Time Magazine
Wall Street Journal
Washington Post

MEMOIRS

Allan, Andrew. *Andrew Allan: A Self-Portrait*. Toronto: Macmillan of Canada, 1974.

Allan, Rev. William. *Memories of Blinkbonnie: A Second Book of Musings*. Toronto: Thomas Nelson & Sons, 1939.

Bailey, Barbara. "*Athenia* Survivor," in *Fragments of War: Stories from Survivors of World War II*, ed. Joyce Hibbert. Toronto: Dundurn Press, 1985, 11–21.

Beschloss, Michael R. *Kennedy and Roosevelt: The Uneasy Alliance*. New York: W. W. Norton, 1980.

Blair, Eva M. *Saved from the* Athenia: *A Personal Testimony to the Indisputable Presence of God during the Torpedoing of the R.M.S.* Athenia *Off the Coast of Ireland on September Third Nineteen Thirty-Nine*. Bangor, N. Ireland: G.H.E. Bamford, 1940.

Campbell, Helen Edna. "Torpedoed at Sea: Aboard the S.S. *Athenia*, 1939." Thunder Bay Historical Museum, *Papers & Records* vol. 21 (1993).

Cass-Beggs, Barbara. *Roots and Wings: A Memoir of My Life with David*. Hull, Quebec: Cass-Beggs Productions, 1992.

Churchill, Winston S. *The Second World War: The Gathering Storm*. Boston: Houghton Mifflin, 1948.

———. *The Second World War: Their Finest Hour*. Boston: Houghton Mifflin, 1949.

Dönitz, Karl. *Memoirs: Ten Years and Twenty Days*. Cleveland: World Publishing, 1959.

Evans, Montgomery. *A Ship Was Torpedoed*. N.p.: Montgomery Evans, 1941.

Gainard, Joseph. *Yankee Skipper: The Life Story of Joseph A. Gainard, Captain of the* City of Flint. New York: Frederick A. Stokes, 1940.

Goodson, James. *Tumult in the Clouds*. New York: New American Library, 2004.

Hale, Patricia. "I Was on the *Athenia.*" *Canadian Home Journal* (December 1939), 8–9, 18, 28–31, 66.

Hull, Cordell. *The Memoirs of Cordell Hull*, vol. 1. New York: Macmillan, 1948.

Ickes, Harold L. *The Secret Diaries of Harold L. Ickes: The Inside Struggle, 1936–1939*, vol. 2. New York: Simon and Schuster, 1954.

———. *The Secret Diaries of Harold L. Ickes: The Lowering Clouds, 1939–1941*, vol. 3. New York: Simon and Schuster, 1954.

Long, Breckinridge. *The War Diary of Breckinridge Long: Selections from the Years 1939–1944*. Edited by Fred L. Israel. Lincoln: University of Nebraska Press, 1966.

Macmillan, Harold. *The Blast of War, 1939–1945*. New York: Harper and Row, 1967.

MacPherson, F. Elwood. *Voyage, Venture and Victory*. Hantsport, NS: Lancelot Press, 1980.

Massey, Vincent. *What's Past Is Prologue: The Memoirs of the Right Honourable Vincent Massey*. Toronto: Macmillan of Canada, 1963.

Nicolson, Harold. *Diaries and Letters of Harold Nicolson: The War Years, 1939–1945*, vol. 2. New York: Atheneum, 1967.

O'Connor, Father Joseph. "I Was Aboard the 'Athenia.'" *The Irish Digest* 6, no. 3 (May 1940): 36–37.

Park, Russell A. "Aboard the *Athenia*," *World War II* (July 1989).

Pearson, Lester B. *Mike: The Memoirs of the Honourable Lester B. Pearson*. Vol. 1, *1897–1948*. Toronto: University of Toronto Press, 1972.

Phillips, William. *Ventures in Diplomacy*. Boston: Beacon Press, 1952.

Richie, Charles. *The Siren Years: A Canadian Diplomat Abroad, 1937–1945*. Toronto: Macmillan of Canada, 1974.

Shirer, William L. *Berlin Diary: The Journal of a Foreign Correspondent, 1934–1941*. London: Hamish Hamilton, 1941.

Stewart, D. G. B. "Homeward Bound on the *Athenia*." *The Canadian Banker*, October 1939, 80–84.

Stork, Charles Wharton. "Sketches by an 'Athenian.'" *Saturday Evening Post*, 4 November 1939, 33.

Sweigard, Dr. Lulu E. "The *Athenia* Disaster—My Story." *The Alumnus*, January 1940, 5–8.

LATER WORKS

Baer, George W. *One Hundred Years of Sea Power: The U.S. Navy, 1890–1990*. Stanford: Stanford University Press, 1994.

Bailey, Thomas A., and Paul B. Ryan. *The Lusitania Disaster: An Episode in Modern Warfare and Diplomacy*. New York: Free Press, 1975.

Bennett, G. H., and R. Bennett. *Hitler's Admirals*. Annapolis, Md.: Naval Institute Press, 2004.

Blair, Clay. *Hitler's U-Boat War: The Hunters, 1939–1942*. New York: Random House, 1996.

Blatz, W. E. *Hostages to Peace: Parents and Children of Democracy*. New York: Willam Morrow, 1940.

Boyne, Walter J. *Clash of Titans: World War II at Sea*. New York: Simon and Schuster, 1997.

Cain, T. M. *H.M.S. Electra*. London: Frederick Muller, 1959.

Carroll, Francis M. "'The First Casualty of the Sea': The *Athenia* Survivors and the Galway Relief Effort, September 1939." *History Ireland* 19, no. 1 (January–February 2011): 42–45.

———. "The First Shot Was the Last Straw: The Sinking of the T.S.S. *Athenia* in September 1939 and British Naval Policy in the Second World War." *Diplomacy & Statecraft* 20, no. 3 (September 2009): 403–13.

Caulfield, Max. *Tomorrow Never Came: The Story of the S.S. Athenia*. New York: W. W. Norton, 1959.

Charman, Terry. *Outbreak 1939: The World Goes to War*. London: Virgin Books, 2009.

Creighton, Donald. *Canada, 1939–1945: The Forked Road*. Toronto: McClelland and Stewart, 1976.

De Bedts, Ralph F. *Ambassador Joseph Kennedy, 1938–1940: An Anatomy of Appeasement*. New York: Peter Lang, 1985.

Divine, Robert A. *The Illusion of Neutrality: Franklin D. Roosevelt and the Struggle of the Arms Embargo*. Chicago: Quadrangle Books, 1969.

Doenecke, Justus D. *Storm on the Horizon: The Challenge to American Intervention, 1939–1941*. Lanham, Md.: Rowman and Littlefield, 2000.

Duggan, John P. *Neutral Ireland and the Third Reich*. Dublin: Gill and Macmillan, 1985.

Dunnet, Alastair. *The Donaldson Line: A Century of Shipping, 1854–1954*. Glasgow: Jackson Son and Company, 1960.

Dwyer, T. Ryle. *Behind the Green Curtain: Ireland's Phoney Neutrality during World War II*. Dublin: Gill and Macmillan, 2009.

Eyman, Scott. *Ernst Lubitsch: Laughter in Paradise*. Baltimore, Md.: Johns Hopkins University Press, 2000.

Fox, Stephen. *The Ocean Highway: Isambard Kingdom Brunel, Samuel Cunard and the Revolutionary World of the Great Atlantic Steamships*. London: Harper Perennial, 2003.

Francis, Daniel. "The Sinking of the *Athenia*." *The Beaver* (April–May 2006), 30–36.

"Gallup and Fortune Polls." *Public Opinion Quarterly* 4, no. 1 (March 1940): 83–115.

Gilbert, Martin. *Churchill and America*. New York: Free Press, 2005.

———. *Winston S. Churchill: Finest Hour, 1939–1941*, vol. 6. London: Heinemann, 1983.

Granatstein, J. L. *Canada's War: The Politics of the Mackenzie King Government, 1939–1945*. Toronto: University of Toronto Press, 1975.

Great Britain Ministry of Defence. *U-Boat War in the Atlantic, 1939–1945: German Naval History*. Edited by Gunter Hessler. London: Her Majesty's Printing Office, 1992.

Grob-Fitzgibbon, Benjamin. *The Irish Experience during the Second World War: An Oral History*. Dublin: Irish Academic Press, 2004.

Hadley, Michael L. *U-Boats Against Canada: German Submarines in Canadian Waters*. Kingston, ON: McGill-Queen's University Press, 1985.

Hall, Christopher. *Britain, America & Arms Control, 1921–37*. New York: St. Martin's Press, 1987.

Heinrichs, Waldo. *Threshold of War: Franklin D. Roosevelt & American Entry into World War II*. New York: Oxford University Press, 1988.

Heydecker, Joe, and Johannes Leeb. *The Nuremburg Trials*. London: Heinemann, 1962. First published in Germany in 1958.

Hibbert, Joyce, ed. *Fragments of War: Stories from Survivors of World War II.* Toronto: Dundurn Press, 1985.

Hyde, Charles Cheney. "Editorial Comment: The City of Flint." *American Journal of International Law.* 34, no. 1 (January 1940): 89–95.

Hyde, Francis E. *Cunard and the North Atlantic, 1840–1973: A History of Shipping and Financial Management.* London: Macmillan, 1975.

Jacob, Philip E. "Influences of World Events on U.S. 'Neutrality' Opinion." *Public Opinion Quarterly* 4, no. 1 (March 1949): 48–65.

Kahn, David. *Seizing the Enigma: The Race to Break the German U-Boat Codes, 1939–1943.* New York: Barnes and Noble, 2001.

Keegan, John. *The Price of Admiralty: The Evolution of Naval Warfare.* New York: Penguin, 1990.

Kennedy, Paul. *The Rise and Fall of British Naval Mastery.* London: Ashfield Press, 1992.

Kimball, Warren F. *Forged in War: Roosevelt, Churchill and the Second World War.* New York: William Morrow, 1997.

Koskoff, David A. *Joseph P. Kennedy: A Life and Times.* Englewood Cliffs, N.J.: Prentice-Hall, 1974.

Langer, William L., and S. Everett Gleason. *The Challenge to Isolation: The World Crisis of 1937–1940 and American Foreign Policy,* vol. 1. Gloucester, MA: Peter Smith, 1970.

Lash, Joseph P. *Roosevelt and Churchill, 1939–1941: The Partnership That Saved the West.* New York: W. W. Norton, 1976.

Lavine, Harold, and James Wechsler. *War Propaganda and the United States.* New Haven, Conn.: Yale University Press, 1940.

Leaming, Barbara. *Jack Kennedy: The Education of a Statesman.* New York: W. W. Norton, 2006.

Legro, Jeffery W. *Cooperation under Fire: Anglo-German Restraint during World War II.* Ithaca, N.Y.: Cornell University Press, 1995.

Link, Arthur S. *Wilson: The Struggle for Neutrality, 1914–1915.* Princeton: Princeton University Press, 1960.

Mallison, W. T., Jr. *International Law Studies, 1966: Studies in the Law of Naval Warfare: Submarines in General and Limited Wars.* Washington, D.C.: Government Printing Office, 1968.

Medlicott, W. N. *Contemporary England, 1914–1964.* London: Longmans, 1967.

Meister, Brian R. "Terror of War: The Tragedy of the *Athenia.*" *Voyage* no. 9 (June 1991), 185.

Middlebrook, Martin. *Convoy.* New York: William Morrow, 1977.

Milner, Marc. *Battle of the Atlantic.* St. Catherines, ON: Tempus Publishing, 2003.

Morison, Samuel Eliot. *The Battle of the Atlantic, 1939–1943.* Edison, N.J.: Castle Books, 2001.

O'Brien, Michael. *John F. Kennedy: A Biography*. New York: St. Martin's Press, 2005.

O'Connell, Robert L. *Sacred Vessels: The Cult of the Battleship and the Rise of the U.S. Navy*. New York: Oxford University Press, 1991.

Padfield, Peter. *War beneath the Sea: Submarine Conflict during World War II*. New York: John Wiley, 1995.

Pickersgill, J. W. *The Mackenzie King Record, 1939–1944*, vol. 1. Toronto: University of Toronto Press, 1960.

Poirier, Michael. "Survivors Recall *Athenia's* Final Voyage." *Voyage* 49 (Autumn 2004): 28.

Preston, Diana. *Wilful Murder: The Sinking of the Lusitania*. London: Corgi Books, 2002.

Rademacher, Cay. *Drei Tage im September: Die letzte Fahrt der Athenia, 1939*. Hamburg: Mare, 2009.

Rauch, Basil. *Roosevelt from Munich to Pearl Harbor: A Study in the Creation of a Foreign Policy*. New York: Creative Age Press, 1950.

Renehan, Edward J., Jr. *The Kennedys at War, 1937–1945*. New York: Doubleday, 2002.

Reynolds, David. *From Munich to Pearl Harbor: Roosevelt's America and the Origins of the Second World War*. Chicago: Ivan R. Dee, 2001.

Rock, William R. *Chamberlain and Roosevelt: British Foreign Policy and the United States, 1937–1940*. Columbus: Ohio State University Press, 1988.

Roskill, Captain S. W. *The Strategy of Sea Power: Its Development and Application*. London: Collins, 1962.

———. *The War at Sea, 1939–1945: Defensive*, vol. 1. London: Her Majesty's Stationery Office, 1954.

Ruge, Friedrich. *Der Seekrieg: The German Navy's Story, 1939–1945*. Annapolis, Md.: United States Naval Institute, 1957.

Shepardson, Whitney H. *The United States in World Affairs: An Account of American Foreign Relations, 1939*. New York: Council on Foreign Relations, 1940.

Shirer, William L. *The Rise and Fall of the Third Reich: A History of Nazi Germany*. New York: Simon and Schuster, 1960.

Simpson, Colin. *Lusitania*. Harmondsworth, England: Penguin, 1983.

Snow, Richard. *A Measureless Peril: America in the Fight for the Atlantic, the Longest Battle of World War II*. New York: Scribner, 2010.

Spector, Ronald H. *At War at Sea: Sailors and Naval Combat in the Twentieth Century*. Harmondsworth, England: Penguin, 2002.

Stegemann, Bernd. "Germany's Second Attempt to Become a Naval Power," in *Germany and the Second World War*, vol. 2, edited by Klaus A.

Maier, Horst Rohde, Bernd Stegemann, and Hans Umbreit. Oxford: Clarendon Press, 1991.

———. "The Submarine War," in *Germany and the Second World War*, vol. 2, edited by Klaus A. Maier, Horst Rohde, Bernd Stegemann, and Hans Umbreit. Oxford: Clarendon Press, 1991.

Taylor, A. J. P. *English History, 1914–1945*. Oxford: Clarendon Press, 1965.

Trefousse, H. L. *Germany and American Neutrality, 1939–1941*. New York: Octagon Books, 1969.

Tusa, Ann, and John Tusa. *The Nuremberg Trial*. New York: Atheneum, 1986.

Uhlig, Frank, Jr. *How Navies Fight: The U.S. Navy and Its Allies*. Annapolis, Md.: Naval Institute Press, 1994.

Van der Porten, Edward P. *The German Navy in World War II*. New York: Thomas Y. Crowell, 1969.

Van der Vat, Dan. *The Atlantic Campaign: World War II's Great Struggle at Sea*. New York: Harper and Row, 1988.

Watt, Donald Cameron. *How the War Came: The Immediate Origins of the Second World War, 1938–1939*. New York: Pantheon Books, 1989.

Whale, Derek. *The Liners of Liverpool, Part II*. Birkenhead, England: Countryvise Press, 1987.

Whalen, Richard J. *The Founding Father: The Story of Joseph P. Kennedy*. New York: New American Library, 1964.

Williams, Andrew. *The Battle of the Atlantic: Hitler's Grey Wolves of the Sea and the Allies' Desperate Struggle to Defeat Them*. New York: Basic Books, 2003.

Willmott, H. P. *The Last Century of Sea Power*. Vol. 2, *From Washington to Tokyo, 1922–1945*. Bloomington: Indiana University Press, 2010.

Wills, Clair. *That Neutral Island: A Cultural History of Ireland during the Second World War*. London: Faber and Faber, 2007.

Woodman, Richard. *The Real Cruel Sea: The Merchant Navy in the Battle of the Atlantic, 1939–1943*. London: John Murray, 2004.

Woodring, Stephen. "Phenylthiocarbamide: A 75-Year Adventure in Genetics and Natural Selection." *Genetics* 172 (April 2006): 2015–23.

INDEX

ABOUT THE AUTHOR

FRANCIS M. CARROLL, Professor Emeritus at the University of Manitoba, was educated at Carleton College, the University of Minnesota, and Trinity College Dublin. He has published ten books and is the winner of the J. W. Dafoe Prize and the Albert B. Corey Prize.